[加] 吉恩-皮尔里·布鲁恩（Jean-Pierre Brun）
[美] 莫莉·西尔弗（Molly Silver） 著
王秀梅　林洁莹　译

走向破产

跨国反腐败资产追查的策略

Going for Broke

Insolvency Tools to Support Cross-Border
Asset Recovery in Corruption Cases

世界银行

法律出版社
LAW PRESS · CHINA
北京

Contents

目　　录

Boxes

方框

Acknowledgments

致 谢

Going for Broke: Insolvency Tools to Support Cross-Border Asset Recovery in Corruption Cases is published by the World Bank–United Nations Office on Drugs and Crime (UNODC) Stolen Asset Recovery Initiative (StAR) in collaboration with the Asset Recovery Committee of the Legal Practice Division of the International Bar Association and is produced by kind permission of the International Bar Association, London, United Kingdom.

The handbook was written and coordinated by Jean-Pierre Brun (Financial Integrity Unit), Molly Silver (Financial Integrity Unit), and practitioners from around the world. Yves Klein, Edward Davis, Martin Kenney, Elizabeth O'Brian, Lynne Gregory, Annette Escobar, Stephane Bonifassi, Victoire Chatelin, Rodrigo Kaysserlian, Andres Federico Martinez, and Will Paterson each contributed to the drafting of the handbook's chapters. Their time and expertise were invaluable in developing a practical tool to assist policy makers and practitioners interested in using insolvency tools to recover the proceeds of corruption.

The authors are especially grateful to Emile J. Van der Does de Willebois (Coordinator, StAR), Mahesh Uttamchandani (Practice Manager, FCI-EFI), and Alfonso Garcia Mora (Global Director, FCI-EFI) for their ongoing support and guidance.

The team benefited from many insightful comments during the peer review process, which was chaired by Yira Mascaro (Practice Manager, FCI-EFI). The peer reviewers were Anthony Fariello (Lead Counsel, World Bank), Fernando Dancausa (Senior Financial Sector Specialist, EFNFI), David Burdette (INSOL International), and James Maton (Cooley LLP).

The handbook also benefited from the guidance and contributions

《走向破产：跨国反腐败资产追查的策略》由世界银行—联合国毒品和犯罪问题办公室（UNODC）与国际律师协会法律实践司追赃委员会合作出版，由国际律师协会（英国）许可出版。

该手册由吉恩－皮尔里·布鲁恩（金融廉政部）、莫莉·西尔弗（金融廉政部）共同编写，同时得力于世界各地的实务工作者——伊夫·克莱因、爱德华·戴维斯、马丁·肯尼、伊丽莎白·奥布莱恩、琳恩·格雷戈里、安妮特·埃斯科巴、斯蒂芬·博尼法西、维克多·沙泰林、罗德里格·凯瑟琳以及安德列斯·费德里科等协作而成。其中，威尔·帕特森等对初稿各章节均有贡献，他们为开发此类工具指南投入了宝贵的时间和专业的知识，极大地帮助了相关决策者和从业人员运用破产策略追回腐败资产。

需要特别鸣谢如下人员的支持和指导，他们是：埃米尔·威勒博伊斯（协调员，StAR）、马赫什·北阿坎丹尼（业务经理，FCI-EFI）和阿方索·加西亚·莫拉（全球主管，FCI-EFI）。

同时，团队从同行评议的过程中汲取了诸多宝贵意见，他们是：伊拉·马斯卡洛（业务经理，FCI-EFI）、审稿人安东尼·法里洛（世界银行首席顾问）、费尔南多·丹卡萨（高级金融专家，EFNFI）、大卫·博迪特（INSOL 国际）和詹姆斯·莫顿（Cooley 有限责任公司）。

另外，下列人员也对本手册有诸多的贡献与指导：斯蒂芬·贝克

of Stephen Baker (Baker & Partners, Chairman of the International Bar Association Asset Recovery Subcommittee), Christopher Redmond (Redmond Law Firm), and Felicity Toube (South Square).

A special thanks to Keesook Viehweg (Program Assistant, FCI-EFI) for administrative support and Sara Balagh (Georgetown University Law Center) for assistance in editing the handbook.

（贝克律所合伙人、国际律师协会资产返还分会主席），克里斯托弗·雷蒙德（雷蒙德律师事务所），以及费力西蒂·图伯（南方分部）。

特别鸣谢基硕·维赫威格（项目助理，FCI–EFI）的行政支持以及莎拉·巴拉（乔治敦大学法律中心）对本册的编辑和协助。

About the Authors

关 于 作 者

Jean-Pierre Brun is a senior financial specialist at the World Bank. He worked as a prosecutor and investigative judge in France and as a director of forensic and fraud investigations at Deloitte Finance in Paris. In 2008, he joined the World Bank, where he works on anti–money laundering, terrorist financing, illicit financial flows, and stolen asset recovery, providing technical assistance and training to investigators, prosecutors, and judges dealing with financial crime. He is the lead author of various publications, including *Asset Recovery Handbook: A Guide for Practitioners*, *Public Wrongs–Private Actions: Civil Lawsuits to Recover Stolen Assets*, and *Identification and Quantification of the Proceeds of Corruption*.

Molly Silver is a consultant in the Finance, Competitiveness, and Innovation Group at the World Bank. She previously served as a presidential management fellow in the departments of Treasury and Defense. She then worked on international policy strategy at technology companies, including Facebook, Inc., and Palantir Technologies. Molly studied political science as an undergraduate at New York University and American foreign policy as a graduate student at the Johns Hopkins School of Advanced International Studies.

吉恩－皮尔里·布鲁恩（Jean-Pierre Brun）是世界银行的高级金融专家，曾在法国担任检察官、调查法官、德勤会计师事务所（巴黎）法证及欺诈调查部主管。2008年，他加入世界银行，从事反洗钱、恐怖分子融资、非法资金流动及腐败资产追查工作，为金融犯罪相关的调查人员、检察官和法官提供技术支持与培训。同时，还著有《资产追回手册：从业者指南》《公职过错，对私诉讼：提起民事诉讼，追回腐败资产》。

莫莉·西尔弗（Molly Silver），世界银行金融竞争力与创新小组顾问，曾担任美国财政部、国防部总统事务管理研究员。随后，在脸书和帕兰提尔科技等技术公司从事国际政策战略研究。莫莉在纽约大学攻读政治学专业，并在约翰霍普金斯大学国际高级研究院研究美国外交政策。

Abbreviations

缩　写

COMI	center of main interest
DOJ	Department of Justice
EBRD	European Bank for Reconstruction and Development
ECHR	European Convention on Human Rights
EU	European Union
FBI	Federal Bureau of Investigation
FCPA	Foreign Corrupt Practices Act
FIU	Financial Intelligence Unit
GDP	gross domestic product
GE	General Electric
IOH	insolvency office holder
MLAT	mutual legal assistance treaty
PEP	politically exposed person
PILA	private international law act
SEC	Securities and Exchange Commission
StAR	Stolen Asset Recovery Initiative
UNCAC	United Nations Convention against Corruption
UNCITRAL	United Nations Commission on International Trade Law

All monetary amounts are in U.S. dollars unless otherwise indicated.

COMI	主要权益中心
DOJ	司法部
EBRD	欧洲复兴开发银行
ECHR	《欧洲人权公约》
EU	欧盟
FBI	美国联邦调查局
FCPA	《反海外腐败法》
FIU	金融情报机构
GDP	国内生产总值
GE	通用电气
IOH	破产管理人员
MLAT	司法互助协定
PEP	政治公众人物
PILA	《瑞士国际私法》
SEC	美国证券交易委员会
StAR	被盗资产返还倡议
UNCAC	《联合国反腐败公约》
UNCITRAL	联合国国际贸易法委员会

除另有说明外，所有金额均以美元为单位。

Glossary

词 汇 表

Administrator: A representative who has been charged with rescuing a business, rather than closing it, unless the context requires otherwise.

Arbitration: A procedure under which parties agree to resolve a dispute by submitting it to one or more private persons who have no financial interest in the outcome. Arbitration clauses can be found in international contracts and bilateral investment treaties.

Assets: Assets of every kind, whether corporeal or incorporeal, movable or immovable, tangible or intangible, and legal documents or instruments evidencing title to or an interest in such assets [United Nations 2005, art. 2(e)]. The term is used interchangeably with "property."

Avoidance actions: The cancellation of transactions that took place during a period before the insolvency of an enterprise. Such transactions can be, for example, fraudulent, gratuitous, preferential, or outside the ordinary course of business.

Bankruptcy: The legal procedure for managing the insolvency of individuals and businesses.

Beneficial owner: The true owner of securities or property who is rightfully entitled to their benefits; the beneficial owner is often different from the title holder, which may be a financial institution holding securities on behalf of clients.

Bona fide purchaser: A third party with an interest in an asset subject to confiscation who did not know of the conduct giving rise to the confiscation or who, on learning of the conduct giving rise to confiscation, did all that reasonably could be expected under the circumstances to terminate the use of the asset. The term is used interchangeably with "innocent owner."

行政管理人员：如无特指，则指致力于挽救而非关闭企业的人员。

仲裁：指各方同意由一个或多个非利益相关人解决争议的程序。仲裁条款可在国际合同或双边投资条约中约定。

资产：任何有形或无形的动产或不动产的总称，以及证明对该资产具有所有权或其他权益的法律文书［联合国，2005 年第 2 条第（e）款］，可与“财产”互换使用。

撤销：取消企业在宣告破产之前一段时间内发生的交易。此类交易往往涉嫌欺诈、无偿转让或非正常低价出售等业务活动。

破产：管理企业和个人破产的法律程序。

实际受益人：证券或财产权益的真正所有权人；其不同于名义持有人，后者通常指代表客户持有证券的金融机构。

善意第三人：对被没收资产享有权益但对可能被没收不知情，或在获悉可能被没收后采取了当时可预期的一切手段停止动用该资产的第三方，可与“无辜所有人”互换使用。

Bribery: Any of the promising, offering, or giving of an undue advantage to a national, international, or foreign public official and the acceptance of an undue advantage by such an official.

Civil action: A noncriminal action brought to enforce, redress, or protect a private or civil right. An action brought by a private person is a private action; an action brought by a government is a public action. The term is used interchangeably with "lawsuit."

Civil forfeiture: The seizure by a government of property upon suspicion of its involvement in illegal activity.

Claimant: A party asserting an interest in an asset, including a third party, innocent owner, defendant, target, or offender. The term is used interchangeably with "plaintiff."

Collateral security: Security given in addition to a senior security, and subordinate to it, intended to guaranty its validity or convertibility or ensure its performance; if the senior security fails, the creditor may recover through recourse to the collateral security.

Compensation: The amount of money that places the victim in the financial position it would have held absent the corruption.

Confiscation: The permanent deprivation of assets by order of a court or other competent authority. The term is used interchangeably with "civil forfeiture." Persons or entities that hold an interest in the funds or other assets at the time of the confiscation lose all rights to those funds or assets.

Contempt of court: Any willful disobedience or disregard of a court order that interferes with a judge's ability to administer justice.

Contract: A covenant or agreement between two or more persons, with lawful consideration or cause, to do, or abstain from doing, some act.

Corruption: The act of an official or fiduciary who unlawfully and wrongfully uses his station or character to procure some benefit for himself

贿赂：任何向本国或外国公职人员承诺提供、实际提供不当利益，以及任何收受不当利益的行为。

民事诉讼：为执行、纠正或保护私人民事权利的非刑事诉讼。私人提起的为民事诉讼；公权力机关提起的为行政诉讼（公共诉讼）。该术语可与“诉讼”互换使用。

没收：对涉嫌从事非法活动而获得的资产进行收缴的行为。

申请人：主张资产权益的主体，包括第三方、善意第三人、辩护人、目标或侵权行为人（犯罪人）。该术语可与“原告”互换使用。

附加担保：除主要担保外的担保，旨在保证主要担保的效力。如果主要担保失效，债权人可通过附加担保追偿。

赔偿：对受害人因腐败行为而产生损失的救济，旨在恢复受害人应有的权益。

没收：法院或其他主管部门对资产进行的永久性剥夺。该术语可与“民事没收”互换使用。没收后，原资产所有人将丧失对该资产的全部权利。

藐视法庭：任何故意不服从、不尊重法庭命令或干扰法官的行为。

合同：两个或两个以上主体之间基于合法目的约定，做出或放弃某些行为的协议。

腐败：公职人员或受托人非法利用职权为自己或他人谋取利益，侵害他人权益的行为。

or for another person, contrary to duty and the rights of others.

Damages: Pecuniary compensation that may be recovered by a plaintiff for loss, injury, or harm caused by a breach of duty, including criminal wrongdoing or immoral conduct. Compensatory damages refer to the monetary harm to the economic position of the person who has suffered the damage. The loss of profits represents the profit that could reasonably have been expected but that was forfeited because of the vitiated contract or the breach.

Defendant: Any party who is required to answer the complaint of a plaintiff in a civil lawsuit before a court, or any party who has been formally charged or accused of violating a criminal statute.

Derivative action or suit: A lawsuit on behalf of a corporation by its shareholders against a director or officer for damages for failure of duty or mismanagement.

Embezzlement: Fraudulent appropriation to his own use or benefit by a clerk, agent, trustee, public officer, or other person acting in a fiduciary capacity of public funds or property entrusted to him by another.

Enforcement (civil judgment): The collection of the value stipulated in a judgment against an asset held by a defendant.

Estate: An interest in land or any other property.

Forum: A court of justice or judicial tribunal; a place of jurisdiction; a place where a remedy is sought; a place of litigation.

Frozen asset: An asset that cannot be sold or used as legal leverage owing to a legal ruling. The asset cannot be sold or used for security until the ruling is satisfied or reversed.

Gag order: An order of a court that restricts the dissemination of information about a pending case.

In personam: Latin for “directed toward a particular person.” In a

损害： 因滥用职权（既包括违反法律也包括违背道德的行为）而造成的损害，可据此要求赔偿。补偿性赔偿金是为弥补受害人经济状况的直接损失。利润性损失则是指可合理预期但因违约或违规而损失的经济收益。

被告： 应在民事诉讼中回应原告指控诉求的一方，或因违反刑法而被正式指控的一方。

派生诉讼：（又称代位诉讼）因公司管理人员怠于履行诉讼职责，公司股东为了公司利益代表公司提起的诉讼。

挪用公款： 代理人、受托人、公职人员或公司职员以欺诈手段利用职权将公共资金或财产挪为己用的行为。

强制执行（民事判决）： 依据判决对被告持有的资产进行征收或执行。

财产： 土地或其他资产所产生的权益。

法庭： 寻求司法救济或诉讼的场所。

资产冻结： 根据司法裁决禁止出售或处分（用作合法杠杆）的资产。在履行裁决或裁决被撤销前，该资产无法用于出售或担保。

禁止披露令： 对待决案件相关信息限制披露的法令。

特定人（拉丁语）： 在诉讼或没收程序中，相关措施所针对的特

confiscation or lawsuit, a legal action against a specific person.

In rem: Latin for "against a thing." In a confiscation or lawsuit, a legal action against a specific asset.

Insolvency: The conditions that support proceedings in court (including liquidation and reorganization) and out of court (including receivership) to conduct the winding up of a company that is bankrupt or was created for fraudulent purposes.

International asset recovery: The process by which the proceeds of corruption transferred abroad are recovered and repatriated to the country from which they were taken or to their rightful owners.

Lawsuit: A private action between two persons in a court of law in which a plaintiff who claims to have incurred loss as a result of a defendant's actions seeks a legal or equitable remedy. The term is used interchangeably with "civil action."

Liquidation: The sale of a debtor's assets, the proceeds of which are used for the benefit of creditors.

Money laundering: The act of taking money obtained illegally and investing it to make it appear as if it was obtained legally.

Mutual legal assistance treaty: The process by which jurisdictions seek and provide assistance in gathering information, intelligence, and evidence for investigations; in implementing provisional measures; and in enforcing foreign orders and judgments.

Personal claim: A claim against a person. A plaintiff who has suffered economic damages can demand to be paid or compensated from the assets of the person who caused the damage.

Prima facie: Legal term meaning that a proposition or claim is accepted as correct until proven otherwise.

Proceeds of crime: Any asset derived from or obtained, directly or

定个体。

特定物（拉丁语）：在诉讼或没收程序中，相关措施所针对的特定资产。

破产：实现公司破产或对以欺诈为目的而成立的公司进行清算的一系列程序，包括法定的破产重整和清算程序，以及其他非法定程序如破产管理等程序。

跨国资产返还：从国外转移腐败收益的过程，将相关收益追回并返还其来源国或合法所有者的行动。

诉讼：特指私权利主体之间在法院进行的争议解决、蒙受损失的原告方寻求司法救济的行为。该术语可与“民事诉讼”互换适用。

清算：变卖债务人的资产用于清偿债权人的行为。

洗钱：对非法所得进行再投资再流转，以达到使其看似合法的目的。

司法互助协定：各司法管辖区之间寻求司法互助的条约，旨在情报搜集、证据调查、信息共享以及在外国判决、法令执行等方面实现互助。

个人诉讼：针对个人的赔偿请求。蒙受经济损失的原告可要求从相关侵权人的资产中获得损害赔偿。

表面证据：法律术语，指除非存在可靠的相抗证据，否则被初步推定成立的证据。

犯罪所得：任何通过犯罪行为直接或间接获得的收益，在多数国

indirectly, through the commission of an offense. In most jurisdictions, commingled assets are included.

Proprietary claim: A claim by the beneficial owner of a piece of property or an asset asking the court to return the item or its equivalent value.

Provisional measure: The temporary prohibition against the transfer, conversion, disposition, or movement of assets or temporary assumption of custody or control of assets pursuant to an order of a court or other competent authority. The term is used interchangeably with "freezing (of an asset)," "restraint," and "seizure."

Receivership: The process through which all property subject to claims is placed under the control of an independent receiver, who operates the company or manages its assets in event of a receivership. Some contracts between borrowers and creditors authorize the appointment of a receiver if a secured creditor is not being paid or if a lender finds the company's management practices dubious. Court action is not required.

Recognition (civil judgment): The acceptance by one court of the conclusion of another court without hearing evidence or engaging in an independent decisionmaking process. The second court issues its own judgment stating substantially the same conclusion.

Reorganization: The restructuring of the debt obligations of a bankrupt or insolvent company. During reorganization, the debtor retains ownership of its assets and continues business operations. The debtor renegotiates the terms of its debt obligations to creditors.

Restitution: A court order directing the (1) return of an item to its legal owner, (2) restoration of damaged property to its original state, or (3) payment of compensation to a victim.

Restraining order: A mandatory injunction issued by a judge or a

家的法律中包括混合资产。

所有权请求：实际权利人对相关资产的主张，可要求法院归还原物或赔偿等价资产。

临时措施：法院或其他主管机构做出的临时禁止资产转移、转换、处置或承担资产的保管或控制的措施。该术语可与“冻结”“限制”“扣押”互换使用。

破产管理：将涉诉资产交由独立破产管理人控制、经营和管理的程序。在债权人未获得相关权益或认为公司的经营管理不善时，可由债权人和债务人共同约定破产管理人，无需法院确定。

承认（民事判决）：无需参与听证或庭审而对其他法院所做判决效力的认可。一般表现为以本院的名义发布与之前判决相同的决定。

重整：对破产公司的债务进行重新整理的程序。在重整期间，债务人仍然保留其资产的所有权与经营权。债务人与债权人可重新协商相关债权债务的条款。

复权：依据法院的指示做出下列行为：（1）将财产归还合法所有权人；（2）将受损财产恢复原状；（3）向受害者支付相应赔偿金。

禁制令：由法官或法院作出的强制性命令，禁止任何人在没收程

court that restrains any person from using or disposing of the assets named in the order, pending the outcome of confiscation proceedings. Court authorization is generally required, but some jurisdictions permit restraining orders to be issued by prosecutors or other law enforcement authorities.

Seizure: Taking physical possession of a targeted asset. Court orders are generally required, but in some jurisdictions law enforcement agencies are entitled to seize assets.

Tort: A civil wrong, giving rise to a claim for damages.

Tracing: The process by which a claimant demonstrates the disposition of his property, identifies its proceeds, and justifies his claim that the proceeds can properly be regarded as representing his property.

Unjust enrichment: The principle according to which a person should not be permitted to unfairly enrich himself at the expense of another, but should be required to make restitution for property or benefits unjustly received.

Winding up: The process of settling the accounts and liquidating the assets of a partnership or company, for the purpose of making a distribution and dissolving the concern.

Witness: Someone who, either voluntarily or under compulsion, provides testimonial evidence, either oral or written, of what he or she knows or claims to know about the matter before a court or before an official authorized to take such testimony. Evidence provided by witnesses, including expert witnesses, is frequently important in both civil and criminal asset recovery cases.

序结束前使用或处置指定资产。该命令一般由法院授权，但在某些国家，也允许检察官或其他执法部门发布限制令。

扣押：对目标资产的实际控制和占有，一般需要法院授权，但在某些国家的立法中，其他执法部门也有扣押权。

侵权：民事纠纷中，因过错引发损害赔偿的行为。

追查：原告（申请人）确定财产并证明对该财产应享有合法处置权的过程。

不当得利：通过损害他人从而获取利益的行为，不被法律所允许，应当要求得利人返还不法财产或进行赔偿。

清算：合伙企业或公司结清账户、盘点资产的过程，旨在解决最终权益分配的问题。

证人：自愿或非自愿地在法庭或其他权威机构前，提供口头或书面的知情信息的人。在民事和刑事资产追查案件中，包括专家在内的证人证言都很重要。

Introduction

简　　介

In her opening statement to the 22nd session of the Human Rights Council in March 2013, Navi Pillay, High Commissioner for Human Rights, stated:

> Let us be clear. Corruption kills. The money stolen through corruption every year is enough to feed the world's hungry 80 times over. Nearly 870 million people go to bed hungry every night, many of them children; corruption denies them their right to food, and, in some cases, their right to life. Bribes and theft swell the total cost of projects to provide safe drinking water and sanitation around the world by as much as 40 percent.[1]

Corruption is the abuse of entrusted power for private gain. It hurts everyone whose life, livelihood, and happiness depend on the integrity of people in a position of authority. Corruption holds back economic development, prevents a free market from operating for businesses and consumers, and further exploits already marginalized groups. In the words of leading anticorruption expert Richard Cassin, "[vulnerable] people—hated because they look or sound different, worship another God, or once came from somewhere else—rely on the rule of law for their safety and survival. When the rule of law is replaced by graft, the outcome for the weakest among us is too often catastrophic."[2]

Economist Daniel Kaufmann has estimated that 2 percent of global GDP is lost to bribery alone every year. But these corrupt proceeds may not be gone forever—nations can use asset recovery to fight corruption, restoring stolen funds to the people for sustainable development and deterring further corruption. Because assets stolen in corruption schemes are often moved to different jurisdictions, recovery efforts demand international

人权事务高级专员纳维·皮莱（Navi Pillay），在 2013 年 3 月第二十二届联合国人权理事会致开幕词时提道：

> 我们需要清楚一点：腐败是极具破坏力的。每年因腐败而流失的资产足以使全世界饥民填饱肚子 80 遍。每晚有近 8.7 亿人饿着肚子睡觉，其中有很多是儿童。腐败剥夺了他们的食物权，甚至是生命权。腐败犯罪造成全球安全饮用水和卫生设施的总成本增加了 40%。[1]

腐败，这种利用职务之便谋取私利的行为，大大伤及了民生。它让民众的生计和幸福交由当权者的品德决定。它阻碍了经济发展和自由市场，并进一步剥削了弱势群体。用知名反腐专家理查德·卡辛（Richard Cassin）的话来说，“弱势群体处境艰难，他们信仰上帝或者其他能使其安身立命的法则。可当法治被腐败玷污时，给民众中最弱势群体带来的，往往是灾难性的后果”。[2]

经济学家丹尼尔·考夫曼（Daniel Kaufmann）估计过，每年仅受贿造成的损失就占全球生产总值的 2%，但所幸，这些贪腐收益并非完全不可追回。各国正利用资产返还来打击腐败，将流失资产归还民众以实现可持续发展，并进一步遏制腐败。由于腐败犯罪中流失的资产通常被转移到不同的国家，由不同的司法制度管辖，因此，追查就需要国际社会通力合作。2003 年的《联合国反腐败公约》（UNCAC）制

cooperation. The international framework governing such cooperation is laid down in the 2003 United Nations Convention Against Corruption (UNCAC), which went into force in 2005. The first article of the extensive chapter on asset recovery declares the return of assets "a fundamental principle of the convention" and obligates states that are party to the convention to "afford one another the widest measure of cooperation" (United Nations 2004).

Despite the great advances in international efforts to recover assets from corrupt officials since the UNCAC went into effect, there is still much work to do. Governments often use criminal prosecution and confiscation, as well as civil lawsuits. However, barriers to successful asset recovery are numerous. They include the lack of political will to investigate and charge corrupt politicians; a dearth of capacity, expertise, and resources to pursue cases or cooperate internationally; and the existence of a global financial system that enables corrupt officials to rapidly move and conceal illicit funds.[3]

These challenges can impede justice in many corruption cases. This book offers a rarely used way to recover the proceeds of corruption—insolvency proceedings—thus contributing to the development of an additional tool for the realization of the UNCAC's principle on asset recovery.

As described in the case study in box I.1, victims of corruption may be able to use insolvency processes to gain control of assets held by or on behalf of debtors. The process typically follows a standard pattern, although it may vary by jurisdiction. An insolvency representative is appointed to take control of the debtor and its assets and can ask the debtor's depository bank for information on the debtor's bank accounts and the debtor's counsel and accountant for files and records. (Once appointed, the insolvency representative is entitled to that information; attorney-client privilege

定了相关国际合作的框架。在资产追查的条款中，第一条就宣布“将资产归还，是本公约的一项基本原则”，同时责成各公约缔约国应“相互承担最广泛的合作措施”（联合国 2004）。

尽管自《联合国反腐败公约》生效以来，国际腐败资产返还的成效取得了长足的进步，但仍存在许多问题有待解决。各国动用了刑事诉讼、民事诉讼、没收等手段，但返还过程依旧障碍重重，具体包括：缺乏调查、指控腐败官员的政治魄力，缺乏国际合作办案的能力、资源和专业知识，以及全球化的金融体系使转移和藏匿腐败资金变得极为容易。[3]

这些挑战都可能在众多腐败案件中妨碍司法公正。而本书另辟蹊径，提供了一种新兴的追查腐败流失资产的工具，即破产程序，以实现《联合国反腐败公约》资产返还的原则。

在方框 I.1 的案例中，腐败案件的受害人能够运用破产程序控制由债务人或其代理人所持有的资产。该过程一般都可依照标准程序，破产程序虽然因国家而异，但其不仅可以任命破产管理人处置债务人的资产，还可要求债务人的银行、律师、会计师等提供相关文件和记录。（破产管理人一旦被任命，即有权获得相关信息，相关机构不再具有客户信息保密的抗辩权。）破产管理人有权解雇董事会、董事长、董事会成员和总裁等，财务官、秘书等不再具有任何权限。破产管理人有权采取措施追回或撤销先前的不当让利或欺诈交易。

no longer applies.) The insolvency representative can fire and terminate employees—the board of directors, the chairman of the board, the president, the treasurer, and the secretary no longer have any authority. The insolvency representative has standing to bring actions to recover preferences and to recover fraudulent conveyances.

The terms "bankruptcy" and "insolvency" have different definitions in different legal systems and are sometimes used interchangeably. In this publication, insolvency is used more broadly as the overarching term to describe court proceedings that include liquidation and reorganization and out-of-court proceedings such as receivership. The term insolvency also refers to bankruptcy unless another meaning is indicated; for example, bankruptcy would be used to refer to the insolvency of an individual as opposed to a corporation. The terms "receiver" and "receivership" refer to the process of taking control of assets or businesses for the benefit of a particular creditor as opposed to a body of creditors; a process designed to preserve assets; or the status of a business pending the resolution of a particular proceeding or the occurrence of a specified event. The term "administrator" refers to a representative who has been charged with rescuing a business, rather than closing it, unless the context otherwise requires.

In this book, the term "insolvency representative" refers to the person fulfilling the range of functions that may be performed in any kind of insolvency proceeding, irrespective of his or her specific goal (liquidation or reorganization). Insolvency representatives may, under local law, be called "administrators," "trustees," "supervisors," "receivers," "curators," "official" or "judicial" managers, or "commissioners." See UNCITRAL (2004, 174) and Flores and Inacio (2016). Insolvency proceedings typically require the replacement, in whole or in part, of the debtor's management authority.

英文中“bankruptcy”和“insolvency”都有“破产”的含义，在很多时候二者也可以互换使用，但在不同的法律体系中，二者的含义仍有所区别。在本书中，“insolvency”通常更广泛地指代法院开展的破产程序，包括破产清算、重整以及其他非法定的破产接管等。如无特别说明，“insolvency”可以替换“bankruptcy”使用，但“bankruptcy”有时指代个人破产而非公司破产。此外，“接收人”（receiver）和“接管人”（receivership）都是代表某一特定债权人而非全体债权人控制资产和业务的人员，是为了在程序终结前保护资产。除非上下文另有提及，否则“行政管理人员”（administrator）一词指挽救企业而非关闭企业的代表。

在本书中，“破产管理人”一词指的是在各类破产程序（清算或重整）中履行职责的人。根据不同国家的法律，破产管理人可以被称为“破产代表”“受托人”“主管”“接收人”“监管人”“公职人员”“司法专员”等。参见联合国国际贸易法委员会（2004，174），以及弗雷罗斯和伊瑞希奥的著作（2016）。破产程序通常要求债务人的管理权限被部分或全部替换。任命后，破产管理人对债务人的业务和资产拥有绝对控制权。（欧洲复兴开发银行 2014）

BOX I.1 Case Study on the Appointment of Insolvency Representatives

Federal Republic of Brazil and Municipality of São Paulo v. Durant International Ltd. and Kildare Finance Ltd. [a]

Paulo Maluf, the former mayor of São Paulo, was convicted of committing fraud against the taxpayers of Brazil and São Paolo. Authorities found that he stole approximately 20 percent of the funds that were intended for the construction of a highway around the city. While in office, he ordered the head contractor on the highway project to inflate invoices, which enabled him to siphon funds without causing alarm. Other false invoices were issued by subcontractors, many of whom did no work. A large amount of cash was generated, laundered through dolleiros (unlicensed money brokers), and then deposited into bank accounts in several U.S. states. From there, the proceeds were transferred to a bank account in New York, and some were transferred to Jersey, where they were held in a complicated trust as well as in two private companies—Durant International Ltd. (Durant) and Kildare Finance Ltd. (Kildare). Some of the funds remained in bank accounts in Jersey, but the bulk was invested through unit trusts in shares in a publicly traded company in Brazil.

Durant and Kildare were incorporated in the British Virgin Islands. After uncovering the scheme, the governments of Brazil and São Paulo sued Durant and Kildare for their involvement in the fraud. They alleged that Durant and Kildare knowingly received the proceeds of a public corruption scheme and dishonestly assisted in the fraud. Brazil and São Paulo won, and the Jersey court ordered Durant and Kildare to pay $30 million to Brazil and São Paulo. The plaintiffs recovered $2.1 million from bank accounts in Jersey.

Brazil and São Paulo were still owed substantial amounts by Durant and Kildare, both of which refused to pay the Jersey judgment. Brazil and São Paulo used a statutory demand for creditor's rights in bankruptcy, an insolvency tool, to recover what was still owed to them. They applied to the British Virgin Islands court for insolvency representatives to be appointed over Durant and Kildare. The British Virgin Islands court agreed and appointed two partners of a large accounting firm as insolvency representatives. The insolvency representatives were recognized in the Jersey court and took control of the trust structure. They have wide powers to demand access to records and to interview witnesses. Because Durant and Kildare have been declared insolvent, the insolvency representatives retain control of the companies and all the powers its directors and officers previously held, as a matter of law.

a. [2015] UKPC 35.

方框 I.1 案例分析：破产管理人的任命

巴西联邦政府和圣保罗市诉杜兰特国际有限公司和基尔代尔金融有限公司案[a]

保罗·马尔福，圣保罗市前市长，被指控贪污了圣保罗城郊高速公路20%的建设资金。任职期间，他命令公路项目的总承包商虚开发票，暗中牟利。许多分包商也虚开了发票，而他们大部分根本没有参与该建设项目。贪污的大量现金，交由无证银行经纪人多雷罗斯进行洗钱，然后存入美国多个州的银行账户，一部分转移到纽约，另一部分转移到泽西岛，再以复杂的信托方式委托杜兰特国际有限公司（以下简称杜兰特）和基尔代尔金融有限公司（以下简称基尔代尔）持有。还有一部分留在泽西岛的银行，但大部分资金通过信托的方式用以购买一家巴西上市公司的股票。

杜兰特和基尔代尔两家公司在维京群岛注册，在计划败露之后，巴西和圣保罗市政府起诉两家公司涉嫌欺诈。诉称杜兰特和基尔代尔在明知该收益为贪腐所得的情况下，还提供洗钱协助，并最终胜诉。法院下令两家公司向巴西和圣保罗市政府赔付 3000 万美元，但原告方从泽西岛的银行账号中仅成功追回 210 万美元。

面对大量欠款，杜兰特和基尔代尔两家公司拒绝履行法院判决。于是巴西和圣保罗市政府通过申请破产成为债权人的方式追回欠款。他们向维京群岛法院提出申请，要求法院指定杜兰特和基尔代尔两家公司的破产管理人。维京群岛法院予以支持并委任一家大型会计师事务所的两名合伙人为破产管理人。破产管理人经过法院授权控制了信托机构，享有查阅资料、会见证人等诸多权利。由于杜兰特和基尔代尔公司已宣告破产，因此，破产管理人依法获得对公司、公司董事及其高级管理人的全部权力。

a. [2015] UKPC 35.

Upon appointment, the insolvency representative has absolute control over the business affairs of the debtor and the debtor's assets (EBRD 2014).

Objective

This guidebook is intended to inform policy makers, public officials, and those who have been entrusted with recovering their nations' stolen assets how insolvency can be used to pursue proceeds of corruption. It may also serve as a quick reference for other practitioners—insolvency professionals, auditors, financial institutions, in-house counsel, and others who deal with corruption.

Although there is no guarantee of success, the use of insolvency in asset recovery provides numerous benefits not readily available in other recovery frameworks. As with any asset recovery effort, however, there are hurdles and challenges.

The insolvency mechanisms described in this book can be used against both bribe takers and bribe payers. Many legal systems have comparable provisions in place, such as the ability to petition for the bankruptcy of an individual, the insolvency of a corporation, and the reversal or voiding of past transactions within a specified time after the initiation of insolvency procedures. Although not all jurisdictions offer equivalent procedures, an in-depth analysis of all jurisdictions is beyond the scope of this publication.[4] The authors speak of insolvency and bankruptcy in general, giving examples of significant differences among jurisdictions when relevant.

Scope

This publication focuses on insolvency as an additional civil remedy for the asset recovery practitioner in large corruption investigations and proceedings. The recovery of proceeds of corruption is often sought through

目标

该指南旨在向决策者、各国政府以及受托追查国家流失资产的相关机构提供指导，说明如何利用破产程序追查腐败资产。同时，也可为破产专业人员、审计师、金融机构的顾问以及其他从事反腐败工作的人员提供快速参考。

同其他资产追查手段一样，破产程序也存在诸多障碍和挑战，虽然无法确保万无一失，但仍不妨碍它与其他措施相比具有独特优势。

本书所介绍的破产制度可同时适用于受贿人与行贿人。许多法律制度都有类似的规定，如个人破产的条件、公司破产的条件以及在启动破产程序后指定时间内撤销先前交易的授权等。尽管各国规定不尽相同，但对差异的分析不在本书的讨论范围之内。[4] 对于书中时常谈到的个人破产和公司破产，作者会在后续相关部分具体解释二者的显著差异。

研究范围

本书聚焦破产，将其作为反腐败从业人员在调查和起诉大型腐败案件时可采用的一种救济措施。通过刑事起诉、民事起诉、没收等手段追查腐败资产。尽管破产作为一种手段不是十全十美的，但破产作

criminal prosecution and confiscation or civil lawsuits. Under appropriate circumstances, an insolvency proceeding can also be an effective mechanism, albeit one with advantages and disadvantages. Insolvency is most likely to be beneficial when bribes and stolen funds have been routed through a special-purpose vehicle for concealment and laundering. Although reference may be made to other civil remedies and theories of recovery when appropriate, this guidebook does not address noninsolvency civil remedies or actions.

This guidebook addresses insolvency-related investigations and litigation for asset recovery stemming from official corruption. We focus in particular on common law systems, such as the United Kingdom, the United States, and many offshore common law jurisdictions, which offer the clearest path for asset recovery through insolvency proceedings. We also refer to civil law systems, such as those in France and Switzerland, whose legal systems often deal with illicit financial flows.

Several offshore jurisdictions are relevant in international insolvency cases and feature prominently in this book. Companies in the British Virgin Islands are frequently used in offshore structures, as are those in other offshore jurisdictions that specialize in corporate formation, such as Bermuda, the Cayman Islands, the Isle of Man, and Panama. Crown Dependencies, including Guernsey and Jersey, which specialize in trusts, feature in the discussion of trustees. The court system of the British Virgin Islands in particular has robust protections for those who have been the victims of fraud and corruption. Similarly, the courts in Jersey also offer protection to victims of fraud through the misuse of financial services. Significant expertise has emerged in Jersey and the British Virgin Islands on these matters, and we highlight several cases that demonstrate the progress made.

为一种有效机制，当腐败资产通过专门的渠道被隐匿和洗钱时，能发挥出极大的作用。除此之外，也可适当参考其他法律救济措施和追查方法，但并不属于本书的研究范围。

本指南重点介绍与破产相关的调查手段和法律规定，以追查腐败资产。我们尤其关注英美法系国家以及许多离岸普通法辖区所运用的破产程序实现资产追查时清晰的操作路径。同时，我们也关注大陆法系，特别是与转移非法资金相关的立法，如法国和瑞士的相关立法。

本书还将着重介绍部分与国际破产案件相关的离岸司法辖区。其中，英属维京群岛的公司常被用作离岸皮包公司，而其他诸如百慕大、开曼群岛、马恩岛和巴拿马等专门用作公司注册地；又如从事信托业务的格恩西岛、泽西岛，曾因受王室成员所托而引发关注。此外，维京群岛和泽西岛的司法体系都为金融诈骗、贪污腐败案件的受害人提供了有力的法律保护。在这类问题上，他们都已经积累了宝贵的经验，我们会重点介绍一些成功的案例。

This publication should provide the reader with a solid understanding of how insolvency procedures can effectively be employed to either complement an existing asset recovery action, whether civil or criminal, or act as a stand-alone procedure for recovery. The guidebook is not designed to be a detailed compendium of law and practices and should be read by practitioners in tandem with the rules of their jurisdiction. The authors hope that practitioners in any jurisdiction affected by corruption will find useful references and ideas for their areas of practice.

Methodology

This publication identifies potential methods of asset recovery in insolvency proceedings. Although the book incorporates examples of legislation, concepts, and practices that are relevant for both civil law and common law jurisdictions, as well as developed or emerging countries, some jurisdictions (including the United Kingdom and some other common law jurisdictions) feature the world's most developed institutional insolvency systems, including highly skilled judges and insolvency practitioners.

Although tools that have been successfully applied in the United Kingdom and other common law jurisdictions are not necessarily applicable in other legal systems, most jurisdictions, including civil law jurisdictions, have equivalent concepts or concepts that enable comparable results. These tools are described as comprehensively as possible for the use of jurisdictions establishing legislation or implementing their own systems.

In addition, applying the tools in some jurisdictions may be challenging. This publication does not recommend legal reforms or mandate implementation of specific tools, but highlights potential strategies or practices that may be similar to those allowed in other legal systems or in other cases of asset recovery. The publication also recognizes that

本书致力于让读者对如何有效地运用破产程序，无论是独立运用还是作为其他资产追查手段（刑事或民事）的补充，都能够有深刻的了解。该指南并非只作为详细的司法实践纲要，还需要从业者结合各国法律规范一并阅读。作者希望各国的反腐败从业人员都能够从中获益。

方法

本书提供了破产程序追查资产的几种可能方法。尽管囊括了大陆法系、英美法系、发达国家、新兴国家的大量法律、概念和案例等，但只有一部分国家和地区（主要是英国和其他一些英美法国家）具备当前最先进的破产制度，并拥有高水平的法官和破产专业人员。

尽管在英国和其他英美法国家的成功并不代表在所有法律体系中都适用，但绝大多数国家的立法（包括大陆法系）都有类似的规定，这些工具被认为可以广泛运用于已有相关立法或实践经验的国家。

此外，对一些国家而言，运用这些方法仍具挑战性，本书不建议专门进行法律修订或强行使用特定方法，而是建议相似度较高的法律体系可以运用这些策略。本书还认识到，破产程序的主要目的是维护破产法所保护的相关利益（包括但不限于债权人的利益），通过破产管理人和其他专业人士的判断，追回腐败资产。但并不代表这些专业人

the main purpose of insolvency proceedings is to preserve the interests protected by insolvency legislation (including, but not limited to, creditors' interests). Using the powers of insolvency representatives or other relevant practitioners to identify, trace, and recover proceeds of corruption does not imply that these practitioners should be regarded as enforcing criminal law.

Overview of Chapters

Chapter 1 describes the role of insolvency representatives in formal insolvency processes, under which they can be appointed by commercial courts and judges to administer or liquidate the estate of a natural or legal person whose liabilities exceed his or its assets. The appointment of an insolvency representative typically triggers a moratorium on any further transfer of assets. If a bankrupt entity has assets within the jurisdiction in which it was declared bankrupt, the insolvency process will prevent any further dissipation of the bankrupt estate. Chapter 1 details the effect of such a moratorium internationally, as well as the investigatory powers of the representative.

Chapter 2 outlines the investigative measures that can be used in insolvency procedures. This chapter examines the tools, both statutory and nonstatutory, available to insolvency representatives, including powers of examination of individuals, discovery or delivery of documents, and orders for the provision of specified information. The chapter also discusses ancillary relief designed to maintain the integrity of an investigation, such as seal and gag orders, as well as the powers of courts to dispense with requirements to give notice to parties and to hear matters without notice and in camera.

Chapter 3 discusses how to recover assets from bribe takers through insolvency proceedings. Although the focus is typically on bribe payers,

员能取代司法人员。

章节内容概览

第一章介绍了破产管理人在破产程序中的作用。根据这些程序，商事法院的法官可以委托其管理或清算资不抵债的自然人或法人的财产。在任命破产管理人之后可叫停资产的进一步转移。如果破产企业在破产宣告地拥有资产，破产程序也能防止相关资产的进一步损耗。第一章还详细介绍了国际上施行临时措施的成效和破产管理人的调查权责。

第二章主要介绍了可用于破产程序的调查措施。本章研究了破产管理人可用的法定工具与非法定工具，包括个人调查、文书查阅以及提供其他特定信息的权力。本章还讨论了其他能够确保调查公平公正的辅助性救济措施，如保密、禁止披露以及法院可在不通知或未通知当事人的情况下的秘密听证权。

第三章首先讨论了如何通过破产程序向受贿人追回资产。虽然通常重点关注行贿人，但许多由中间机构协助完成的行贿，也可以通过

agents and facilitators, who are often used as intermediaries to solicit and pay bribes, can also be targeted through the insolvency process. The chapter examines the various causes of action against parties, both criminal and civil, explaining the difference between those causes of action that accrue prior to the insolvency and those that accrue after. The chapter details the options available to insolvency representatives, including taking over the conduct of existing proceedings, commencing proceedings on behalf of the estate, and assignment of causes of action in exchange for value. Derivative actions are also explained and discussed, as are issues concerning the legal standing of insolvency representatives to bring particular types of actions. Finally, the chapter examines the notion of piercing the corporate veil.

Chapter 4 explains the implications of legal privilege in insolvency proceedings in the United Kingdom, the United States, and France. The rules on legal professional privilege can impair the insolvency representative's ability to obtain or use information. Common law jurisdictions have historically recognized privilege as a fundamental principle of justice and grant wide-ranging protection against the disclosure of both lawyer-client communications and, when litigation is contemplated, a wider class of documents with third parties.

Chapter 5 deals with additional issues in the use of insolvency proceedings for asset recovery, including critical differences between developed and developing jurisdictions and cross-border issues that may arise when corrupt assets or defendants are located in other jurisdictions. Legal frameworks are available to ensure the enforcement of insolvency legislation or orders made by the jurisdiction of the insolvency proceeding and the resolution of insolvencies that involve two or more jurisdictions. This chapter also explains how to address the conflict between state confiscation of criminal assets and the recovery of funds through insolvency

破产程序加以确定。其次，探讨了对不同当事人提起不同种类诉讼（民事或刑事）的案由，并对比了在破产前和破产后不同案由的差别。再次，详细介绍了破产管理人的策略选择，包括接管现有资产、代表债权人启动程序、依据不同案由追查收益等。同时，还讨论了派生诉讼和各诉讼种类的法律地位。最后，本章考察了“揭开公司面纱”的概念。

第四章介绍了英国、美国和法国的破产程序中一些与信息保密相关的抗辩特权的含义。这些特权会妨碍破产管理人获取、使用信息。英美法系自古以来就将此类保密特权视为司法的一项基本原则，并给予广泛的保护，以防止律师、当事人的信息以及其与第三方之间的文件在尚未提起诉讼时被提前泄露。

第五章讨论了运用破产程序追查资产可能涉及的其他问题，包括发达国家与发展中国家之间司法体系的重大差异，以及腐败资产或被告人位于其他国家时出现的跨国追查问题。当破产申请地和执行地分属不同国家或地区时，各国或各地区法律可以确保相关破产法令的执行。本章还解释了如何通过破产程序解决犯罪资产没收和返还之间的冲突，并提出了在此过程中针对恶意拖延的应对策略。

proceedings and proposes tactics for dealing with the delays that arise in criminal proceedings.

Notes

1. Opening Statement by Navi Pillay, High Commissioner for Human Rights. Panel on "The Negative Impact of Corruption on Human Rights" (March 27, 2013), www.ohchr.org/Documents/Issues/Development/GoodGovernance/Corruption/HRCaseAgainstCorruption.pdf.

2. Richard L. Cassin, "Rampant Graft and the Risk of Atrocities: Are Whistleblower Reward Programs Really a Good Idea?" *The FCPA Blog* (May 15, 2014) (accessed December 26, 2018). http://www.fcpablog.com/blog/2014/5/15/rampant-graft-and-the-risk-of-atrocities.html.

3. For a detailed discussion of the types of problems encountered in international asset recovery, see Brun et al. (2011).

4. See appendix A for jurisdiction-specific analyses of a selection of relevant procedures and regulations.

References

Brun, Jean-Pierre, Gabriele Dunker, Larissa Alanna Gray, Melissa Panjer, Richard John Power, and Kevin Mark Stephenson. 2011. *Barriers to Asset Recovery*. Washington, DC: World Bank.

EBRD (European Bank for Reconstruction and Development). 2014. *Assessment of Insolvency Office Holders: Review of the Profession in the EBRD Region*. London: EBRD.

Flores, Marta, and Emmanuelle Inacio. 2016. "Report on the Regulation of Insolvency Office Holders", Insolvency Office Holders Forum, INSOL Europe, May 4.

IMF (International Monetary Fund). 2016. "Corruption: Costs and

注释

1. 人权事务高级专员纳维·皮莱（Navi Pillay）的开幕词《腐败对人权的负面影响》（2013 年 3 月 27 日），www.ohchr.org/Documents/Issues/Development/GoodGovernance/Corruption/HRCaseAgainstCorruption.pdf。

2. 理查德·卡辛（Richard L. Cassin）:《贪腐的猖獗与风险：吹哨人奖励计划真的是个好主意吗?》，FCPA 博客（2014 年 5 月 15 日，访问时间：2018 年 12 月 26 日），http://www.fcpablog.com/blog/2014/5/15/rampant-graft-and-the-risk-of-atrocities.html。

3. 有关国际资产追回中遇到的各类问题的详细探讨，请参见布伦等（2011）。

4. 了解对不同国家相关破产程序选择的具体分析可参见附录 A。

参考文献

Brun, Jean-Pierre, Gabriele Dunker, Larissa Alanna Gray, Melissa Panjer, Richard John Power, and Kevin Mark Stephenson. 2011. *Barriers to Asset Recovery*. Washington, DC: World Bank.

EBRD (European Bank for Reconstruction and Development). 2014. *Assessment of Insolvency Office Holders: Review of the Profession in the EBRD Region*. London: EBRD.

Flores, Marta, and Emmanuelle Inacio. 2016. "Report on the Regulation of Insolvency Office Holders", Insolvency Office Holders Forum, INSOL Europe, May 4.

IMF (International Monetary Fund). 2016. "Corruption: Costs and

Mitigating Strategies." IMF Staff Discussion Note No. 16/05, IMF, Washington, DC.

UNCITRAL (United Nations Commission on International Trade Law). 2004. *Legislative Guide on Insolvency Law*. Vienna: UNCITRAL.

United Nations. 2004. *United Nations Convention Against Corruption.* Vienna: United Nations Office on Drugs and Crime.

Mitigating Strategies." IMF Staff Discussion Note No. 16/05, IMF, Washington, DC.

UNCITRAL (United Nations Commission on International Trade Law). 2004. *Legislative Guide on Insolvency Law*. Vienna: UNCITRAL.

United Nations. 2004. *United Nations Convention Against Corruption.* Vienna: United Nations Office on Drugs and Crime.

Going for Broke

走向破产

1. Insolvency Proceedings and Representatives

The ability to commence an insolvency proceeding is crucial for asset recovery. Typically, there are two standard tests for commencement of insolvency proceedings: (1) illiquidity, or the inability to pay existing obligations as they become due in the ordinary course of business; and (2) the balance sheet test, when liabilities exceed assets. Countries will generally use one or both tests. These two tests are discussed in World Bank Principle C4.2 (box 1.1), one of the World Bank's Principles for Effective Insolvency and Creditor/Debtor Rights Systems, which set out a range of benchmarks, based on international best practices, for evaluating the effectiveness of domestic insolvency systems.

The traditional commencement tests, while internationally recognized as best practices for opening a standard insolvency case, may be insufficient to recover stolen assets through insolvency proceedings. This guidebook discusses a third method of commencement, just and equitable grounds (see chapter 3 for more details). Some jurisdictions addressed in this book, such

BOX 1.1 World Bank Principle C4.2: Commencement

Commencement criteria and presumptions about insolvency should be clearly defined in the law. The preferred test to commence an insolvency proceeding should be the debtor's inability to pay debts as they mature, although insolvency may also exist where the debtor's liabilities exceed the value of its assets, provided that the values of assets and liabilities are measured on the basis of fairmarket values.

1. 破产程序及破产管理人

能否启动破产程序对资产追查至关重要。通常，启动破产程序有两种判定标准：（1）资产流动性不足，在一般情况下无法及时偿还已到期的债务。（2）资产负债表明确显示负债已超过资产价值。各国通常会使用其中一项或两项判定标准。世界银行准则 C4.2（见方框 1.1）探讨了这两项标准，这也是世界银行《关于有效破产和债权人 / 债务人权利制度的原则》中的内容。该原则从国际最优实践方案中提炼而成，用以评估国内破产制度的成效。

虽然传统的启动判定标准被国际上认为是运行一般破产案件最好的操作，但通过破产程序可能并不足以追回腐败流失资产。本指南讨论的第三种启动方法，更为公平合理（详见第三章）。在本书中提到的一些地区，如英属维京群岛、开曼群岛和英国本土等，[1] 当非法行为一经发现时，则以违背“公平公正”原则为由对债务人宣告破产。[2]

方框 1.1	世界银行准则 C4.2：启动

法律中应明确规定启动破产程序的标准与条件。启动破产程序的首选标准应是债务人无力偿还到期债务。如果债务人的负债价值超过其资产价值，也可以启动破产程序，前提是资产和负债的价值是由市场公平定价机制决定的。

as the British Virgin Islands, the Cayman Islands, and the United Kingdom,[1] permit a declaration of insolvency on just and equitable grounds when business has been conducted illegally.[2]

Winding up a company is a legal tool (see box 1.2). Should an insolvency framework not provide just and equitable grounds for winding up, the enterprise will have to meet one of the standard tests for commencement of insolvency proceedings before any action can be taken. Although insolvency is not generally relevant in corruption cases, insolvency representatives can play a key role in the subsequent asset recovery process, even when their primary role is to protect the interests of creditors and other parties. They have a duty to report to criminal agencies and supporting institutions any illegal or irregular conduct uncovered in the administration of an estate and thus can aid the detection and identification of illicit assets. In cases of embezzlement of public funds, the main creditor of an estate is the government; therefore, insolvency representatives should coordinate with the investigative authorities to recover illicit assets. In other circumstances, companies may be created, either domestically or overseas, for the sole purpose of holding illicit assets stolen from the government or

BOX 1.2 Just and Equitable Winding Up

A court may order the winding up of a company, even if the company is not technically bankrupt or insolvent, if the court believes that there are just and equitable grounds for doing so—a decision that is largely at the discretion of the court. Reasons for ordering the just and equitable winding up of a company have varied from country to country. They can include deadlock within a company's management, loss of substratum (the loss of the reason for a company to exist), or abuse of power by a company's leadership (often by the suppression of minority owners). This type of ruling has been used to wind up companies that were created for fraudulent purposes.

清算是一种合法手段（见方框 1.2）。如果相关立法并无“公平公正”原则，则企业必须至少符合两项判定标准中的一项，才能启动破产程序。虽然通常破产与腐败案件无关，但破产管理人可在随后的资产追查中发挥重要作用。即便其主要职责在于保护债权人或其他当事人的利益，但其有义务向相关刑事司法机构报告在破产资产管理时发现的非法或异常行为，帮助追查相关资产。在挪用公款的案件中，破产资产的主要债权人是政府。因此，破产管理人应配合调查机构追回涉案资产。除此之外，犯罪分子也可能通过成立公司的方式持有和运营腐败所得，破产管理人可运用下列两种方式追回损失：

方框 1.2 “公平公正”的破产清算

即便公司不存在技术意义上的破产指征或资不抵债的情况，只要法院认为存在明显违背“公平公正”原则的交易，也可对其宣告破产。破产决定很大程度上取决于法院的判断且因国家而异，可以包括公司僵局、公司成立的初始原因灭失或公司高层滥用职权（一般体现为压制少数股东）等。实践中许多涉嫌商业欺诈的公司已被清算。

purchased with the proceeds of corruption. Insolvency representatives can use their powers to recover proceeds of corruption in two ways:

- The insolvency representative acts as the representative of an insolvent person or entity that was deprived of assets following corrupt activities conducted by one of its directors or managers, that is, the insolvent entity is the victim.
- The insolvency representative acts on behalf of the person or entity that perpetrated or assisted in the corruption.

For example, an investigation may demonstrate that a company's only activity was to issue fictitious invoices to justify the transfer of funds used to pay bribes to directors or managers of another company. Other cases involve the use of companies to transfer or manage assets purchased with proceeds of corruption. Companies that are used as instruments of corruption or for the laundering of illicit proceeds can be targeted as insolvent companies or on just and equitable grounds, when available. If prosecutors or victims of corruption demonstrate that these companies do not have sufficient assets to cover their liabilities or claim not to have assets, hide assets, or simply refuse to pay what is owed, the claimant can ask the court to appoint an insolvency representative who will use his investigative and legal powers to identify information or assets that are essential to the recovery process.

For a government seeking to recover proceeds of corruption that a former official invested, managed, or laundered through businesses or companies, insolvency can be a productive strategic step, especially if the government can show that the entity is liable for unpaid taxes, or when, as is the case in some civil law countries, the insolvency legislation allows prosecutors to petition courts to open a bankruptcy case. Not all countries have insolvency regulations that allow prosecutors to do so.[3]

As shown in box 1.3, when a person or an entity effectively defaults, a

- 破产管理人代表受腐败行为侵害的公司行使权利。

- 破产管理人代表实施腐败行为或协助实施腐败行为的公司行使权利。

例如，一项调查表明，某公司的唯一业务就是虚开发票掩盖行贿支出，或者通过其他方式运营腐败所得，若证据充分，就可认定该公司违背“公平公正”原则从事非法交易而对其申请破产（如果该国确有这一原则）。检察官或受腐败侵害的一方若能证明该公司资不抵债或隐瞒资产拒绝清偿债务，也可向法院申请委认破产管理人，调查、确定、恢复相关重要的信息或资产。

对政府而言，追查经过洗钱后的腐败资产，破产策略往往有效，特别是在偷税、漏税的情况下。就像某些大陆法系国家的破产法规定，检察院可向法院申请破产。[3]

如方框 1.3 所示，当一方违约时，债权人可以向法院或其他主管

creditor can apply to a court or another competent authority and request that the person or entity be declared insolvent. In insolvency proceedings, the first step is usually a moratorium, or freeze, on all transactions, followed by the appointment of an insolvency representative to manage the assets and ensure that they are used fairly to reimburse creditors. In corruption cases that are pursued through insolvency proceedings, the appointment of an

BOX 1.3 Using Insolvency Proceedings in Asset Recovery

In this hypothetical example, a Latin American country has been the victim of substantial theft by corruption. A government official in the country entered into a series of contracts on behalf of a state-owned bus service provider with bus manufacturing companies in France, Germany, Italy, and the United Kingdom. The contractual sums due were paid by the state-owned bus service provider into bank accounts held by the bus manufacturers in each of the four European countries.

Shortly before each of the contracts was signed, offshore companies owned by the bus manufacturers entered into contracts for consulting services with four Isle of Man companies. The Isle of Man companies billed the manufacturers for substantial sums, which were paid from bank accounts, held in the names of subsidiaries of the bus manufacturers, in Singapore. The funds were then transferred into a variety of complex investment holdings. Anticorruption officers in the Latin American country learned of the scheme and successfully sued three of the consultants in the Isle of Man.

Because there were evidentiary issues with the case against the fourth consultant, it was not included in the initial legal proceeding. However, the judgment in the other three cases was so heavily in favor of the claimant that anticorruption officers decided to evaluate other options to pursue a case against the fourth consultant. All four consultants were part of a scheme to defraud the Latin American country. The companies had no commercial rationale. Representatives of the Latin American government, attempting to recover the stolen assets, petitioned for the fourth consultant to be wound up on just and equitable grounds because it existed only for demonstrably fraudulent purposes. The Isle of Man court ordered that the company be wound up, and an insolvency representative was appointed. The assets held by the company were recovered and repaid to the Latin American country.

部门提出破产申请。在破产程序中，第一步一般为中止或冻结所有交易，然后任命破产管理人管理资产，确保公平公正地清偿债权人。在破产程序介入的腐败案件中，委任破产管理人至关重要。

方框 1.3 资产返还中适用的破产措施

假设某拉美国家一直深受腐败所害，某政府贪腐官员代表国有巴士营运公司与法国、德国、意大利和英国的四家巴士制造商签订了侵害国家利益的合同，以从中牟利。该巴士营运公司将合同款打入四国巴士制造商的银行账户。

在每份合同签署之前，巴士制造商拥有的离岸公司都与四家马恩岛公司签订了咨询服务合同。马恩岛公司向制造商收取大笔款项，并以制造商新加坡子公司名下的账户支付。随后，又投资许多复杂的项目和股票。拉美国家的反贪官员了解了该计划后，成功起诉了其中的三家马恩岛咨询公司。

由于涉案的第四家咨询公司存在证据问题，因此未将其纳入最初的起诉范围中，但其他三起案件，法院都判决原告胜诉。鉴于此，反贪官员追加了对第四家咨询公司的诉讼，申请宣告其破产，因为他们都以明显不正当的手段参与了欺诈该国的计划。马恩岛法院裁定对这四家公司进行了破产清算，并委任了破产管理人对拉美国家进行清偿。

insolvency representative is a crucial step.

The purpose of insolvency proceedings for asset recovery is to seize and sell assets of the debtor-defendant and distribute the money equitably to creditors and other injured parties, thereby protecting their rights. Proceedings are generally conducted, monitored, or decided in court, through liquidation or reorganization, in similar out-ofcourt proceedings.

The appointment of an insolvency representative and, more generally, the launch of insolvency proceedings have an immediate legal effect on the asset recovery process.

Cross-border effects may allow the representative to seek the identification and recovery of the bankrupt entity's assets in foreign jurisdictions. Finally, insolvency representatives have two types of power that are relevant and crucial for the asset recovery process: investigatory powers and legal powers to claim assets.

The elements of insolvency proceedings are addressed in the remaining sections of chapter 1.

Moratorium

Moratorium refers to the suspension of activity, especially the suspension of collection of debts by a private business, government, or under a court order. In insolvency law, it means a halt to the right to collect a debt from the insolvent company as soon as the insolvency proceedings have commenced.

Appointment of an Insolvency Representative

The insolvency representative's main role is to maximize the interests of creditors and other parties harmed by the insolvency or the fraudulent activity. Policy makers and practitioners should keep in mind that the

破产程序的目的是没收并出售债务人的资产，将所得收益公平分配给债权人及其他受害方，维护他们的权益。一般来说，清算或重整等程序在法庭上进行，但也存在其他类似的庭外程序。

任命破产管理人、启动破产程序对资产追回具有即时的法律效力。

而跨国破产程序可以使破产管理人在域外管辖区对破产资产进行识别和追索。总的来说，破产管理人具有调查权和诉讼权这两种资产追查的重要权力。

在第一章的剩余各节还讨论了破产程序的其他要素。

延期支付

延期支付，是指中止或暂停赔付，特别是私营企业或政府等作为债权人，依据法院裁定暂停要求债务人清偿债务。在破产法中，是指在破产程序开始后暂停向破产公司索赔。

破产管理人的任命

破产管理人的主要作用是将债权人的权益最大化以弥补损失。政策制定者和从业人员应谨记，破产管理人在清算程序中的权力与重整程序中的权力可能不同。例如，在英国，破产管理人具有对脆弱交易

powers of insolvency representatives in terminal insolvency proceedings, which wind up a business, may differ from those in rescue proceedings, which reorganize a business. In the United Kingdom, for example, the representative will have powers under a rescue proceeding similar to those available for vulnerable transactions and powers of examination.

To retrieve stolen assets, the insolvency representative will be required to identify and retrieve the illegally obtained proceeds stolen by bribe takers or others committing fraud. Although insolvency laws have much in common across jurisdictions, the position of insolvency representative varies considerably between jurisdictions.[4]

Insolvency representatives generally have the benefit of broad powers to access information and to demand testimony from individuals such as directors or managers. The availability of a statutory mandate to investigate, often under the protection of secrecy, has proven to be a powerful weapon in large asset recovery cases. The declaration of insolvency and the ensuing appointment of an insolvency representative has the automatic effect of freezing the status quo and empowering the insolvency representative to act on behalf of the bankrupt entity. Among other things, an insolvency representative is generally entitled to bring claims against a company's former directors for their wrongdoing in involving the company in a corruption scheme. Claims for restitution or damages can also be made against third parties dishonestly assisting with or participating in that wrongdoing. If defendants or assets are located in a foreign jurisdiction, the powers of an insolvency representative may be more easily enforced abroad than those of a creditor.

Insolvency representatives can also be appointed to take control of and manage a debtor's assets as either a general receiver or a special receiver. A general receiver is analogous to an insolvency representative: upon

进行救济以及检查的权力。

为了追回腐败流失资产，破产管理人应按要求查明和追索受贿人或其他相关人员的非法所得。尽管各国破产法存在许多共通之处，但各法域破产管理人的地位仍然具有很大差异。[4]

破产管理人需要经过充分的授权才能获取相关信息或要求董事或经理作证。实践证明，在大型资产追查案件中，有法定的调查任务，而且往往是在保密状态下进行时，是一种强有力的武器。宣告破产之后，任命破产管理人冻结资产，代表破产公司行使经营管理权将自动生效。除其他事项外，破产管理人通常有权对腐败、渎职的前公司董事或其他涉案第三方作出的不当决策提起诉讼。如果被告人或资产位于域外司法管辖区，相较债权人，破产管理人更容易在国外行使职权。

破产管理人还可以被任命为一般接管人或特殊接管人来控制、管理债务和资产。一般接管人类似于受全权委托的破产管理人，被任命后，控制所有资产，经营债务人的所有业务，直到出售或清算为止。

appointment, the general receiver takes control of all assets and operates the businesses of the debtor until either sale or liquidation. In a special or limited receivership, the receiver takes possession only of designated assets or businesses of the debtor.

Liquidation, compulsory proceedings to sell and dispose of assets for distribution to creditors, might result from a creditor's petition to a court seeking the winding up of the company. The creditor will likely prevail if the company is unable to pay its debts. In liquidation, the insolvency representative conducts all proceedings, including the sale of remaining assets.

Jurisdictions differ as to the authorities that have the power to select and appoint insolvency representatives; these differences may depend on the type of insolvency proceeding (World Bank Principle C17 2016; UNCITRAL 2004, 176; EBRD 2014, 55).

The Different Authorities that May Appoint Insolvency Representatives

In general, there is a public model and a private-professional model for insolvency representatives. In developed jurisdictions, a professional from an international accounting firm is commonly appointed as an insolvency representative. In the public model (more common in low- and middle-income countries), an employee of the state is appointed as the insolvency representative.[5] Some jurisdictions also allow legal professionals to serve as insolvency representatives.

In most jurisdictions, depending on the type and the purpose of the insolvency proceeding, insolvency representatives are appointed by: (1) the court; (2) the court with creditor input or at the direction of the creditors; or (3) independent appointing authorities (EBRD 2014, 55). Some jurisdictions use an electronic random selection system to select and appoint representatives.

而特殊接管人则拥有特殊或有限的接管权，仅管理和占有债务人指定的资产或业务。

当公司资不抵债时，债权人向法院申请盘点、出售和处置公司资产以获得清偿的强制性程序称为清算程序。在此过程中，破产管理人全权参与所有程序，包括出售破产资产。

依据破产程序的种类不同，各国对破产管理人的选择权和任命权也有所差异（世界银行准则 C17 2016；联合国国际贸易法委员会 2004，176；欧洲复兴开发银行 2014，55）。

破产管理人的不同任命机构

通常，破产管理人的任命有大致统一的标准，有时也需要特别的专业技能。在发达国家，一般会聘请国际会计师事务所的专业人士担任，在中低收入国家，公务员常被委任为破产管理人。[5] 有些国家也允许法律专业人士担任破产管理人。

在大多数国家，根据破产程序的类型和目的，破产管理人由以下机构任命：（1）法院；（2）债权人参与或指定的法院；（3）独立任命机构（欧洲复兴开发银行 2014，55）。也有一些国家使用电子系统随机任命破产管理人。

In some jurisdictions, creditors play a role in recommending and selecting the insolvency representative, provided that the person recommended meets the qualifications for serving in the specific case. In other jurisdictions, insolvency representatives are designated by the company or its directors or, in other cases, by the court at the request of a creditor. In some jurisdictions a government to which taxes are owed may have a say in the selection of the insolvency representative.

Using an independent appointing authority to select the insolvency representative has the advantage of enabling the choice of professionals with the expertise and knowledge to handle a specific case (EBRD 2014, 55). This can be particularly useful when dealing with banks, as discussed in the following section.

One or more of these approaches may be available to victims of political corruption, including the government, or other persons harmed by corruption. Which approach is correct will depend upon the facts of the case and the jurisdiction in which the debtor and the assets are located.

Although less visible, the supervision and disciplinary control of insolvency representatives is also important, and it varies considerably from jurisdiction to jurisdiction. The World Bank Principles recommend an independent system to oversee the profession, establish who is competent to act as a representative, and provide standards of conduct. Boxes 1.4 and 1.5 set out World Bank Principles D7 and D8, which identify key best practices for insolvency representative regulation.

在某些国家，债权人可以推荐和选择符合条件的破产管理人。在另一些国家，破产管理人则由公司或其他董事指定或由法院根据债权人的要求指定。还有些国家，当债务人偷税漏税时，政府对破产管理人的任命也有发言权。

选用独立的任命机构委任破产管理人，有利于选择具有专门知识和技能的相关从业人员来处理特定的案件（欧洲复兴开发银行 2014，55）。如下一节所述，这在与银行打交道时特别有用。

以上方法中的一种或几种都可能适用于政治腐败的受害方，包括政府和个人。具体哪种方法更为适用，取决于案情本身以及债务人、资产所在的司法管辖区。

虽然对破产管理人的监督并不常受到关注，但也同样重要，且不同国家之间存在很大的差异。《世界银行准则》建议建立一个独立的体系来监督破产管理人，以便于确定其从业资格、行为标准等。方框 1.4 和方框 1.5 列出了《世界银行准则》D7 和 D8，提供了对破产管理人监督的最佳范例。

BOX 1.4 World Bank Principle D7: Role of Regulatory or Supervisory Bodies

The bodies responsible for regulating or supervising insolvency representatives should:

- Be independent.
- Set standards that reflect public expectations of fairness, impartiality, transparency, and accountability.
- Have appropriate powers and resources to enable them to discharge their functions, duties, and responsibilities effectively.

In addition to the World Bank Principles, the EBRD Insolvency Office Holder (IOH) Principles set out 12 more detailed principles, including those for the qualification, remuneration, and supervision, as well as a code of ethics, for insolvency representatives. Officials establishing or reforming an insolvency representative regulatory regime should take these IOH Principles into account. These principles would also enable interested parties (such as governments, commercial banks, and law firms) to analyze the regulatory environment in the country from which they are seeking asset recovery to understand any weaknesses in the system regulating insolvency representatives.

Source: EBRD 2007.

BOX 1.5 World Bank Principle D8: Competence and Integrity of Insolvency Representatives

The system should ensure that:

- Criteria as to whom may be an insolvency representative are objective, clearly established, and publicly available.
- Insolvency representatives are competent to undertake the work to which they are appointed and to exercise the powers given to them.
- Insolvency representatives act with integrity, impartiality, and independence.
- Insolvency representatives, where acting as managers, are held to director and officer standards of accountability, and are subject to removal for incompetence, negligence, fraud, or other wrongful conduct.

Specific Rules and Practices for an Insolvent Bank

In the case of an insolvent bank, the power to manage both the assets and the bank itself is frequently given to bank guarantee funds, which guarantee the interests of creditors, specifically depositors.[6] For example,

方框 1.4　世界银行准则 D7：监管机构的职责与监管主体

负责监管破产管理人的机构应满足：

- 独立。
- 制定的标准满足公众期待，公平、公正、透明且可被问责。
- 具有一定的职权和资源，能够切实履行职责和义务。

除《世界银行准则》之外，欧洲复兴开发银行《破产管理人守则》还提出了 12 项细则，涵盖了从业资格、薪酬、监督和职业操守等内容。制定破产管理人监管制度的有关部门应参考上述细则。这些细则还有助于为政府、商业银行或律所等机构分析资产所属国的监管环境，以便于更好地发现破产管理人制度中的缺陷。

资料来源：欧洲复兴开发银行，2007。

方框 1.5　世界银行准则 D8：破产管理人的从业资格与职业操守

破产管理人的监管制度应该做到：

- 破产管理人的任命标准应该客观、明确及公开。
- 破产管理人具备胜任工作、行使职权的能力。
- 破产管理人应遵循公正、公平、独立的职业操守。
- 破产管理人在担任公司董事、经理时应遵循同样的问责标准；若其不能胜任或存在过失、欺诈等行为，应被罢免。

银行破产的细则和实践

对于无力偿债的银行，由存款担保基金支持银行管理和资产担保，以保证债权人和储户的利益。[6] 例如，2012 年 9 月乌克兰的一项法律将存款担保基金的任务范围从偿还储户存款扩大到支持临时或正式的

in Ukraine, a law enacted in September 2012 extended the mandate of the Deposit Guarantee Fund beyond reimbursing depositors of failed banks to acting as their provisional administrator or insolvency representative. Thus, the government agency manages the operations of the failed bank before liquidation is complete and has the power necessary to collect financial and transaction information, identify and collect information on suspicious transactions, cooperate with criminal investigators, and launch civil or commercial lawsuits on behalf of the company to recover funds and other assets.

In other countries, for example, Moldova, the insolvency representative of an insolvent bank is appointed by the central bank or by a supervisory authority. This approach has many advantages, most significantly that the appointed insolvency representative is familiar with banking. The second advantage is that the insolvency representative enjoys legal protection as a central bank employee. This is especially important in a jurisdiction with a corrupt legal system, where debtors can initiate legal suits against the insolvency representative to jeopardize the recovery process. The appointment and remuneration of the insolvency representative by the central bank also solves the problem of an insolvent bank that does not have sufficient funds to pay the insolvency representative's salary.

The insolvency representative appointed by the central bank has the power to initiate civil cases against debtors, former managers, or other third parties if he believes that the bank was affected by their actions (or inaction). In some jurisdictions, the insolvency representative can request that the prosecutor's office initiate criminal cases.

The appointment of an insolvency representative by a central bank was used recently in Moldova after an extensive bank fraud. After the fraud was discovered, the National Bank of Moldova played a key role in the liquidation of the banks, including appointing an insolvency representative,

破产管理人。因此，政府可以在清算程序结束之前运营倒闭银行，收集财务信息、可疑交易信息，与犯罪调查人员合作以及代表公司提起民商事诉讼追回相关资产。

在其他国家，如摩尔多瓦，破产银行的管理人由中央银行等监管机构委任。此举具有如下优点：第一，指定的破产管理人熟悉银行业务，这点至关重要。第二，中央银行的公职人员担任破产管理人受到法律保护，这在司法不健全的国家尤其关键。在这些国家，债务人可以对破产管理人提起诉讼以干扰破产程序。同时，中央银行负责破产管理人的任命和薪酬，也解决了破产银行缺少足够资金支付破产管理人报酬的问题。

如果中央银行任命的破产管理人认为债务人、前公司管理人员或其他第三方存在不法行为，则有权提起民事诉讼。在某些国家，破产管理人还可以要求检察机关提起刑事诉讼。

在一次大规模的银行欺诈案之后，摩尔多瓦施行了由中央银行任命破产管理人的做法，对相关银行清算起到了显著的作用。具体行动包括任命破产管理人、批准破产管理人执行重大交易以及宣告清算程序完成等。最终清算了三家银行，包括一家政策性银行。而其前总理

approving significant transactions executed by the insolvency representative, and declaring the liquidation process closed. Three banks were ultimately liquidated, including one of systemic national importance. The former Prime Minister was sentenced to nine years in prison on corruption charges.

Liquidation is not demonstrably more efficient than the use of a Deposit Guarantee Fund in Ukraine for winding up an insolvent bank. Although the administrative resources allocated for the liquidation and recovery process are important, the legal framework determining the powers of the insolvency representative and the functioning of the legal system in practice, which is often related to the level of systemic corruption, are critical.

Effects of the Appointment of an Insolvency Representative

Box 1.6 provides a brief overview of the powers afforded to insolvency representatives in many jurisdictions.

BOX 1.6 Overview of the Powers of an Insolvency Representative

Insolvency representatives are appointed to manage the assets of an institution that has been declared insolvent. They generally have the power to do the following:

- Act on behalf of the bankrupt entity, sometimes jointly with the debtor
- Take possession of assets related to the insolvent entity and manage them
- Gain access to all books, transaction records, accounting documentation, or financial information relevant to the management of the company
- Conduct or order a comprehensive audit of financial statements and suspicious transactions to find information that can lead to recoverable assets
- Use all investigative and provisional measures available in civil litigation, including seizure of property and records, public examination, and freezing of assets
- Exercise discovery and examination of interested parties and third parties
- Compel testimony from individuals, such as directors or managers, and bring claims against them for wrongdoing in any corrupt scheme
- Bring claims against third parties for participating in any wrongdoing
- Act to prevent any further movement of assets out of the insolvent estate.

也因贪污罪被判入狱九年。

很显然，没有比乌克兰这种用存款担保基金清算破产银行更有效的做法了。除清算、复权程序的行政资源分配以外，确定破产管理人、保证执法成效（通常与系统腐败的程度有关）的相关立法也至关重要。

指定破产管理人的效力

方框 1.6 简要概述了许多国家破产管理人的权力。

方框 1.6　破产管理人权力概览

破产管理人有权对宣告破产的机构实行管理，并享有以下职权：

- 代表破产公司行使职权，有时可与债务人共同行事
- 接管、占有破产公司的资产
- 获得所有与公司运营相关的账簿、交易记录、会计凭证等财务信息
- 对财务报表和可疑交易进行全面审计，以收集有助于涉案资产的信息
- 有权采取民事诉讼中所有的调查措施和临时禁令，包括扣押财产、扣押文书、公开检查、冻结资产等
- 对利益相关方和第三方机构进行检查
- 有权强制公司董事、经理等个人作为证人作证，并就其中任何不法行为提请损害赔偿
- 针对第三方的不当行为开展索赔
- 采取必要措施防止资产转移

Once the insolvency process has commenced and an insolvency representative is appointed, an automatic or court-imposed moratorium against any action, execution, or other legal process against the bankrupt person or entity takes effect.[7] If a bankrupt entity has assets within the jurisdiction in which it was declared bankrupt, insolvency regimes will in principle prevent any further movement of assets out of the insolvent estate. The effect of such a moratorium internationally can be complex, but international regimes—such as the Council of the European Union's Regulation on Insolvency Proceedings[8] and the United Nations Commission on International Trade Law (UNCITRAL) Model Law on Cross-Border Insolvency[9]—often give this stay of proceedings extraterritorial effect.

In most insolvency cases, the insolvency representative gets access to all books, transaction records, accounting documentation, and financial information relevant to the company. Often, the insolvency representative will conduct or order a comprehensive audit of financial statements and suspicious transactions to find information that can lead to recoverable assets. These audits are generally the starting point of an investigation, when specific actions or transactions that resulted in the transfer of assets of value out of the company are identified. As representatives of the company or the bankrupt estate, insolvency representatives are able to use all investigative and provisional measures available in civil litigation, including seizure of property and records, public examination, and freezing of assets.

In addition, insolvency laws often give the insolvency representative powers of discovery and examination of interested parties and third parties. Government officials seeking to recover assets should remember, however, that conducting forensic investigations and other legal actions can be extremely expensive, and creditors may not support these investigations financially in the absence of a good chance of success. If the chance

一旦破产程序启动并任命了破产管理人，针对破产公司的所有行动、法令会即刻生效。[7] 如果破产公司在宣告破产地拥有资产，破产程序原则上可将资产转移出去。该禁令的国际效力往往很复杂，但是欧洲联盟理事会《破产程序条例》[8] 和联合国国际贸易法委员会（UNCITRAL）《跨国界破产示范法》[9] 通常认为这一诉讼程序具有域外法律效力。

在大多数破产案件中，破产管理人可以审查与公司有关的所有账簿、交易记录、会计凭证等财务信息，对财务报表和可疑交易进行全面审计，以搜集追查资产的线索。审计特定的资产转移，往往是调查的起点。作为公司的代表，破产管理人可以运用民事诉讼中所有的调查和诉讼措施，包括没收财产和相关记录、公开检查、冻结资产等。

此外，破产法还赋予破产管理人识别、审查当事方和第三方的权力。但是，追查资产的相关人员应注意，司法调查往往成本高昂，若胜算不大，债权人一般不会提供资金支持，此时破产管理人可与执法部门合作调查。

of success is weak, insolvency representatives can coordinate with law enforcement on transactions that appear suspicious.

Insolvency laws generally authorize the insolvency representative to take possession of and manage assets from the bankrupt individual or company. These powers give the insolvency representative direct access to recoverable property. In most cases, asset recovery is complex, and financial investigations as well as provisional measures are necessary to identify, trace, and secure recoverable funds or property.

Cross–Border Recognition and Conducting Insolvency Actions Abroad

Assets are often hidden in financial centers where local secrecy rules or banking opportunities are abused by criminals. Countries pursuing asset recovery efforts often have to work across borders to identify and repatriate their stolen funds, including in insolvency cases. In criminal cases, law enforcement authorities have tools that facilitate the exchange of information with their foreign counterparts. (See appendix A for countryspecific regulations and UNCAC for the international framework governing such cooperation.) Coordination with law enforcement authorities may be useful to insolvency practitioners.

Insolvency representatives who seek to exercise their powers in foreign countries must keep in mind the variations in legal recognition and enforcement of foreign judgments in cross-border insolvency proceedings. Under domestic legislation and applicable multilateral or bilateral treaties, a number of foreign jurisdictions support insolvency representatives appointed in the jurisdiction where the insolvency proceedings were initiated. In the British Virgin Islands, for example, a foreign representative appointed in "relevant countries"[10] may apply to the court for orders to restrain any

破产法授予破产管理人占有、管理资产以便其直接追查资产的权力。在大多数情况下，追查资产的过程较为复杂，需要财务调查、临时禁令来识别、追踪和保全相关财产。

破产程序的跨国承认与执行

涉案资产一般隐藏在金融中心，犯罪分子借着保密条款常有可趁之机。资产原属国必须跨国开展追查工作，破产案件也不例外。在刑事案件中，执法部门拥有更多便于与外国同行交换信息的工具。（有关国家的法规，请参见附录 A；有关此类合作的国际协议，请参见 UNCAC。）因此，和执法部门通力合作，有助于破产案件的侦办。

在国外行使职权的破产管理人必须注意跨国破产程序的域外法律效力以及在实践中的差异。根据国内立法或国际双边或多边条约，许多国家对程序启动国所任命的破产管理人予以承认。比如，在英属维京群岛，“相关国家”[10]中委任的破产管理人可以向法院提起针对债务人及其资产的禁令，针对债务人或与债务人的任何财产，限制或禁止相关程序的进行；可要求任何相关主体将债务人的所有相关财产交付给外国破产管理人，并任命债务人相关财产的临时接管人。

proceedings against a debtor or in relation to any of the debtor's property, to require any person to deliver any property of the debtor to the foreign representative, and to appoint an interim receiver of any property of the debtor.

In some jurisdictions, courts can recognize foreign bankruptcy proceedings and issue orders at the request of a foreign representative authorized to act on behalf of the debtor. In the Cayman Islands, such orders include prohibiting the commencement of legal proceedings against the debtor, staying the enforcement of a judgment against the debtor, and ordering the turnover to the foreign representative of any property belonging to the debtor. The foreign representative can also request an order requiring a person in possession of information relating to the business of the debtor to be examined and to produce documents.

In other jurisdictions (including the United Kingdom and the United States), crossborder insolvency legislation gives the UNCITRAL Model Law the force of local law. Expert meetings have shown that jurisdictions that adopted this model handled cases quickly and routinely, with no difficult issues. Requests for legal recognition could be resolved within hours.[11] In the United Kingdom, foreign insolvency proceedings and foreign representatives must be recognized by courts if certain formal documents are provided and an application is issued by the Business and Property Courts (Insolvency and Companies List) of the High Court.

Other systems to ensure that insolvency representatives and foreign representatives can exercise the rights and act on behalf of the estate in foreign jurisdictions include the Regulation (EU) 2015/848 on Insolvency Proceedings (Recast Insolvency Regulation), which gives primacy to the law of the country that opens insolvency proceedings if the company has its center of main interest (COMI) in that country. The insolvency

在某些国家或地区，法院认可外国破产程序的效力，并依照外国破产管理人的申请签发法令。在开曼群岛，此类法令包括：禁止启动针对债务人的诉讼，中止对债务人的判决执行以及将债务人的所有资产、营业额等移交外国破产管理人等。破产管理人还可以申请对债务人业务相关的文件进行查阅。

在其他国家（包括英国和美国），跨国破产相关的法律赋予联合国国际贸易法委员会《跨国界破产示范法》以本国法律效力。许多专家表明，适用该示范法的国家可以快速、例行处理案件，没有阻力。法律的授权在数小时内就能获得。[11] 在英国，破产管理人必须向英国高等商业财产法院递交所需文件（如破产公司清单），申请获批后，跨国破产程序、外国破产管理人的效力才得以承认。

其他保证外国破产代理人在境外行使代表权的法律还包括《破产程序条例》（EU2015/848，修订版），如果破产程序启动国是破产公司的主要权益中心，则承认其效力。这样，破产管理人可以在资产所在的所有欧盟成员国行使管理权。该法规还确立了对位于非主要权益中心的成员国的企业提起二级诉讼的基础。但有一个前提，外国管理人必须证明破产程序中的债务人符合英国现行的普通法，才能在英国执

representatives are then able to exercise their powers in all other European Union (EU) Member States where assets are located. Regulation 2015/848 also establishes the basis for opening secondary proceedings against businesses located in a Member State that is not the company's COMI. However, there is a premise that in order to enforce foreign insolvency orders in England, foreign representatives must show that the debtor in the insolvency proceeding falls within the existing U.K. common law rules.[12] The case discussed in box 1.7 illustrates the application of this principle. See the section in chapter 5 titled *United Kingdom Cross-Border Insolvency Regulations* 2006 for more detail.

BOX 1.7 **U.K. Supreme Court Rules on Cross-Border Insolvencies: The Limits of Universalism in *Rubin v. Eurofinance S.A.*** [a]

Eurofinance S.A. created Consumers Trust, an English law trust governed by English law, with a jurisdiction clause selecting English courts. The scheme of Consumers Trust ran into financial difficulties and the Trust decided to seek protection by entering bankruptcy under the U.S. Bankruptcy Code. The U.S. bankruptcy court appointed Rubin, a foreign representative, to serve on behalf of the Trust to seek aid, assistance, and cooperation from the English High Court to enforce the U.S. bankruptcy court's judgments against persons and entities residing in or owning property in the United Kingdom.

In the U.S. bankruptcy court, Rubin commenced proceedings that were equivalent to the insolvency claims under the U.K. Insolvency Act 1986. The defendants, who were not resident in the United States and did not submit to the jurisdiction of the bankruptcy court, did not present a defense in those proceedings.

Default and summary judgment were entered against them. Rubin then sought to enforce these judgments.

The main issue before the U.K. Supreme Court was whether the English courts would recognize and enforce insolvency orders under common law. By the usual common law rules, for a claimant to enforce a foreign order in the United Kingdom, the defendants would have had to be present in the foreign country at the time

行外国破产令。[12] 方框 1.7 中讨论的案件就阐释了这一原则。更多详细信息，可参见第五章“英国跨国破产条例 2006”部分。

方框 1.7　英国高等法院跨国破产规则：鲁宾诉欧洲金融集团案[a]中普遍主义的局限

欧洲金融集团创立了一家消费者信托公司，选定英国法院管辖，所以这是一家受英国法律管辖的信托公司。该公司由于陷入财务困境，决定根据《美国破产法》申请破产。随后，美国破产法院委任了破产管理人鲁宾，向英国高等法院寻求协助，执行美国破产法院对位于英国的财产的判决。

在美国破产法庭上，鲁宾根据英国 1986 年《破产法》提起了破产诉讼，非美国居民或不属于美国破产法院管辖的被告则未被列入本次诉讼中。

法院适用简易程序并判决公司违约，鲁宾随后申请执行判决。

英国最高法院面临的主要问题是，是否依据普通法承认并执行他国的破产判决。根据一般的习惯法规则，要在英国执行外国判决，在诉讼时，被告应属于外国的司法管辖范围，同时外国诉讼中的原告或被告必须参与该国的诉讼。

continued

proceedings were instituted and to have been a claimant or counterclaimant in the foreign proceedings. They would also have to have participated in the proceedings or submitted to the jurisdiction of the foreign court..

The U.K. Supreme Court held that insolvency proceedings do not form a separate category of judgment outside the common law rules, and foreign officeholders would have to show that the debtor met the criteria under the existing common law rules to enforce foreign insolvency orders in England.[b] The UNCITRAL Model Law (see the section in chapter 5 titled *The UNCITRAL Model Law on CrossBorder Insolvency*), which is implemented by the Cross-Border Insolvency Regulations 2006, makes no mention of the recognition or enforcement of foreign judgments against third parties. Accordingly, the Cross-Border Insolvency Regulations 2006 were not designed to provide for reciprocal enforcement of judgments. Because there is no expectation that foreign courts will mutually enforce U.K. court decisions, existing rules governing courts' common law and statutory powers regarding foreign judicial enforcement are deliberately limited in scope. It is a matter for the legislature, rather than the judiciary, to expand the rules on when foreign insolvency judgments can be enforced in U.K. proceedings. Finally, as a matter of policy, the rules for foreign insolvency judgments should be no more liberal than those for judgments made in proceedings other than insolvency proceedings.

Prior to *Rubin*, the most relevant case law suggested that, in insolvency proceedings, an English court did not have to follow the normal common law rules on enforcing a judgment. *Rubin* returns the law to classic principles on jurisdiction and enforcement. *Rubin* establishes that in order to enforce foreign insolvency orders in the United Kingdom at common law, the foreign office holder must show that the judgment debtor: (1) was present in the foreign jurisdiction at the time the proceedings were instituted; (2) was the claimant or the counter-claimant in the foreign proceedings; (3) had submitted to the foreign proceedings by appearing voluntarily; and (4) had submitted to the foreign proceedings by agreement.

a. Rubin v. Eurofinance S.A. [2012] UKSC 46. For a discussion of the case, see Lexology, "Enforcing Orders Made in Insolvency Proceedings" (October 24, 2012), https://www.lexology.com/library/detail.aspx?g=a2f57317-5f4f-4f19-b5c2-49e9a043f684; Financier Worldwide, "U.K. Supreme Court Rules on Cross-Border Insolvencies" (January 2013), https://www.financierworldwide.com/uk-supreme-court-rules-on-cross-border-insolvencies/#. Wflu9jdqFBr.

b. See Stephanie Woods, Case Comment, "Rubin & Anor v. Eurofinance S.A. & Ors [2012] UKSC 46," U.K. Supreme Court Blog (October 29, 2012), http://ukscblog.com/case-comment-rubin-and-another-respondents-v-eurofinance-sa-and-others-appellants-new-cap-reinsurance-corporation-in-liquidation-and-another-respondents-v-a-e-grant-and-others-as-members-of/.

续表

英国最高法院裁定，该破产程序并不符合普通法规则中独立判决的情形。外国破产管理人必须证明债务人符合现行普通法规则，才能在英国执行外国破产判决。[b]2006 年《跨国界破产条例》实施的联合国国际贸易法委员会示范法（见第五章联合国国际贸易法委员会《跨国界破产示范法》部分）并未提及承认或执行外国判决。由此可见，2006 年的《跨国界破产条例》并不支持国际互相执行判决。所以，现行普通法的规定以及外国法院的司法执行受到了明显的限制。但如何扩大适用范围，使英国执行外国破产判决，是立法机关而非司法机关的职责。最后，作为一项政策问题，审理外国破产案件的原则不应比其他审判程序更宽松。

在鲁宾案之前，最相似的判例认为，在破产程序中，英国法院执行判决时不必遵循普通法的一般原则。鲁宾案的判决将法律还原为管辖权和执行权的经典原则。鲁宾案显示，为了按照普通法在英国执行外国破产判决，外国当事人必须证明判决中的债务人符合：（1）提起诉讼时属于该国司法管辖；（2）是该国诉讼中的原告或被告；（3）自愿出庭参与该国诉讼；（4）通过协定参与该国诉讼。

a. Rubin v. Eurofinance S.A. [2012] UKSC 46. For a discussion of the case, see Lexology, "Enforcing Orders Made in Insolvency Proceedings" (October 24, 2012), https://www.lexology.com/library/detail.aspx?g=a2f57317-5f4f-4f19-b5c2-49e9a043f684; Financier Worldwide, "U.K. Supreme Court Rules on Cross-Border Insolvencies" (January 2013), https://www.financierworldwide.com/uk-supreme-court-rules-on-cross-border-insolvencies/#. Wflu9jdqFBr.

b. See Stephanie Woods, Case Comment, "Rubin & Anor v. Eurofinance S.A. & Ors [2012] UKSC 46," U.K. Supreme Court Blog (October 29, 2012), http://ukscblog.com/case-comment-rubin-and-another-respondents-v-eurofinance-sa-and-others-appellants-new-cap-reinsurance-corporation-in-liquidation-and-another-respondents-v-a-e-grant-and-others-as-members-of/.

In the United States, chapter 15 of the Bankruptcy Code incorporates the Model Law on Cross-Border Insolvency to encourage cooperation between the United States and foreign countries on cross-border insolvency cases (Goffman 2017). Under chapter 15, "foreign representatives" of debtors who have initiated insolvency proceedings abroad, where the debtor has its COMI, are allowed to seek recognition of the proceedings abroad, as either a foreign main proceeding or a foreign nonmain proceeding in the United States (Goffman 2017). Debtors can block chapter 15 recognition if they offer evidence of corruption in the case against them. A general allegation that the foreign judiciary is corrupt is not sufficient. The case in box 1.8 describes evidence of corruption in a foreign insolvency proceeding that is sufficient to block chapter 15 recognition.

Finally, in those jurisdictions that have not adopted the Model Law, insolvency representatives may have to seek cross-border recognition through the international private law of the country. They may be able to use their power to request specific measures on behalf of the debtor by using existing legislation on asset recovery, civil proceedings, and investigation measures. Insolvency representatives may have to request that the specific measures ordered by the courts where the insolvency proceedings took place be recognized by the courts of the jurisdiction where assets are located. Insolvency representatives may request, directly or by using their own judicial system, the exequatur, or the execution of specific measures using treaties on legal assistance and recognition or execution of court decisions. Generally, this method of securing the extraterritorial effect of insolvency proceedings is time-consuming and uncertain.

美国将《跨国界破产示范法》纳入了《破产法》第十五章，以鼓励美国与外国破产案件的合作（考夫曼，2017）。根据《破产法》第十五章的规定，如果债务人的主要权益中心在破产程序启动国，则外国破产管理人可以向美国寻求承认该国破产程序作为主要程序或非主要程序（考夫曼，2017）。但如果债务人提供了该国司法腐败的证据，则可以阻却第十五章中的承认程序。不过，对于外国司法腐败，一般强度的指控是不够的。方框 1.8 的案例阐释了外国破产程序中，被认定为足够阻却承认程序的腐败证据的强度。

最后，在那些未通过示范法的国家中，破产管理人可通过该国的国际私法寻求跨国承认；还可利用有关资产追回民事诉讼、调查措施的现行法律，代表债务人申请特定措施。破产管理人在程序启动国获得的判决，必须由资产所在地的法院承认才能执行。破产管理人也可以直接利用本国司法系统，寻求法律援助，以执行相关措施。通常，这种认定破产程序域外法律效力的方法，往往既费时，效果也不确定。

BOX 1.8 U.S. Court Grants Recognition of Former Russian Business Owner's Bankruptcy

The Commercial Court of the Moscow Region appointed a financial administrator in the insolvency proceeding of Sergey Petrovich Poymanov pursuant to Russian bankruptcy law. In a U.S. bankruptcy court, the administrator moved for recognition of the Russian insolvency proceeding as a "foreign main proceeding" against a Delaware company, PPF Management LLC (PPF), under chapter 15 of the U.S. Bankruptcy Code. Counsel for PPF challenged the recognition of the Russian bankruptcy proceedings against Sergey Poymanov.

PPF alleged extensive corruption in the Russian judicial system but was unable to provide evidence that the Russian insolvency proceeding had been tainted.

In *In re Sergey Petrovich Poymanov*,[a] the U.S. bankruptcy court stated that the bar to block chapter 15 recognition is high, explaining that PPF would have to show that such an order would be manifestly contrary to the public policy of the United States. To do so, PPF would have had to present evidence of corruption in the present case, rather than merely claiming that corruption exists generally in the Russian judiciary. The court said that there was "simply no evidence" of the improprieties, bad faith, and criminal corruption that PPF alleged had tainted the Russian bankruptcy.

a. In re Sergey Petrovich Poymanov, No. 17-10516 (Bankr. S.D.N.Y. July 31, 2017), https://www.leagle.com/decision/inbco20170801684. For a discussion of the case, see "Bid to Block Ch. 15 Recognition Scrutinized in Russian Case," LAW360 (July 19, 2017), https://www.law360.com/articles/946123/bid-to-block-ch-15-recognition-scrutinized-in-russian-case; "Russian Ex-Biz Owner's Bankruptcy Granted U.S. Recognition," LAW360 (August 1, 2017), https://www.law360.com/articles/950228?scroll=1.

In Brazil, despite significant reforms, the law has no provision for the recognition of court decisions issued in foreign insolvency proceedings and does not address crossborder issues (Felsberg n.d., 2–3). The Constitution, the Introductory Law to the Civil Code, and the Code of Civil Procedure of Brazil provide the general rules that require an exequatur for the recognition of foreign judgments (Felsberg n.d., 3). In the absence of detailed rules, recognition and enforcement of foreign judgments of insolvency proceedings are theoretically possible in Brazil under certain conditions

方框 1.8　美国法院对某前俄罗斯企业所有人破产程序的承认

根据俄罗斯破产法，莫斯科商事法院在谢尔盖·米诺舍维奇·伯曼诺夫一案中任命了一名破产管理人。根据美国《破产法》第十五章，在美国破产法庭上，管理人申请针对特拉华州 PPF 公司的俄罗斯破产程序为“外国主要程序”。而 PPF 公司的代理律师对这一认定有所质疑。

PPF 公司声称俄罗斯司法系统存在广泛的腐败行为，但无法提供确凿的证据。

美国破产法院在该案的裁决[a]中指出，第十五章阻却认定的标准很高，并解释说明了 PPF 公司必须证明这一破产判决明显违反了美国的公共利益，要求 PPF 公司必须在本案中提供确凿的腐败证据，而非以声称俄罗斯司法体系普遍存在腐败了事。而法院最终认定“几乎没有证据”证明 PPF 公司所指控的腐败行为。

a. In re Sergey Petrovich Poymanov, No. 17-10516 (Bankr. S.D.N.Y. July 31, 2017), https://www.leagle.com/decision/inbco20170801684. For a discussion of the case, see “Bid to Block Ch. 15 Recognition Scrutinized in Russian Case,” LAW360 (July 19, 2017), https://www.law360.com/articles/946123/bid-to-block-ch-15-recognition-scrutinized-in-russian-case; “Russian Ex-Biz Owner’s Bankruptcy Granted U.S. Recognition,” LAW360 (August 1, 2017), https://www.law360.com/articles/950228?scroll=1.

在巴西，尽管开展了重大的司法改革，但该国法律仍然没有关于承认外国破产判决的相关规定，也无法解决跨国执行的问题（费尔斯伯格 d.2–3）。巴西《宪法》、《民法典》和《民事诉讼法》仅仅提供了一般原则，要求对外国破产程序的承认必须提交领事证书（费尔斯伯格 d.3）。在没有细则的情况下，若满足一定条件，巴西理论上允许承认和执行国外破产判决（费尔斯伯格 d.3）。而其中执行的最重要条件之一，是将外国判决提交高级法院，即巴西司法系统中的第二高级联邦法院。[13]

(Felsberg n.d., 3). One of the most important conditions for an exequatur to be enforceable in Brazil is the requirement that a foreign judgment be submitted to the Superior Court of Justice (the second highest federal court in the Brazilian judiciary system).[13]

The Swiss Federal Supreme Court ruled that a worldwide freezing order issued by the High Court of London (often still referred to by their former name, Mareva injunctions) could be enforced by Swiss courts.[14] These worldwide freezing orders are generally not enforceable in the United States, although exceptions exist.

Powers of Insolvency Representatives in Asset Recovery

Tools Available to Collect Information and Evidence

Once insolvency representatives have identified and analyzed the suspicious transactions that may lead to stolen or recoverable assets, they will be able to use a range of measures to collect information and evidence to ensure effective asset recovery and bring actions to bankruptcy or other civil courts. These measures will be briefly presented in this section and are discussed in more detail in chapter 2.

The powers of insolvency representatives often include the ability to compel the production of books and records, including from lawyers, accountants, and banks, and to conduct audits. In addition, whether in common or civil law systems, the insolvency representatives, acting on behalf of the insolvent entities, can use existing legal tools to trace, secure, and recover assets.

In civil cases, such tools include disclosure and "no-say" or "gag" orders (especially in common law jurisdictions), search orders, freezing orders, and proprietary injunctions. Witness interrogations can be used to pursue civil corruption cases. Provisional measures may include worldwide

瑞士联邦最高法院裁定，瑞士法院可以执行由伦敦高等法院签发的全球冻结令（通常被称为玛瑞瓦禁令，Mareva injunctions）。[14] 而这类全球冻结令一般无法在美国执行，尽管也有例外。

破产管理人在资产追回中的权力

调查取证的措施

一旦破产管理人识别、分析了以转移资产为目标的可疑交易，就能够采取措施调查取证，确保追回资产并向破产法院或其他民事法院提起诉讼。这些措施将在本节中简要介绍，更详细的讨论参见第二章。

破产管理人有权查阅、审计包括律师、会计师、银行等在内的相关文件与信息。此外，无论在普通法系还是大陆法系国家，破产管理人都可以代表破产公司运用法律工具跟踪、保护及追讨相关资产。

在民事诉讼中，可用的法律工具包括禁止披露令（特别是在习惯法国家）、搜查令、冻结令以及其他专有禁令。证人证言也可用于民事腐败案件。还有一些临时措施，诸如全球范围内的冻结令（玛瑞瓦禁令）等。

freezing orders (Mareva injunctions) and similar measures.

Initiating criminal proceedings by reporting transactions to law enforcement authorities may also be an effective tool for collecting evidence of fraudulent activity, identifying assets, and enforcing judgments. The use of the criminal law provides prosecutors with the power to compel third parties to provide material that may be relevant to their investigation or prosecution; this material may also reveal the existence or amount of assets. In many jurisdictions, particularly common law jurisdictions, a complainant (who may be an insolvency representative acting on behalf of an insolvent entity) has a constitutional or common law right to commence a private prosecution.

Insolvency representatives should consider a range of criminal offenses for a criminal prosecution. For example, many individuals and companies seek voluntary arrangements with their creditors to avoid the scrutiny that follows from insolvency. When submitting a voluntary proposal, debtors have an obligation to provide accurate and truthful information. Failure to do so is a criminal offense, for which an insolvency representative or complainant may bring a criminal prosecution to compel the sharing of information and documents from third parties that may reveal evidence and assets.

Legal Actions that Authorize Insolvency Representatives to Claim Assets

Once insolvency representatives have identified recoverable assets and collected evidence to prove their cases in court, they can use a number of different legal actions to obtain effective recovery orders. This section provides a brief overview of these tools; more details are discussed in chapters 2 and 3.

Asset Tracing and Other Proprietary Claims

In general, insolvency representatives can assert a proprietary interest

在实践中，为了搜集罪证、追查资产、执行判决，启动刑事诉讼也是非常有效的方法。检察官有权要求第三方提供与案件相关的材料，其中可能含有与资产数量有关的信息。在很多国家，特别是普通法国家，申请人（可以是破产管理人）甚至具有宪法或普通法赋予的自诉权。

破产管理人还需要小心过程中可能存在的违法行为，比如，许多破产公司为了避免破产后的审计，要求自行与债权人进行资产分配。当债务人申请自行分配时，有义务提供准确真实的信息，否则将构成犯罪。破产管理人可以提起刑事诉讼，要求第三方披露与证据、资产有关的信息和文件。

破产管理人追查资产可采用的法律措施

一旦破产管理人将掌握的充分证据递交法庭，便可以采取多种法律措施申请支付令。本节简要概述了这些工具，更多细节可参考第二章和第三章的内容。

资产追查及所有权诉讼

一般来说，破产管理人可以对公司侵吞的资产主张所有权。这里

over a company's misappropriated assets. Misappropriation may result from various activities, including embezzlement, bribery, abuse of power, and theft. Claims may also extend to any subsequent assets into which the original property was converted. In court, the plaintiffs will need to show enough evidence to conclude that assets are derived from the debtors. In many common law jurisdictions, the concept of "beneficial ownership" allows courts to apply the theory of "constructive trust" when third parties have paid bribes to agents of principals. Under the theory of constructive trust, the bribes paid to agents are considered to be the proceeds of the breach of a fiduciary duty. The insolvency representative will be able to claim that the state is the beneficial owner of the funds or of the assets purchased with the bribes.[15]

Actions on the theory of constructive trust generally do not exist in civil law countries, which may hinder the recovery of bribes that never become property of the state. Plaintiffs may need to use personal claims instead to recover the funds (Brun et al. 2015, 51–55). The insolvency representatives in civil law countries will also be able to exercise "revindication" actions to recover embezzled or stolen assets. Some of these actions may be outside the scope of the insolvency law and may need to be sought in the broader legal system, such as in the civil courts.

Claims Available to Void, or Avoid, Suspicious or Fraudulent Transactions

The ability to cancel transactions that took place before the insolvency of the enterprise is an important tool for asset recovery in corruption cases. Such transactions may be fraudulent, gratuitous, preferential, or outside the ordinary course of business. Many countries' insolvency frameworks provide for a look-back or suspect period—a timeframe close to the company's insolvency during which payments are presumed to be

的“侵吞”具体可以包括挪用公款、贿赂、滥用职权、贪污等不法行为，还可以主张原始财产后续产生、转化的收益。在庭审中，原告需要提供充足的证据证明相关收益和资产属于债务人。在许多普通法国家，规定了“实际所有人”的概念，即如果第三方有行贿行为，法院可以运用“推定信赖”原则，将贿赂金视为违反信赖义务的不法收益。此时，破产管理人可将该收益收归国家。[15]

在大陆法系国家中，通常不存在“推定信赖”原则，因为它们认为，追讨的不法收益本就不属于国家。处理这种情况，一般由个人起诉代替资产追讨（布伦等，2015，51–55）。大陆法系的破产管理人也可以采用“返还原物之诉”的方法追讨资产。其中一些措施未必属于破产法的范畴，而是在更广泛的法律体系中，如民事法院中解决。

对无效交易、可撤销交易、可疑交易、欺诈交易的诉讼

撤销破产程序开始前的交易行为是追查腐败资产的重要手段。这类交易通常涉嫌欺诈、无偿转让或提前清偿等非正常业务。许多国家或地区的破产法都设计了回溯期，是指在破产程序开始前设定一个期限，允许撤销该期限内的可疑交易。大部分发达国家，如法国、意大利、西班牙、英国和美国的回溯期都不超过破产程序启动前两年（古里亚·马丁内斯，2016，21）。提前清偿，是指债务人提前向债权人赔付，

preferential. The suspect period in most developed jurisdictions (such as France, Italy, Spain, the United Kingdom, and the United States) is no longer than two years prior to the commencement of the insolvency process (Gurrea-Martinez 2016, 21). Preferential payments can involve a debtor's transfer to a creditor for an existing debt or, as the result of the transaction, a creditor's receiving a share of its claim from the debtor's assets higher than that received by other creditors of the same class or rank. The suspect period is often longer for transfers to affiliated persons (that is, those with a family or corporate relationship) or are gratuitous (consisting of payment with no proper consideration). Additional detail is provided in chapter 3. Box 1.9 presents the World Bank Principle on Avoidable Transactions.

BOX 1.9 World Bank Principle C11: Avoidable Transactions

C11.1 After the commencement of an insolvency proceeding, transactions by the debtor that are not consistent with the debtor's ordinary course of business or engaged in as part of an approved administration should be avoided (cancelled), with narrow exceptions protecting parties who lacked notice.

C11.2 Certain transactions prior to the application for or the date of commencement of the insolvency proceeding should be avoidable (cancelable, including fraudulent and preferential transfers made when the enterprise was insolvent or that rendered the enterprise insolvent).

C11.3 The suspect period, during which payments are presumed to be preferential and may be set aside, should be reasonably short in respect to general creditors to avoid disrupting normal commercial and credit relations, but the period may be longer in the case of gifts or when the person receiving the transfer is closely related to the debtor or its owners.

Some jurisdictions focus on voiding, or avoiding, fraudulent, dishonest, or undervalued transactions, and other jurisdictions have specific provisions allowing or facilitating the avoidance of transfers made by the debtor within a certain period before the bankruptcy filing.

An action for a declaration of invalidity, which restores the assets of

或债权人获得的实际份额比同等级其他债权人更高。这些都是可疑期内需要注意的。而对转移到其他关联人（家庭成员，或与公司有关系的成员）的资产的可疑审查期会更长。第三章提供了更多详细的信息。方框 1.9 介绍了世界银行关于可撤销交易的规定。

方框 1.9　世界银行准则 C11：可撤销交易

C11.1 破产程序开始后，应取消与债务人日常业务不符的交易或自行核准的交易，只有少数为保护善意第三人的例外可被允许。

C11.2 发生在破产程序开始当天或之前的某些交易应被撤销，包括在企业破产时或导致破产的财产转移、提前清偿等行为。

C11.3 对一般债务人而言，在可疑期内的交易都应先推定为提前清偿，搁置处理，但搁置期不应过长，以免干扰正常的商业活动。但如果是对债务人的密切关系人无偿赠与的操作，则需要更长的搁置期。

一些国家侧重于避免欺诈交易、低价交易发生；而其他一些国家则是将破产之前一定期间内已产生的交易作废。

通常而言，破产管理人、其他法定代表、专员或检察官可以提起

the debtor, is usually brought by the administrator, the legal representative, the commissioner for the execution of the plan, or the public prosecutor. In some jurisdictions, specifically in common law systems, insolvency representatives may apply for a broader range of remedies. Courts often have discretion as to the types of remedies, including undoing transactions in whole or in part, or ordering compensation or any measure that would restore the debtor to the position it would have had had it not entered into the transaction.

If a country's insolvency legislation does not enable insolvency representatives or creditors to look back at transactions that occurred close to the time of insolvency and cancel them, the insolvency representative may have difficulty acquiring resources that were dispersed prior to the insolvency. Some insolvency legislation does not clearly define a voidable transaction. Therefore, it is important to develop a clear understanding of what the legislation and case law of a country has determined constitutes a voidable transaction before using this method, even if it is broadly available within the legislative framework. Further discussion of preferential and fraudulent transactions is found in chapter 3 in the sections titled *Proceedings for Fraudulent or Wrongful Trading* and *Preferences and Transactions at Undervalue*, which describe specific mechanisms for recovery of stolen assets and provide examples of how they have been used.

Undervalued transactions or preferences are not necessarily proof of corruption, but, when corruption is suspected, they should be investigated to determine whether corporate entities are being used to conceal the value and the beneficial ownership of money flows.

Liability Actions

In some jurisdictions, the insolvency representative or the public prosecutor can carry out actions against legal (or de facto) directors when,

宣告交易无效的程序，恢复债务人的资产。在一些国家特别是普通法国家，破产管理人也可申请更广泛的救济措施，法院可酌情决定对其撤销全部或部分交易、命令赔偿或采取其他任何能使债务人资产恢复的措施。

如果一国的破产法不允许破产管理人或债权人回溯查看或撤销破产程序启动前产生的可疑交易，那么破产管理人将难以追索被提前转移的资产。另外，尽管大部分国家都有相关立法，但一些破产法并没有明确定义何为“无效交易”。因此，清楚了解一个国家的立法和判例，确定何为“无效交易”也变得极为重要。有关提前清偿和欺诈交易的进一步讨论，请参见第三章针对欺诈交易、提前清偿、低价交易等不当行为的程序等内容，其中具体阐释了资产追回的机制并提供了实践范例。

低价交易和提前清偿未必涉嫌欺诈，但若有嫌疑，则应开展调查，确定是否属于假借公司名义而掩护实际受益人的情况。

责任诉讼

在一些国家，破产程序启动时，如果债务人的资产不足以清偿债务，破产管理人或检察官可以对法定（或实际的）董事提起诉讼。法

at the date of the commencement of the bankruptcy case, the assets of the debtor are not sufficient to pay the company's liabilities. Courts can hold a director liable for all or part of the difference based on evidence that the position of the creditors has deteriorated following the misconduct (whether mismanagement or fraud) of the director. In France, insolvency representatives may have to show that the mismanagement or fraud has directly caused an increase in liabilities that contributed to the insufficiency of assets. As in typical tort cases, insolvency representatives must demonstrate fault (mismanagement, fraud, or any action that should not have been performed by a normally diligent director), damages (insufficiency of the assets or an increase in the shortfall of assets), and causation (the damages were caused by the fault) to sustain the claim. Winning a judgment of personal liability against directors requires a good deal of evidence of gross negligence or dishonesty, and we emphasize the point. Negligence or dishonesty of directors is sometimes obvious, especially in cases in which directors agree to abuse companies they manage to enable corruption or money laundering. For example, there may be evidence that a company was created for the purpose of buying and managing real estate purchased with proceeds of corruption on behalf of a corrupt official. For more information, see chapter 3.

Piercing the Corporate Veil

In principle, a registered corporation is a legal entity separate from those who own or control it. Shareholders, managers, directors, or beneficial owners of a company are generally not liable for the expenses or debts incurred by it. In some legal systems, however, legislation or courts may find it appropriate to "pierce the corporate veil" and to treat the rights or liabilities of a company as the rights or liabilities of its shareholders, directors, or agents. This is particularly relevant when the company was

院可以根据董事的不当行为（管理不善或欺诈等）认定债权人权益受损，该董事须对全部或部分债务的差额承担责任。在法国，破产管理人必须证明，公司的经营不善、欺诈行为与负债增加、资不抵债的后果存在明确的因果关系。要强调的是，与一般的侵权案件一样，破产管理人必须证明：（1）过错（包括管理不善、欺诈或渎职等行为）；（2）资不抵债的损害结果；（3）二者之间的因果关系，即损害是由过错造成的；只有举证上述三项才能支持自己的主张。有时公司董事存在明显的过错、欺诈行为，或滥用职权利用公司洗钱等，比如，某一证据表明，公司设立的目的就是替涉贪的公职人员购买和管理不动产。更多信息，详见第三章。

揭开公司面纱

一般来说，注册公司是一种独立于其实际所有人、控制人的法人实体。公司的股东、经理、董事或实际所有人一般不负担公司的债务或成本。但是，在一些国家，“揭开公司面纱”，指将公司的权利或义务等同于股东、董事或代理人的权利或义务，特别是当公司成立的目的就是掩盖不法交易或洗钱时。当公司不能支付因股东、董事或实际所有人的非法行为而产生的债务被宣告破产时，破产管理人完全有可能将公司股东、董事或实际拥有人的其他合法财产用于清偿。（参见第

created or used as a device or a façade for fraud or money laundering. The company may be placed under receivership or another insolvency proceeding if it cannot or will not pay judgments or other debts arising from the fraudulent activities conducted by its shareholders, directors, or beneficial owners. In these circumstances, it will be possible for insolvency representatives to recover assets legally owned either by the entity or its shareholders, directors, and beneficial owners. (See the section titled *Piercing the Corporate Veil* in chapter 3.)

Key Points from this Chapter

- The purpose of an insolvency proceeding is to seize and sell assets of the debtor-defendant and distribute the money equitably to creditors and other injured parties, thus protecting their rights.
- In insolvency proceedings, certain jurisdictions allow a business to be wound up on just and equitable grounds, which can be valuable in cases of corruption, embezzlement, or any type of fraudulent activity. Other jurisdictions rely on more traditional definitions of insolvency.
- Insolvency representatives can, through their efforts to retrieve assets of the estate, recover illegally obtained proceeds stolen by corrupt officials.
- In the pursuit of assets stolen for corrupt purposes, insolvency representatives have a variety of tools available to them to identify and immobilize assets belonging to the insolvent estate.
- Some corruption crosses borders; insolvency representatives are often called upon to exercise their powers in foreign countries, where they must keep in mind the variations in the legal rules for recognition and enforcement of foreign judgments in insolvency proceedings.

Notes

1. Just and equitable grounds is generally a common law concept; although the concept is not clearly defined in many legislative frameworks that provide for it, it has evolved through case law. For example, in the

三章中“揭开公司面纱”的相关内容。)

本章要点

- 破产程序是为了获得或出售债务人的资产，并将其公平分配给债权人以维护他们的合法权益的过程。
- 某些国家的破产法制定了“公平公正”原则，十分有利于打击腐败或其他诈骗犯罪。而有些国家则更依靠较为传统的破产概念。
- 破产管理人有权追回涉贪公职人员以不法方式获取的资产。
- 为了追回腐败资产，破产管理人可以采取多种方法识别、冻结破产财产。
- 在跨国腐败案件中，破产管理人需要在国外行使权力，而各国破产程序均有差异，此时破产管理人牢记这些差异就显得尤为重要。

注释

1. “公平公正”原则一般是习惯法的概念。提出这个概念的许多法律制度并没有对其明确界定，它通过判例演变而来。例如，在英国，以欺诈目的成立的公司，在成立之初就可被下达清算令。See Anglo-

United Kingdom, windingup orders have been made when a company was formed for fraudulent purposes. See, for example, Anglo-Greek Steam Co. [1866] LR 2 Eq 1; In re West Surrey Tanning Co. [1866] LR 2 Eq 737; In re London and County Coal Co. [1867] LR 3 Eq 355.

2. See, for example, In re International Securities Corp. [1908] 99 LT 581.

3. In Belgium and France, prosecutors can petition a court to open a bankruptcy proceeding. In the United Kingdom and the United States, only a creditor may petition to open a case.

4. If a country has no or very limited rules and regulations for who can become an insolvency representative, the quality and reliability of those representatives will vary. Moreover, should a country not have a mechanism for monitoring and training representatives, holding them to account and ensuring continued quality will be difficult.

5. In the private-professional model, the primary obligation is the recovery of assets for creditors and injured parties. In the public model, the employee has a state salary, so the incentives are slightly different.

6. Some countries have insolvency laws that exclude financial institutions from their scope and application. In this section, we focus on countries that include them.

7. The moratorium can sometimes be initiated as early as the filing of the originating insolvency process.

8. Regulation (EU) 2015/848 of the European Parliament and of the Council of May 20, 2015, on Insolvency Proceedings (Recast Insolvency Regulation).

9. Forty-four jurisdictions have adopted the Model Law on Cross-Border Insolvency.

10. The "relevant countries" are Australia, Canada, Finland, China,

Greek Steam Co. [1866] LR 2 Eq 1; In re West Surrey Tanning Co. [1866] LR 2 Eq 737; In re London and County Coal Co. [1867] LR 3 Eq 355.

2. See In re International Securities Corp. [1908] 99 LT 581.

3. 在比利时和法国，检察官可以向法院申请启动破产程序。在英国和美国只有债权人具有申请资格。

4. 若一个国家的破产法对破产管理人的任职资格缺乏相关立法或立法不完善时，则破产管理人的资质无法保证。此外，若一国缺乏对破产管理人的监督和培训，则难以确保他能尽职尽责。

5. 对于非国家公职破产管理人而言，其主要目的是为债权人和受害方追回资产。对于公职破产管理人而言，具有国家薪资保障，因而激励机制略不相同。

6. 有些国家的破产法将金融机构排除在适用范围之外，在本节，我们将重点介绍这些国家。

7. 有时候，在破产程序启动之前，就可以申请延期支付。

8. 2015 年 5 月 20 日，欧洲议会和理事会 2015/848 号条例修订后的破产条例）。

9. 44 个国家、地区通过了《跨国界破产示范法》。

10. “相关国家或地区”具体包括澳大利亚、加拿大、芬兰、中国、

Japan, Jersey, New Zealand, the United Kingdom, and the United States.

11. UNCITRAL-INSOL-World Bank Report, 12th Multinational Judicial Colloquium, Sydney, March18–19, 2017. http://www.uncitral.org/pdf/english/colloquia/insolvency-2017/twelfthJC.pdf.

12. See case comment at https://www.lexology.com/library/detail.aspx?g=b952eefc-e9c9-4687-b9a9-3950f0db4e02.

13. Brazil will not recognize foreign courts' rulings, however, if the law provides for exclusive Brazilian jurisdiction (Felsberg n.d., 3).

14. Swiss Federal Supreme Court, 94A_366/2011 (October 31, 2011).

15. For example, in *Attorney General v. Reid,* the government of Hong Kong SAR, China was recognized as the owner of properties purchased with bribes because the funds were obtained through a breach of fiduciary duty. The dishonest official was deemed to hold the funds (and the properties purchased with them) as a constructive trustee; the government was their true owner. Similarly, in *Kartika Ratna Thahir v. Pertamina* (Singapore), https://star.worldbank.org/corruption-cases/sites/corruption-cases/files/documents/arw/Pertamina_Singapore_Appeals_Court_Aug_25_1994.pdf, an Indonesian state-owned energy enterprise sued its former executive to recover bribes he received from two contractors. The former executive had deposited the bribes in a bank in Singapore. The court found that the former executive owed a fiduciary duty to the enterprise and that he held the bribes as a constructive trustee for the true owner.

References

Brun, Jean-Pierre, Pascale Helene Dubois, Emile van der Does de Willebois, Jeanne Hauch, Sarah Jais, Yannis Mekki, Anastasia Sotiropoulou, Katherine Rose Sylvester, and Mahesh Uttamchandani. 2015. *Public Wrongs, Private Actions*. Washington, DC: World Bank.

日本、泽西岛、新西兰、英国和美国。

11.《联合国国际贸易法委员会—国家反腐协会—世界银行报告》，第十二届多边国家司法学术研讨会，悉尼，2017 年 3 月 18 日至 19 日，http://www.uncitral.org/pdf/english/colloquia/insolvency-2017/twelfthJC.pdf。

12. 案件评论详见：https://www.lexology.com/library/detail.aspx?g=b952eefc-e9c9-4687-b9a9-3950f0db4e02。

13. 然而，如果法律规定巴西具有专属管辖权，巴西可以拒绝执行外国法院的裁决（费尔斯伯格 d.3）。

14. 瑞士联邦高等法院 94A_366/2011（2011 年 10 月 31 日）。

15. 例如，在香港特别行政区总检察长诉里德案中，中国政府才是涉案资产的所有人，因为这些资金是通过违反信赖义务获取的，涉贪官员以推定受托人的身份持有相关资产，但政府才是真正的所有权人。同样，在新加坡的卡迪卡 · 拉特纳 · 塔希尔诉佩塔米纳案中，印度尼西亚一家国有能源企业起诉前高管以追讨他从两名承包商处收受的贿赂。这位前高管将贿赂金存放在新加坡的一家银行。法院认为，前任高管对企业负有信赖义务，对于真正所有权人而言，他只是贿赂金的推定受托人。（详见 https://star.worldbank.org/corruption-cases/sites/corruption-cases/files/documents/arw/Pertamina_Singapore_Appeals_Court_Aug_25_1994.pdf。）

参考文献

Brun, Jean-Pierre, Pascale Helene Dubois, Emile van der Does de Willebois, Jeanne Hauch, Sarah Jais, Yannis Mekki, Anastasia Sotiropoulou, Katherine Rose Sylvester, and Mahesh Uttamchandani. 2015. *Public Wrongs, Private Actions*. Washington, DC: World Bank.

EBRD (European Bank for Reconstruction and Development). 2007. "EBRD Insolvency Office Holder Principles." EBRD, London. https://www.ebrd.com/documents/legal-reform/ebrd-insolvency-office-holder-principles.pdf.

———. 2014. "Assessment of Insolvency Office Holders: Review of the Profession in the EBRD Region." EBRD, London.

Felsberg, Thomas Benes. n.d. "Cross-Border Insolvency in Brazil: The Need for Rules." Unpublished.

Goffman, Jay M. 2014. Panel discussion at the International Insolvency & Restructuring Symposium: America Now!, London, October 30–31.

Gurrea-Martinez, Aurelio. 2016. "The Avoidance of Pre-Bankruptcy Transactions: An Economic and Comparative Approach." Working Paper Series 10/2016, Instituto Iberomaericano de Derecho y Finanzas (IIDF), Madrid, Spain.

UNCITRAL (United Nations Commission on International Trade Law). 2004. *Legislative Guide on Insolvency Law*. New York: UNCITRAL.

World Bank. 2016. "C17: Insolvency of International Enterprise Groups." In *Principles for Effective Insolvency and Creditor/Debtor Regimes*. Washington, DC: World Bank.

EBRD (European Bank for Reconstruction and Development). 2007. "EBRD Insolvency Office Holder Principles." EBRD, London. https://www.ebrd.com/documents/legal-reform/ebrd-insolvency-office-holder-principles.pdf.

———. 2014. "Assessment of Insolvency Office Holders: Review of the Profession in the EBRD Region." EBRD, London.

Felsberg, Thomas Benes. n.d. "Cross-Border Insolvency in Brazil: The Need for Rules." Unpublished.

Goffman, Jay M. 2014. Panel discussion at the International Insolvency & Restructuring Symposium: America Now!, London, October 30–31.

Gurrea-Martinez, Aurelio. 2016. "The Avoidance of Pre-Bankruptcy Transactions: An Economic and Comparative Approach." Working Paper Series 10/2016, Instituto Iberomaericano de Derecho y Finanzas (IIDF), Madrid, Spain.

UNCITRAL (United Nations Commission on International Trade Law). 2004. *Legislative Guide on Insolvency Law*. New York: UNCITRAL.

World Bank. 2016. "C17: Insolvency of International Enterprise Groups." In *Principles for Effective Insolvency and Creditor/Debtor Regimes*. Washington, DC: World Bank.

2. Investigative Measures Potentially Available in Insolvency and Civil Cases

International insolvency and cross-border asset recovery efforts to combat corruption entail complicated processes. To right the wrongs and ensure that the culprits do not enjoy their illicit gains, investigators charged with investigating corruption or misappropriation in insolvency proceedings need both judicial and nonjudicial resources.

Experienced investigators of corruption are accustomed to using both, enabling them to develop a complete picture, target available resources, and form a plan. In cases of corruption, nonjudicial tools, such as investigative measures and examination of witnesses, can be crucial in establishing the purported insolvency that leads to the appointment of an insolvency representative, who can then assist in the recovery of assets. Chapter 2 provides an overview of the various tools available to professionals charged with recovering the proceeds of corruption.

Investigative measures to identify and trace assets that could be the proceeds of corruption and targets for civil actions are available in both civil law and common law jurisdictions. Depending on the legal system, litigants, including insolvency representatives acting on behalf of the insolvent entity, can exercise powers provided for by commercial or civil legislation or insolvency legislation, including obtaining court orders authorizing disclosure of information and searches of premises. This chapter lays out the range of legal tools using examples drawn primarily from common law systems.

2. 民事破产案件的调查手段

跨国反腐败资产追查的破产行动需经过复杂的程序，为了打击犯罪并追回不法资产，腐败案件的调查员需要司法和非司法资源的充足支持。

经验丰富的反腐败调查人员擅长双管齐下，将这两类资源结合使用，以便全面掌握信息并制定可行计划。在腐败案件发生时，调查手段和证人取证等非司法手段对于破产程序的启动至关重要，影响到破产管理人的委任和后续的追查行动。第二章介绍了反腐败追查资产常用的几种调查措施。

大陆法系和普通法系都有相关的调查措施，用以追踪、识别腐败资产和民事诉讼的标的。根据法律制度的不同，申请人、破产管理人可以行使商法、民法和破产法等规定的权利，包括申请授权披露信息、搜查场所等。本章主要采用普通法的示例列明各项法律工具。

Many of these tools exist under different names and concepts in other legal systems. For instance, authorization to search private premises in the course of civil litigation can be granted by French judges through application of the French Code of Civil Procedure. Policy makers and practitioners in different legal systems should investigate the legislation and jurisprudence in their jurisdictions that might enable them to reach solutions similar to those described in this chapter.

Extrajudicial Investigative Tools

In addition to the investigative measures available in an insolvency case, meaningful information can be gathered through extrajudicial investigative activities, including:

- Examination of all available records and other documentary evidence
- Liaison with known sources of information, both open and confidential, including sources within official police and government circles when appropriate
- Attempts to develop additional confidential and open sources
- Covert gathering of intelligence and evidence
- Retrieval of pertinent information from various electronic and other databases
- Surveillance of principal targets and, if appropriate, potential targets
- Initiation of covert evidence and intelligence gathering and the commencement of discreet inquiries to accomplish, among other things, the reverse tracing of concealed assets
- Interviews with selected witnesses.

Overt, extrajudicial investigative activities, coupled with judicially assisted investigations, when appropriate, may be used to develop information on the assets and ultimate beneficial ownership of entities that may have been used

其中许多法律工具的名称、概念因国家而异。例如，在法国，法官适用的是《法国民事诉讼法》授权对私有企业场所的搜查。不同国家的政策制定者和执行者都应了解本国的立法，从中获得与本章所述相似的解决方案。

法外调查工具

除了破产程序中规定的可用调查措施外，还可以通过其他法定程序之外的调查措施收集信息，包括：

- 查阅相关文件、记录等证据；
- 与公开或机密的信息源保持联络，可能的话，包括警方和政府内部人士提供的信息；
- 尝试拓展其他公开或机密的信息来源；
- 秘密搜集情报和证据；
- 充分利用多个数据库检索信息；
- 监视主要目标以及潜在目标；
- 谨慎验证情报，对隐匿资产反向追踪；
- 获取特定的证人证言。

显然，在适当的时候，法外调查手段配合法定调查程序，能够获得更多可能被用作转移、隐藏或持有的腐败资产和真正受益人的信息。

to move, conceal, or hold assets that were corruptly obtained.

Information relevant to building a case is often available online, including judgments, liens, and bankruptcy filings; property records; business registrations (cross-referenced in various ways); oil and gas partnerships; motor vehicle and drivers' license registrations; regulatory proceedings and filings; thoroughbred horse ownership; lists of all former addresses; property tax rolls; information relating to divorce proceedings; and details of boat or plane ownership. Social media are also powerful sources of public information.

Discovery Databases as a Source of Information

Search engines can locate and decipher information that may appear insignificant to the untrained eye. Asset recovery investigations require access to computer records and analysis of digital information. The programs available to assist an investigator are potentially helpful but complex. Computer forensic professionals will be needed.

Computer databases were an invaluable tool for the investigative team that searched for dormant accounts left by Holocaust victims in Swiss banks. A team of dedicated accountants combined old-fashioned investigative methods with the capabilities of a large relational database to find and sort through reams of files and recover almost $1 billion in funds deposited by individuals who died in Nazi-era concentration camps. These funds were placed in escrow to pay claims brought by lawful heirs.

Electronic evidence has often shaped the outcome of high-profile insolvency and civil asset recovery investigations, ranging from the theft of intellectual property and insider trading that violates U.S. Securities and Exchange Commission (SEC) regulations to proof of employee misconduct that results in termination of employment for cause. Critical electronic

与案件相关的信息通常都能在从网上获得，例如，判决信息、留置权信息、破产申请、财产记录和商业登记等（彼此印证参照）；又如，石油天然气合作供应商、机动车驾驶执照注册、有关监管备案程序、纯种马的所有权、所有先前地址列表、纳税记录、婚姻状况、船只和飞机所有权信息等。此外，社交媒体也是公开信息的重要来源。

充分发掘数据库信息源

搜索引擎可以定位和解密一些常人看来不重要的信息。资产追查则需要访问计算机系统并分析相关数据。开发相关程序能帮助调查人员获取信息，但通常难度较大，需要计算机专业人士协助完成。

为了检索纳粹大屠杀受害人在瑞士银行的休眠账户，一支专业技术团队将大型关联数据库的功能和传统调查方法相结合，通过对大量文件的查找和分类，追回了纳粹集中营被屠杀的受害者们近 10 亿美金的存款。这些资金将交由托管机构，用于后续支付法定继承人的相关赔偿。

在一起知名的与破产相关的民事纠纷中，电子证据为调查提供了重要支持。一名雇员涉嫌窃取公司知识产权，违反美国证券交易委员会（SEC）法令，实施了内部交易等不当行为而最终被解雇。重要证据是在该雇员的网页浏览历史记录中找到的，包括收到的电子邮件、访问的站点和相关网页的搜索记录等。

evidence is often found in a suspect's web-browsing history in the form of received emails, sites visited, and attempted Internet searches.

What is saved on a computer hard drive can provide invaluable information, but often what is not saved—or to be more precise, what has been deleted—will prove critical. Often a hard drive retains information that a user has tried to delete; computer professionals may be able to retrieve this information.

Examination of Witnesses under Standard Insolvency Practices

Insolvency laws often specify the duties and functions of insolvency representatives upon their appointment and the powers available to them to perform those duties and functions efficiently and effectively.

Insolvency representatives are generally empowered to conduct examinations of witnesses who may have information likely to assist the representative in determining the state of affairs or assets of a debtor, whether in a personal or corporate insolvency.

Obtaining information concerning the debtor, its assets, liabilities, and past transactions (especially those taking place during the period immediately preceding the commencement of insolvency or bankruptcy) is one of the core duties of the insolvency representative. The powers available to obtain that information generally include examining the debtor and any third person who had dealings with the debtor.

In the United Kingdom, insolvency representatives may make application to the court for orders against any officers of the company or any persons whom they think capable of providing information concerning the business, dealings, and affairs of the company.

An English court enjoys unfettered discretion whether to issue the order, but the exercise of that discretion involves a balancing of the needs of

另外，保存在计算机硬盘上的内容可以提供宝贵的信息，但没保存的内容，确切地说，被删除的内容更加重要。硬盘通常会保留用户删除的信息，计算机专业人员能够将其恢复。

标准化破产实践中的证人取证

破产法通常规定了破产管理人的职责与义务，也规定帮助其高效履行职责所拥有的权力。

在个人破产或公司破产程序中，破产管理人通常有权对相关证人进行调查，这些证人往往掌握着债务人及相关资产的信息。

获取关于债务人及其相关资产、负债和先前交易（特别是临近破产程序期间所发生的交易）的信息是破产管理人的核心任务。获取这些信息通常需要管理人对债务人进行调查，或者对与债务人存在交易关系的第三方进行调查。

在英国，破产管理人可以向法院申请调查令，对公司的高级管理人员，或任何破产管理人认为掌握公司交易、业务相关信息的人员开展调查。

英国法院可以自由裁量是否发布调查令，行使自由裁量权主要考量的是，如何在破产管理人的需求与可能存在的对被调查者的压迫、

insolvency representatives against any possible oppression, unfairness, or prejudice to examinees. The process of examination is not intended to enable the representatives to, nor will they be permitted to, conduct a "fishing expedition." Courts might also, in the exercise of their discretion, consider the risk of collusion between the insolvency representatives and the debtors' management, resulting in a settlement that isn't in the best interest of the creditors.

Targets of Examination

Examination powers are generally used to inspect or obtain documents from directors; in most jurisdictions, other persons and entities—including a company's solicitors, accountants, auditors, and bank managers—may also be examined if they are believed to have information about the business, dealings, and affairs of the company. In applying for examination power with regard to a particular person, the onus is on the insolvency representative to establish a reasonable need for the information sought. Relevant information may be held by individuals and corporate entities, as well as governmental bodies.

In a corporate insolvency that consists of a winding up in the United Kingdom, an examinee could be:

- Any officer or director of the company
- Any person known or believed to have in his or her possession any property of the company or any person supposed to be indebted to the company
- Any person whom the court believes capable of giving information about the promotion, formation, business, dealings, affairs, or property of the company.

In a bankruptcy (personal insolvency) in the United Kingdom, an examinee could be:

- The bankrupt person or his or her spouse or former spouse

偏见和不公平之间取得平衡。调查过程不希望也不允许破产管理人“审前非法调查”（fishing expedition）（也有译作“远距离求证”）。法院也还需要考虑破产管理人与债务人合谋的风险，避免对债权人权益造成损害。

调查对象

调查对象一般是指公司董事及其掌握的相关文件。在大多数国家，如果个人或机构被认为掌握与公司业务、交易相关的信息，就可对其开展调查。这里的个人或机构也包括公司的律师、会计、审计师或银行经理等。在申请对某个证人开展调查时，破产管理人有责任确保此调查是合理需求。这里的信息掌握人可以是个人、公司或政府机构。

在英国公司破产程序中，被调查者可以是：

- 任何公司董事、管理人员、雇员等；
- 任何已知或被认为掌控公司财产的人，或任何可能因公司而受益的人；
- 法院认为任何掌握与公司扩张、成立、交易、业务、资产等事务相关信息的人。

在英国个人破产程序中，被调查者可以是：

- 破产人本人、配偶或前任配偶；

- Any person known or believed to have in his or her possession any property belonging to the estate of the bankrupt person or any person supposed to be indebted to the bankrupt person
- Any person whom the court believes capable of giving information about the bankrupt person or his or her dealings, affairs, or property.

Although corporate insolvency processes would be initiated where the company maintains its center of main interest (COMI), personal insolvency cases are likely to be initiated within the debtor's home jurisdiction. Therefore, it is less likely that a personal insolvency, as opposed to a corporate insolvency, would take place in an offshore jurisdiction.

In the United Kingdom, the power of examination is not restricted to persons situated or resident there. Questions of jurisdiction and recognition of the order may arise, however, when an examination order is sought against a foreign entity. In some cases, a foreign court may be willing to grant to a recognized foreign insolvency representative powers that are the same or equivalent to those available to local insolvency representatives. Box 2.1 provides an example of how a court in Australia, which has adopted the United Nations Commission on International Trade Law (UNCITRAL) Model Law, dealt with a request for assistance from a British Virgin Islands court.

The examination of corporate officers is considered less likely to be oppressive than an examination of third parties, because officers have a statutory duty to cooperate and, by virtue of their position, are more likely to be in possession of relevant information.

Generally, no examination will be permitted once the insolvency representative has commenced or has resolved to commence legal proceedings against the person in question, because such information would ordinarily come to light in the process of discovery during those proceedings.

- 任何已知或被认为持有破产人财产的个人，或因破产人而受惠的个人；

- 法院认为任何掌握有关破产人交易、个人事务、或财产信息的个人。

公司破产程序一般在债务人主要权益中心（COMI）所在地启动，但个人破产案件则一般在债务人本国启动。所以，与公司破产程序不同，个人破产程序在国外发生的可能性较小。

在英国，调查并不限于位于或居住于英国的人；但申请涉外调查时，可能引发对其他司法管辖区的法令进行效力认定的问题。在一些情况下，国外法院愿意将本国破产管理人的权力同等赋予外国破产管理人。方框 2.1 提供了一个示例，表明澳大利亚法院如何运用联合国国际贸易法委员会的《跨国界破产示范法》，处理英属维尔京群岛法院的请求。

与对第三方人员的调查相比，对公司高级管理人员的调查通常不被认为具有压迫性，主要是因为公司高管原本就负有配合调查的法定义务，并且因职务关系，也更可能掌握有关信息。

一般而言，一旦破产管理人开始启动或已经决定启动破产程序，所有的非法定调查措施都不再被允许。因为在诉讼过程中自然能够获取所需要的信息。

BOX 2.1 ***Crumpler ex rel. Global Tradewaves Ltd. v. Global Tradewaves, in re Global Tradewaves Ltd.***[a]

The applicants (Crumpler) had been appointed as insolvency representatives of Global Tradewaves Ltd. (Global Tradewaves), a company registered in the British Virgin Islands pursuant to an order of the Eastern Caribbean Supreme Court's High Court of Justice, the British Virgin Islands Commercial Division (the British Virgin Islands Court).

Even though there was no evidence that Global Tradewaves carried on business in Australia or had any Australian creditors, its insolvency representatives sought recognition in an Australian court of the British Virgin Islands liquidation as a foreign main proceeding. The insolvency representatives also sought an ancillary order that a former director of Global Tradewaves be summoned for examination.

The Federal Court of Australia was satisfied that the statutory winding-up regime that operates in the British Virgin Islands is similar to that of the Australian Corporations Act and, accordingly, that the liquidation of Global Tradewaves was a foreign proceeding and that its insolvency representatives were foreign representatives. The court was also satisfied that the British Virgin Islands was the COMI of Global Tradewaves.

Recognition of the British Virgin Islands liquidation enabled the insolvency representatives to seek ancillary orders for the examination of the former director, who they believed was resident in Australia.

A public examination of the former director could be ordered on three bases:

- Article 21(1)(d) authorized the court to provide for the examination of a witness on information concerning the company's assets, affairs, rights, obligations, or liabilities.
- Article 21(1)(g) authorized the court to make an order for a public examination pursuant to division 1 of part 5.9 of the Corporations Act.
- Having received a letter of request from the British Virgin Islands Court, the court also had discretion to order an examination under section 581 of the Corporations Act.

The court was satisfied that the former director was a person likely to have an intimate knowledge of the affairs of Global Tradewaves and that the insolvency representative was entitled to summon the former director for public examination.

a. [2013] FCA 1127.

方框 2.1　环球贸易有限公司（一家在英属维尔京群岛注册的公司）的克朗普勒（作为清算人兼联合代表）诉环球贸易有限公司（清算中）[a]

申请人克朗普勒被任命为环球贸易有限公司的破产管理人，该公司是根据东加勒比最高法院英属维尔京群岛商业高等法院的命令在维尔京群岛注册的公司。

尽管没有证据表明环球贸易有限公司在澳大利亚开展过业务或在这有任何债权人，但它的破产管理人仍然在澳大利亚申请对英属维尔京群岛破产判决的承认并将其作为“外国主要程序”审理。同时，破产管理人还附加申请了调查令，要求传唤一名 GT 公司的前主管接受调查。

由于英属维京群岛的破产制度与澳大利亚公司法律规定类似，所以澳大利亚联邦法院对 GT 公司的清算适用的是外国程序，认定克朗普勒为外国破产管理人，还认可英属维京群岛为该公司的主要权益中心地。

对英属维京群岛破产裁决的认可使破产管理人能够申请附加令，调查澳大利亚籍的公司前董事。

对公司前任董事的公开调查权基于如下三个条款：

- 第 21(1)(d) 条：法院有权就公司资产、业务、权利或义务对证人调查取证。
- 第 21(1)(g) 条：法院有权依据《公司法》第 5.9 条第 1 款下令进行公开调查。
- 收到英属维京群岛法院的请求后，法院有权依据《公司法》第 581 条签发调查令。

法院认为该前任董事很可能对环球贸易有限公司的事务有深入的了解，且破产管理人有权申请传唤他接受公开调查。

a. [2013] FCA 1127.

Whether the examination of a person outside the jurisdiction will be ordered depends on the statutory mechanisms available in the forum or local jurisdiction and in the target jurisdiction. Courts generally have no power to summon a foreign resident. In the United Kingdom, section 237(3) of the Insolvency Act 1986 provides that persons who are not within the jurisdiction (but could be summoned to appear before the court under section 236 of that Act) may be subject to an order for examination either within or outside the United Kingdom. Section 236, which deals with inquiries into a company's dealings, does not have extraterritorial effect.

If an appropriate mechanism for such an order exists in the jurisdiction in which the examination target resides, however, an English court may make such an order under section 237(3) of the Act.[1] Applications to obtain information from foreign residents can be technically complex. Expert advice is often needed in such situations.

Range of Examination

In practice, an examination is confined to information concerning the corporation's promotion, formation, management, administration, winding up, or any other affairs of the corporation or related entities. Questions concerning matters relating to the "property" of a corporation are also within the ambit of an examination. In theory, this could extend to any potential right to compensation for malfeasance of its officers, including its directors, and the general right of action for breach of directors' duties.

The range of an examination must be seen in the context of assisting insolvency representatives in carrying out their duties. To enable creditors to be repaid, insolvency representatives are required to take possession of, protect, liquidate, and distribute the assets or the proceeds of the liquidation of the assets of the debtor to the creditors, in accordance with applicable statutory priorities. To fulfill those functions, insolvency representatives

是否下令对司法管辖区外的人员进行调查取证取决于本国法院、本国法律及目标国相关的法律制度。法院通常无权传唤外国居民作为证人出庭。但根据英国《1986 年破产法》第 237（3）条，不属于本国司法管辖范围的人员（除根据第 236 条可被传唤出庭的外），无论在英国境内或境外，皆可被传唤出庭。第 236 条是规范与公司破产相关的证人质证，但不具有域外效力。

如果被调查者所属司法管辖区的法律并不排斥这条法令，则英国法院可依据上述第 237（3）条发布传唤令。[1] 从技术上来说，申请外国居民作证的过程比较复杂，通常需要专家的特别建议。

调查的范围

在实践中，调查范围一般为有关公司扩张、组建、管理、行政、清算或公司与其他相关机构事务的信息。与资产相关的信息也在调查范围之内。从理论上讲，这些可以延伸到后续对董事、高管的渎职行为提起诉讼，并要求损害赔偿。

调查范围结合破产管理人的职责而考量确定，为了使债权人获得清偿，破产管理人可拥有、保留、清算以及依据法定优先权分配债务人资产。为履行该职能，破产管理人需要先确定资产的种类、数量、性质，有形或无形等，再从相关人士处获取其他信息。调查范围包括银行经理、会计师、公司高管、业务伙伴或其他关联的个人或机构。破产管理人的调查权也可强制要求不愿提供信息的知情人员配合调查

must determine what assets exist, both tangible and intangible. Determining what assets are available will invariably involve obtaining information about such assets from those in a position to provide it, such as bank managers, accountants, officers, even business associates or affiliated persons or entities. Insolvency representatives may use powers of examination to obtain information from those who are unwilling to provide it voluntarily.

In *Re Gold Co. Ltd.*, Sir George Jessel, referring to a section that provided for the power to examine, wrote:

> [T]he whole object of the section is to assimilate the practice in winding up to the practice in bankruptcy, which was established in order to enable assignees, who are now called trustees, in bankruptcy to find out facts before they brought an action, so as to avoid incurring the expense of some hundreds of pounds in bringing an unsuccessful action, when they might, by examining a witness or two, have discovered at a trifling expense that an action could not succeed.[2]

Justice Buckley, in *Re Rolls Razor Ltd.*, wrote, in relation to the comparable provision in the Companies Act 1948 (U.K.):

> The powers conferred by [section] 268 are powers directed to enabling the court to help an insolvency representative to discover the truth of the circumstances connected with the affairs of the company, information of trading, dealings, and so forth, in order that the insolvency representative may be able, as effectively as possible and, I think, with as little expense as possible and with as much expedition as possible, to complete his function as insolvency representative, to put the affairs of the company in order and to carry out the liquidation in all its various aspects, including, of course, the getting in of any assets of the company

提供信息。

在里卡淘金公司案中，乔治·塞耶尔在关于调查权的一节中写道：

> 本节的目的是吸收破产实务中的经验，让破产受托人（现在被称为破产管理人）能够在起诉前查明事实，避免因败诉而承担数百英镑的不必要的损失。如果他们通过向一两个证人取证后发现无法胜诉，所负担的成本就相对小很多。[2]

大法官巴克利在劳斯剃刀公司案中就1948年《英国公司法》相对应的条款写道：

> 第268条是为了让法院能够帮助破产管理人及早发现与公司事务、交易相关的真相，以便破产管理人履行自己的义务，完成破产程序。我认为，应该以尽可能少的费用和尽可能多的调查，使破产管理人行使职权，以便厘清公司事务完成清算，并获取清算中的所有资产。

available in the liquidation.

> It is, therefore, appropriate for the insolvency representative, when he thinks that he may be under a duty to try to recover something from some officer or employee of a company, or some other person who is, in some way, concerned with the company's affairs, to be able to discover, with as little expense as possible and with as much ease as possible, the facts surrounding any such possible claim.[3]

Any question designed to elicit information concerning assets of the debtor, even intangible assets or assets that have been misappropriated, should fall within the range of the examination. Information that may enable the insolvency representative to reach an informed decision also falls within the scope of what is considered permissible.

In general, an examination will be permitted as long as an insolvency representative is not seeking information merely to pressure a potential litigation adversary for an improper purpose. An applicant who seeks an examination order for the purpose of obtaining a forensic advantage not otherwise available, however, may be committing an abuse of process.

Use of Information

Information obtained during an examination can be used only to further the exercise of the functions and duties of insolvency representatives. The nature, scope, and purpose of their power are relevant to how the information will be used. As long as the information is sought for a proper purpose, examinees, particularly officers and former officers and directors of the debtor, have no privilege against self-incrimination when responding to requests for information. The answers provided, however, may not be used in criminal proceedings.

Even in the absence of a privilege against self-incrimination, the

因此，破产管理人认为他有责任从公司高管、雇员或其他利益相关人处获取信息，以尽可能少的费用、尽可能省力的方法挖掘相关事实，这是很合理的。[3]

任何债务人的资产信息，包括无形资产和被转移资产的信息，以及其他能够影响破产管理人做决定的信息，都在调查范围之内。可以帮助破产管理人作出明智决策的信息，也都应在可调查之列。

一般而言，只要不是破产管理人基于专门给对手施加压力等不正当目的而开展的调查，就应该被允许。但为获取证据优势而申请调查令可能存在滥用司法资源的风险。

信息使用

调查获取的信息只能在破产管理人的职权范围内使用。它的性质、范围、目的都与信息的使用方式息息相关。只要是基于正当目的开展的调查，被调查者，特别是债务人的管理人员、前管理人员以及公司董事，在接受调查时都不享有豁免自证其罪的特权。但是，被调查的信息不被允许用于刑事诉讼中。

即便没有豁免自证其罪的特权，也仍然需要考虑保密问题。从第

maintenance of confidentiality is an important consideration. Information that comes from third parties may be subject to privacy protection and secrecy provisions, such as those applicable to banks. The insolvency representative is generally permitted to use that information only for the insolvency proceeding in which the examination was permitted, unless the court decides otherwise. Confidentiality issues may also be relevant to the provision and obtaining of information in criminal proceedings against the debtor.

It is a general principle of law that the use of information or material obtained under compulsion authorized by statute is limited by the provisions of the statute.

In *Johns v. Australian Securities Commission*, a case concerning statutory powers of investigation conferred on the police, Justice Brennan wrote:

> [W]hen a power to require disclosure of information is conferred for a particular purpose, the extent of dissemination or use of the information disclosed must itself be limited by the purpose for which the power was conferred. In other words, the purpose for which a power to require disclosure of information is conferred limits the purpose for which the information disclosed can lawfully be disseminated or used. In *Marcel v. Commissioner of Police of the Metropolis*, Sir Nicolas Browne-Wilkinson V.-C. said, in reference to a statutory power conferred on police to seize documents: "Powers conferred for one purpose cannot lawfully be used for other purposes without giving rise to an abuse of power. Hence, in the absence of express provision, the Act cannot be taken to have authorized the use and disclosure of seized documents for purposes other than police purposes."[4]

三方获取信息还可能受到隐私权等其他保密条款的限制，如部分银行的类似规定。所以，除非另有法令，破产管理人通常只能将调查到的信息运用于授权调查的破产程序中。刑事诉讼的调查取证也会遇到这样的保密问题。

经授权强制获得的信息使用必须受到相应的法律限制，是法律的一般原则。

布伦南大法官在约翰诉澳大利亚证券委员会案中授权警察依法开展调查：

> 当出于特定目的被授权调查取证时，所获信息的使用范围要与调查目的相一致。换句话说，调查取证的目的限制了信息使用、传播的目的。在马可诉首府警务人员一案中，尼古拉斯法官提到警察没收文件的权力，他说："为了调查权不被滥用，获取的信息只能用于开展调查时的最初目的，不得用于其他目的。因此，在没有明确规定的情况下，该案不能认为警察可以将发现的文件用于其他目的。"[4]

These principles apply in insolvency investigations. The use of the information obtained is generally confined to enabling the insolvency representative to locate, preserve, and liquidate assets for the benefit of creditors, or to take any other steps in furtherance of those objectives.

Insolvency representatives who become aware of activity that might constitute a fraud on the company may pursue information that may ultimately lead to the institution of proceedings against those involved. Thus, in carrying out asset recovery in a case of corruption, insolvency representatives could seek an examination of any persons likely to have information regarding the acts of corruption themselves, the location of any proceeds of corruption, and the identity of any persons who facilitated those acts, whether the corruption itself or the assistance in laundering the proceeds.

Costs of Examination

Examinees may be ordered to pay the costs of the insolvency representative's application if they are ordered to produce assets as a result of an examination, evidence contained in an affidavit, or the production of documents. Examinees may also be ordered to pay the costs of an examination if they unjustifiably refuse to provide the information sought. Some jurisdictions impose criminal sanctions in more serious cases of withholding of information.

Discovery

Discovery (sometimes called "disclosure") refers to the process of obtaining information within the context of pending proceedings. Discovery may be requested from the opposing party or, in certain circumstances, from third parties to the litigation. Discovery of information is generally limited to information relevant to the issues between the parties. When the

以上原则都适用于破产调查。一般而言，所获取信息只能用于追讨、保管和清算破产资产，服务于为债权人争取权益的目的。

破产管理人认为公司可能存在欺诈交易等行为时，会搜集诉讼所需的相关信息。因此，在追查腐败资产时，破产管理人可以对潜在腐败行为、腐败所得的存放地，以及其他可能与腐败或洗钱活动相关的人员开展调查。

调查的费用

当被要求出示在证明文件或书面证词中提及的资产时，被调查者也可能需要向破产管理人支付调查费用。如果被调查者无正当理由拒绝提供信息，也可能被强制要求支付调查费用。部分国家还会对严重隐瞒信息的行为施以刑事制裁。

信息披露

信息披露，也可被称为信息发掘，是指从待决诉讼中获取信息的过程，可以要求相对方或第三方（在某些情况下）提出。披露的范围通常限于争议相关的信息。在明确哪些事实存在争议后，可以申请信息披露以发掘事实真相。申请书应当全面、清晰地列出案情的主要信息。

pleadings in a case have made clear what facts are at issue, discovery can be sought, and ordered, to produce the information necessary to determine the truth. Pleadings set out the basis of the case; they must be as clear and comprehensive as possible.

Nonstatutory Tools

Anton Piller (Search and Seizure) Orders

The *Anton Piller* (search and seizure) order takes its name from a decision of the English Court of Appeal in *Anton Piller K.G. v. Manufacturing Processes Ltd.*[5] It permits the applicant's solicitors to enter premises, without notice, and to search for and remove all items covered by the order. The usual purpose of an *Anton Piller* order is to preserve evidence or property. Although not commonly used in civil or insolvency cases, an *Anton Piller* order may be available.

In insolvency cases, an *Anton Piller* order is particularly useful when an insolvency representative has reason to believe that documents or property belonging to a debtor, or concerning a debtor, its affairs, or its assets, may be destroyed. It may be used against lawyers, accountants, and other service providers who may possess information relevant to the debtor's assets and business. Because such orders are executed without notice, the potential for concealment or destruction of records prior to the arrival of the insolvency representative is reduced.

In *Anton Piller*, Lord Justice Ormrod of the English Court of Appeal set out the following requirements for granting this form of relief:

- There must be an extremely strong prima facie case against the respondent.
- The damage, potential or actual, to the applicant must be very serious.
- There must be clear evidence that the respondents have in their

法外调查工具

安东·皮勒令（Anton Piller，搜查与羁押令）

安东·皮勒搜查令的名称源于英国安东·皮勒诉MP有限公司的判决。[5]该令允许申请人的律师不经通知进入被申请人的住所搜查和扣押申请令上列明的所有物品。安东·皮勒令通常旨在保全证据及涉案资产，虽然在民事和破产案件中不常用，但依然不失为可用的调查工具之一。

在破产案件中，如果破产管理人认为与债务人相关的文件或资产存在被销毁的风险时，安东·皮勒令就能派上用场。它可用来对付可能掌握与债务人资产或业务有关的律师、会计师以及其他服务提供商等。由于该令允许在事先不通知的情况下直接执行，因此大大降低了相关文件和记录被提前销毁的风险。

对安东·皮勒令，英国上诉法院大法官奥姆罗德对此做了如下阐明：

- 对被调查者必须有足够充分的表面证据。
- 对申请人造成的实际或潜在的损害必须足够严重。
- 必须有明确的证据表明被调查者持有相关文件或财产并极有可

possession relevant documents or property and that there is a real possibility that they may destroy such material before an inter partes application can be made.

The Court of Appeal also laid out safeguards against abuse of *Anton Piller* orders and placed the responsibility on the applicant's solicitors for ensuring that the orders are carried out meticulously and carefully with the greatest respect for the defendants' rights.

In recognition of the drastic nature of the relief and its potentially serious consequences, courts have developed further safeguards to prevent injustice.

In *Universal Thermosensors Ltd. v. Hibben*,[6] the Chancery Division laid down the following guidelines for the execution of an *Anton Piller* order:

- Orders should be executed on working days during normal office hours to ensure that the defendant has access to legal representation.
- A detailed record of materials or property removed at the time of execution of the order must be made.
- The solicitor executing the order should be neutral and experienced (in serving and executing the order, there should be a supervising solicitor present who should explain the order to the defendants and give them the opportunity to consult their own solicitors. If the defendants wish to apply to discharge the order as having been improperly obtained, they must be allowed to do so. If the defendants refuse permission to enter or to inspect, the plaintiff must not force its way in. It must accept the refusal and bring it to the court's attention, if need be, on an application to commit for contempt of court).
- The order should be carried out in the presence of the defendant or his representative.

能在当事人申请之前将之销毁。

上诉法院还制定了防止安东·皮勒令被滥用的保障措施，并要求申请人及其律师必须确保认真、谨慎地执行，最大限度地尊重被调查者的权利。

考虑到该禁令的特殊性和潜在的严重后果，法院进一步制定了保障其公平公正被执行的措施。

在通用温度传感器有限公司诉希本案[6]中，法院为执行安东·皮勒令制定了以下原则：

- 该法令应在工作日的正常办公时间执行，确保被告人有权获得法律代理。
- 执行该法令时，必须详细记录被扣押的材料、财产清单。

- 执行该法令的律师应具有一定经验并保持中立。在执行该法令时，应配备一名监督律师在场，负责向被告解释该法令，并给予他们同自己律师磋商的机会。如果被告希望以法令获取不当为由解除该法令，应该得到允许。当被告拒绝被介入、被调查时，原告不得强行介入，否则在必要时可以藐视法庭为由向法院提起诉讼。

- 执行法令时，被告或其代理人应在场。

- Where the premises are likely to be occupied by an unaccompanied woman, if the supervising solicitor is a man, he must be accompanied by a woman.

Further, in *Canadian Bearings Ltd. v. Celanese Canada Inc.*[7] in 2006, the Canadian Supreme Court laid down the following additional safeguards:

- The scope of an *Anton Piller* order should not be wider than necessary, and material that is not spelled out in the order should not be removed.
- The number of persons who are to execute the search should be limited, and their names should be specified in the order.
- The order should state explicitly that the defendant is entitled to return to court on short notice to discharge the order.
- The order should contain a limited-use clause stating that the documents seized may only be used for the pending litigation.
- A list of all evidence seized should be prepared and provided to the defendant for inspection and verification at the end of the search and before the removal of the evidence.
- If a list of evidence cannot be provided to the defendant at the time of the search, the documents seized should be placed in the custody of the independent supervising solicitor.

In the United Kingdom, the High Court's power to grant search and seizure orders (*Anton Piller*) is derived from section 7(1) of the Civil Procedure Act 1997, and the relevant procedural requirements are set out in *Civil Procedure Rule 25* and *Practice Direction 25A.*

Common law jurisdictions that permit this type of relief include Australia, India, Ireland, Jersey and other British common law financial centers, and New Zealand. Similar relief is also available in Belgium, France, and Germany, and, for the enforcement of intellectual property rights, throughout the EU.[8]

- 搜查女性独居场所时，监督律师为男性的，须有一名女性陪同。

另外，在 2006 年的加拿大轴承有限公司诉塞拉尼斯加拿大有限公司案[7]中，加拿大最高法院制定了以下附加保障措施：

- 执行安东·皮勒令时，不应超出必要范围，不允许调查或转移法令中未列明的材料。
- 应限制执行人数，并在法令中列明人员名单。
- 法令应清楚表明被告有权在接到通知后立刻前往法院申请解除该法令。
- 法令应包含限制使用的条款，查获的文件只能用于待决诉讼。
- 在搜查取证结束之前，应备好所有查获证据的清单，并交由被告确认核实。
- 在搜查时无法向被告提供证据清单的，应将查获的文件交由独立的监督律师保管。

在英国，高等法院签发安东·皮勒令，源自《1997 年民事诉讼法》第 7(1) 条,《民事诉讼法》第 25 条和《实务指南》第 25A 条的规定。

澳大利亚、印度、爱尔兰、新西兰等英美法系国家，以及包括泽西岛在内的其他英国普通法域下的金融中心都提供了该项救济。在比利时、法国、德国以及整个欧盟，在执行相关知识产权案件时也适用该项法令。[8]

Norwich Pharmacal (Disclosure) Orders in Common Law Jurisdictions

United Kingdom and commonwealth courts have jurisdiction to grant prelitigation discovery orders known as *Norwich Pharmacal* orders, based on common law and equitable principles. In the English case that gave this order its name—*Norwich Pharmacal v. Customs and Excise Commissioners*[9]—Norwich Pharmacal Co. (Norwich) owned the patent for a chemical compound that was being illegally imported without a license by unknown third parties. Norwich wanted to identify the third parties to take action against them. Norwich brought a court action against defendants known to have records of the importers to force them to disclose the importers' identities. The court granted the order, stating that, although usually only parties to litigation have an obligation to disclose, the defendants had a duty to assist Norwich, the party who was wronged, by giving it any information that could identify the wrongdoers.

Lord Reid formulated the jurisdiction as follows:

> The [authorities] seem to me to point to a very reasonable principle that if through no fault of his own a person gets mixed up in the tortious acts of others so as to facilitate their wrongdoing he may incur no personal liability *but he comes under a duty to assist the person who has been wronged by giving him full information and disclosing the identity of the wrongdoers.* I do not think it matters whether he became so mixed up by the voluntary action on his part or because it is his duty to do what he did. It may be that if this causes him expense the person seeking information ought to reimburse him. But justice requires that he should cooperate in righting the wrong if he unwittingly facilitated its perpetration.[10]

The jurisprudence on disclosure orders has been extensively developed.[11] The categories of cases in which the order may be granted are

英美法中的第三方披露令（Norwich Pharmacal Orders）

英国联邦法院根据英美法公平原则，发布了“第三方披露令”。该令源于诺里奇药业诉海关官员案。[9] 诺里奇药业公司拥有一项化合物的专利，但被另一公司非法进口。诺里奇药业对此开展维权行动，向法院申请，要求对掌握进口商信息的第三方披露其进口商的身份。法院予以批准并指出，尽管通常只有诉讼的当事方才有披露义务，但被告有义务向原告诺里奇药业公司提供任何有助于识别不法行为的信息，协助诺里奇药业公司维权。

里德大法官对此评论：

> 在我看来，如果一个人虽无过错却卷入了他人的侵权行为中，尽管无意，但也变相协助了侵害行为。尽管他不需因此承担任何责任，但他仍然有义务通过披露侵害人信息的方式协助受害人维权，这是非常合理的。对于他卷入其中是无意为之还是不可避免的职责所在，我认为这一点也不重要。信息披露可能产生的相关费用，可向申请人报销，但基于公平和正义的要求，只要这个人在事实上助长了侵害的发生，那么他就有义务配合执法。[10]

披露令在实践中得到了广泛的发展。[11] 该令的适用范围也不完全局限于法庭诉讼。

neither closed nor confined to litigation. For example, in *CHC Software Care v. Hopkins & Wood*,[12] Justice Mummery ordered a firm of solicitors to disclose the names and addresses of persons to whom a letter making allegedly false allegations had been sent to enable CHC to write to the same persons correcting the alleged false statements.

The English Court of Appeal recently clarified the circumstances under which *Norwich Pharmacal* relief is available in *NML Capital Ltd. v. Chapman Freeborn Holdings Ltd.* While recognizing the need for flexibility in *Norwich Pharmacal* jurisdiction, to avoid its becoming "wholly unprincipled," the Court of Appeal said that it was essential for the third party to be "involved in the furtherance of the transaction identified as the relevant wrongdoing."[13]

Omar & Ors, R (on the application of) v. Secretary of State for Foreign & Commonwealth Affairs[14] clarified that *Norwich Pharmacal* jurisdiction may not be used to obtain information for use in a foreign proceeding if the foreign jurisdiction has a statutory process for obtaining evidence. The court dismissed the application, finding that the English courts do not have jurisdiction to order the provision of evidence for foreign proceedings using *Norwich Pharmacal* orders if the provision of that evidence is prohibited by the Evidence (Proceedings in Other Jurisdictions) Act 1975:

> [T]he power of the courts to use *Norwich Pharmacal* proceedings must, in our view, be developed within the confines of the existence of the statutory regime through which evidence in proceedings overseas must be obtained. *Norwich Pharmacal* proceedings are not ousted, but where proceedings, such as the present proceedings, are brought to obtain evidence, the court as a matter of principle ought to decline to make orders for the provision of evidence, as distinct from information, for use in

例如，在 CHC 软件维护公司诉霍普金斯与伍德案中[12]，某人被寄送了错误的指控信，穆墨里法官下令某律所向 CHC 软件维护公司披露该收信人的姓名和地址，以便 CHC 软件维护公司及时更正这个错误。

在 NML 资本有限公司诉普查曼·富力伯恩控股有限公司案中，英国上诉法院澄清了签发的第三方披露令的情况。法院认为，应保持该法令的灵活性以避免其变得“毫无原则”，同时认为，第三方“继续协助认定不法交易”是非常必要的。[13]

奥马尔等（申请中）诉外交联邦大臣案[14]则说明，当外国法律有法定的取证制度时，不得将第三方披露令用于域外程序的获取信息。在该案中，法院驳回了申请，理由是，即使《1975 年证据法案》（有关外国程序）禁止该国的取证制度，英国法院也无权要求该国承认第三方披露令：

> 我们认为，法院运用第三方披露令的权力，应该受到外国取证制度的限制。这项程序依然存在，但当它用于涉外案件时，法院原则上应加以区别并予以驳回。

> overseas proceedings.
>
> ...
>
> In our judgment it matters not that there may be no procedure in Uganda for obtaining evidence from the UK to be used in those courts.[15]

This approach was confirmed more recently in *Ramilos Trading Ltd. v. Buyanovsky*,[16] in which the court also emphasized that *Norwich Pharmacal* relief would not be ordered to further a fishing expedition.

Although *Norwich Pharmacal* jurisdiction is no longer considered exceptional and has been used in many common law jurisdictions, the approach to granting the relief is not always consistent. Some jurisdictions, such as Ireland, will permit discovery only to identify the wrongdoer, not to obtain factual information concerning the alleged wrong.[17] Other jurisdictions have not confined the information to the identity of wrongdoer only.

Norwich Pharmacal orders cannot be obtained against persons who are likely to be witnesses (or are prima facie defendants) in any proceeding instituted on the basis of an alleged wrong. This was reemphasized in *Hilton v. D IV LLP*.[18] In his judgment, Judge Pelling, Q.C., referred to the statement of principle in the speech of Lord Reid in *Norwich Pharmacal* as the origin of the jurisdiction. He highlighted, however, Lord Reid's limitations on the use of the jurisdiction:

> [Lord Reid noted that:] "It is not available against a person who has no other connection with the wrong than that he was a spectator or has some document relating to it in his possession." He pointed out that "the reason why the respondent in those proceedings was treated differently was because "without certain action on their part the infringements could never have been

> ……
>
> 据我们判断，乌干达应该没有任何关于在英国取证的程序规定，但这并不影响本案。[15]

拉米罗斯贸易有限公司诉布亚诺夫斯基案[16]也证实了这一做法，在该案中，法院强调不会授权披露令。

第三方披露令制度尽管并非独创，且被推行到许多普通法国家，但彼此之间还是存在一定的差别。例如，在爱尔兰等地，只允许将其用于确认不法行为人的身份，而不能用于获取与指控事实有关的所有信息。[17]其他国家或地区并没有这样的限制。

若指控对象有误，如针对仅仅是可能的证人或只是表面证据显示的被告而申请第三方披露令的，法院不予支持。希尔顿诉DIV有限责任合伙企业案[18]再次强调了这一点。佩林法官在判决中提到了里德大法官的评论是该原则的由来，但也提到了里德对该原则使用范围的限制：

> 里德大法官指出：“对于一个与不法行为无关的人，除非他是目击者或者掌握了相关的文件，否则任何人不得对其动用披露令。”他还指出：“区别哪些被调查者适用该法令，主要看若没有他们的参与，侵权行为是否一定会发生。”正是这些条件组成了里德大法官所提出的申请原则：“如果一个人虽无过错却卷入了他人的侵权行为中，尽管无意，但也变相协

> committed." It was these qualifications that led Lord Reid to formulate the principle that the claimants seek to rely on in this case in these terms: "[I]f through no fault of his own, a person gets mixed up in the tortious acts of others so as to facilitate their wrongdoing he may incur no personal liability but comes under a duty to assist the person who has been wronged by giving him full information." However, as Lord Reid said in *Norwich Pharmacal*, "information cannot be obtained by discovery from a person who will in due course be compellable to give that information... on a subpoena duces tecum." Hence the remedy, which is an exceptional procedural device made available to avoid injustice, is available only against those who won't or shouldn't be liable for the wrong but have nevertheless become mixed up in its commission. Outside that limited class the remedy is not available.[19]

Credit Suisse Trust v. Intesa San Paulo SpA and Banca Monte dei Pasche di Siena[20] was the first reported case of an English court ordering *Norwich Pharmacal* disclosure against two London branches of an Italian bank, even though the banking activity took place in Italy and all the information sought was held in Italy. Credit Suisse had obtained a judgment in Guernsey against a customer of Intesa and Banca Monte for dishonest breach of fiduciary duty. Credit Suisse took steps to enforce that judgment and to obtain further information about the client's assets.

The key question was whether the Italian banks could be forced to disclose information about the client's assets, because the relevant banking activity took place in Italy and was therefore governed by Italian law, in particular, Italian banking confidentiality rules. The evidence before the judge in respect of Banca Monte was that its London branch was able to access the relevant information in Italy so as to ensure compliance with

助了侵害行为，尽管他不需因此承担任何责任，但他仍然有义务通过披露侵害人信息的方式协助受害人维权。”但是，也正如里德大法官在该案中所说：“当信息无法从被调查者那里获取时，被调查者可能被法院强制传唤而提供信息。因此，这项补充是一种保障公平的例外规定。它只能针对那些没有过错但却卷入不法行为中的人，除此之外，其他人概不适用。”[19]

瑞士信托公司诉意大利联合圣保罗银行和意大利西雅那银行集团案[20]是英国法院第一起适用第三方披露令的案件，针对的是意大利一家银行在伦敦的两个分部。尽管该银行的主要活动在意大利，并且所有申请披露的信息都在意大利保存。瑞士信托公司在根西岛以违反忠实信托义务为由起诉了两家分部的一个客户并胜诉，瑞士信托公司为了执行判决，申请披露更多有关该客户资产的信息。

这里的关键问题是，意大利银行是否能被强制披露有关客户的信息。相关业务发生在意大利，因此受意大利法律特别是意大利银行保密规则的约束。为了确保相关法令得以执行，庭前调查的证据显示，意大利西雅那银行集团伦敦分行可以获取客户在意大利的相关信息，而关于意大利联合圣保罗银行是否具备这样的能力，法院无从查明。

the order being sought. The availability of evidence from Intesa's London branch was less clear.

The judge held that, because this was a fraud case, there was nothing in earlier case law to prevent him from making an order merely because the information sought was held by the banks in Italy. The court found that Banca Monte was willing to provide at least some of the information but considered that an order of the English court might be necessary to protect it from Italian confidentiality laws. With respect to Intesa, the judge believed that if Banca Monte's London branch was able to obtain the information from Italy, it should be possible for Intesa's London branch to do so. The judge was also aware that, if either Banca Monte or Intesa did not comply, Credit Suisse would not pursue those banks in England for contempt of court. Rather, Credit Suisse would apply to have the Guernsey judgment or the English *Norwich Pharmacal* order, or both, recognized in Italy. On that basis, the judge granted the *Norwich Pharmacal* relief against the London branches of the two Italian banks.

Norwich Pharmacal relief will not be ordered if the information is sought for the purpose of obtaining an advantage in another litigation, as opposed to enabling the bringing of a suit. In *Orb A.R.L. v. Fiddler*,[21] Mr. Justice Popplewell discharged a *Norwich Pharmacal* order that he had made previously, ruling that the information had not been sought for legitimate purposes but to discredit a party in a separate litigation to obtain an advantage in that case. The judge also found that there were several breaches of the duty to make full and frank disclosure that would have been sufficient to discharge the order.

When preaction disclosure is sought but the facts do not necessarily support *Norwich Pharmacal* relief, court rules of procedure in a particular jurisdiction might be interpreted to provide it. In Jamaica, for example, although

法官认为，由于这是一起欺诈案件，除了申请披露的信息是由意大利银行掌握的以外，在较早的判例中没有任何理由阻止法官授权该法令。法院认为，至少意大利西雅那银行集团愿意提供一些信息，但也意识到英国法院需要作出其他法令以免受意大利保密法的制约。同时，法官认为，如果意大利西雅那银行集团分行能够从意大利总部获取信息，那么意大利联合圣保罗银行分行应该也能做到。法官还意识到，如果这两家分行都不服从法令的话，那么瑞士信托公司也无法在英国指控他们藐视法庭。取而代之的是，瑞士信托公司将在意大利申请对根西岛判决的承认，或在英国申请第三方披露令，或者两者兼而有之。在此基础上，法官批准了针对这两家银行的第三方披露令。

如果当事人获取信息的目的是在另一项诉讼中获得利益，而非提起诉讼，则法官不会批准披露令。在当事人 Orb 公司诉费德勒案[21]中，波普尔维尔法官撤销了先前作出的披露令，他认为当事人并非出于正当目的而申请披露信息，而是为了在另一项诉讼中抹黑另一方当事人。同时，法官还发现有几项违反充分及诚实披露义务的行为，这些都足以使得法院撤销该法令。

在不符合第三方披露令的申请条件时，法院也可能采用其他特殊规则提供救济。比如，在牙买加，尽管没有专门的程序规定可提供事前披露救济，但有类似于英国《民事诉讼程序法》第 31 条的条款，最

there is no specific rule or procedure providing for preaction discovery, such as an equivalent to Civil Procedure Rule Part 31 in the United Kingdom, the Supreme Court of Judicature in *Clarke v. Bank of Nova Scotia Jamaica Ltd.*[22] held that the existing rules gave the court jurisdiction to make orders for discovery even before a case had been filed (see box 2.2).

BOX 2.2 ***Clarke v. Bank of Nova Scotia Jamaica Ltd.***

In *Clarke v. Bank of Nova Scotia Jamaica Ltd.*,[a] the Supreme Court of Judicature in Jamaica referred to rule 8.1(5) of the Civil Procedure Rules, which permits the filing of an application for a remedy before proceedings have started, that is, before a claim form has been filed. The application must be made pursuant to part 11 of the Civil Procedure Rules, which, in part, authorizes the court to exercise any power which it might exercise at a case management conference. The court noted that a court has many powers in a case management conference and that rule 27.9(1)(a) obliges a court to consider whether to give directions for standard disclosure and inspection. Rule 28.6(2) allows a court to order specific disclosure on or without application, and rule 28.6(3) allows an application for specific disclosure to be made at a case management conference. The court's assessment of these rules was, among other things, that they conferred jurisdiction to make orders for discovery even before a claim has been filed.

The court further concluded that rule 17.2 (which governs the grant of interim remedies) allowed the making of preclaim orders for inspection, detention, and preservation of relevant property.

The Supreme Court of Judicature also disagreed with the proposition that *Norwich Pharmacal* jurisdiction is not applicable when the target of discovery is itself a wrongdoer, highlighting a difference of approach to this particular question across jurisdictions.

a. [2012] JMCA Civ 8.

Similarly, if an applicant presents a prima facie case that his funds have been subject to fraud or other misappropriation, and that the funds or their proceeds have been paid by or through the bank or other entity from which disclosure is sought, a *Bankers Trust* order can be used to require a bank to disclose relevant banking documentation.[23] In most British international

高法院在克拉克诉牙买加新斯科舍省银行案[22]中认为，在案件提交之前仍能依据现有的规则批准该法令（见方框2.2）。

方框2.2　克拉克诉牙买加新斯科舍银行案

在克拉克诉牙买加新斯科舍银行案[a]中，牙买加最高法院提到了《民事诉讼程序规则》第8.1（5）条，该条允许在诉前，也就是提交起诉书之前，提出披露申请。该申请必须根据《民事诉讼程序规则》第11部分的内容提出，这部分内容是授权法院行使在案件审理会上能行使的任何权力。法院指出，在案件审理会中所拥有的诸多权力，例如：第27.9（1）（a）条规定法院有义务考量是否为披露和调查提供必要的指导；第28.6（2）条中允许法院在有或没有披露申请的情况下，批准特定披露；而规则第28.6（3）条则允许在案件管理会议上批准对特定披露申请。除其他规定外，这些规定表明，即便在起诉前，法院也有权批准披露令。

法院进一步认为，第17.2条（准予临时救济令）允许法院在起诉前作出关于检查、拘留和财产保全的法令。

而牙买加最高法院并不认同“当披露对象是不法行为人本人时，诺里奇披露令则不适用”的主张。这表明各国在处理该问题上的差异。

a. [2012] JMCA Civ 8.

同样，如果申请人提出初步证据证明其资金已经遭受欺诈或侵吞，并且已由披露令中的银行或其他机构支付，则“美国信孚银行令”可用于要求银行披露更多的相关文件。[23]在大多数的英国离岸金融中心，如泽西岛，法院可在必要时签发针对第三方的大范围的披露令，用于追查资产、执行判决、维护司法公平正义。

financial centers (such as Jersey), the courts will issue broad disclosure orders against third parties if necessary to plead a claim, trace assets, or enforce a judgment, or if disclosure is in the interest of justice.

Ancillary Sealing and Gagging Orders

Common law courts (and many civil law courts) have the power to seal a court's file and prohibit the disclosure of the fact or nature of its orders. Ancillary orders sealing the court record and "gagging" persons with knowledge of it (preventing them from disclosing the existence or subject matter of the proceedings) are complementary to an order permitting the proceedings to be heard in camera (in private). A court must be able to enforce its own rules of practice and to guard against any abuse of its processes. Publication of the fact or details of proceedings to locate and identify concealed assets (or to identify the beneficial ownership of companies holding assets) may enable an apparent wrongdoer to take steps to put those assets beyond the claimant's reach.

An ancillary secrecy order—a compulsory nondisclosure order against a bank or offshore company formation agent under the protection of utmost secrecy—is one of the most powerful tools available to an insolvency representative or other claimant searching for concealed assets or proof of their ultimate beneficial ownership. If a dishonest debtor or corrupt politician has no notice of the gathering of his or her bank and company ownership secrets, assets may be effectively found and frozen.

In *Connelly v. DPP*,[24] Lord Morris of Borth-y-Gest explained the jurisdiction:

> There can be no doubt that a court which is endowed with a particular jurisdiction has powers which are necessary to enable it to act effectively within such jurisdiction. I would regard them as powers which are inherent in its jurisdiction. A court must enjoy such powers

附属的禁止披露令（也有译作“禁言令”或“缄默令”）

对非公开审理的一些案件，英美法院（也有许多大陆法法院）有权封存法院的文件，禁止披露相关诉讼的信息。封存法院文件和“禁言”知情人，防止他们将诉讼本身或诉讼的目标公开。为了让判决得到有效执行，法院必须防止钻程序漏洞的行为。一些案情信息涉及追查和确认隐匿资产或其实际所有人，若将相关案情信息或部分程序细节公开，则可能使不法行为人将资产转移到债权人无法企及的地方。

禁止披露令（强制要求银行或离岸代理公司保密，是最高级别的保密要求）对破产管理人搜查隐匿资产及实际所有权人而言，无疑是最有效的工具之一。债务人、涉嫌腐败的公职人员对此并不知情，有助于破产管理人追查和冻结相关资产。

在康纳利诉 DPP 案[24]中，莫里斯法官解释如下：

> 毫无疑问，案件管辖的法院应该拥有必要的权力使得案件能够顺利进行。法院应有权制止对程序的任何恶意利用，排除对程序的任何妨碍。[25]

> in order to enforce its rules of practice and to suppress any abuses of its process and to defeat any attempted thwarting of its process.[25]

The power to order that proceedings be sealed or that all those with knowledge of those proceedings be prohibited from disclosing the fact or details thereof must be weighed against the principle that justice must be administered in public. Article 6(1) of the European Convention on Human Rights and Fundamental Freedoms (ECHR) provides: "In the determination of his civil rights and obligations or of any criminal charge against him, everyone is entitled to a fair and public hearing within a reasonable time by an independent and impartial tribunal established by law. Judgment shall be pronounced publicly…" (ECHR 1950).

Furthermore, Article 10 of the ECHR guarantees the right of freedom of expression, which may also be infringed by a prohibition on the disclosure of information. A significant overriding interest must justify any restriction on the publication of proceedings or the principle of open justice. The issue of a court's jurisdiction to anonymize and restrict publication of its proceedings was considered by the U.K. House of Lords in *Scott v. Scott.*[26] Viscount Haldane, Lord Chancellor, stated:

> While the broad principle is that the Court of this country must, as between parties, administer justice in public, this principle is subject to apparent exceptions such as those to which I have referred. But the exceptions are themselves the outcome of yet a more fundamental principle that the chief object of the Courts of Justice must be to secure that justice is done.[27]

Viscount Haldane then went on to explain the necessity of protecting the subject matter of litigation as a justification for restricting publicity in a particular class of proceedings. He stated:

> The other case referred to, that of litigation as to a secret

禁止披露案情信息的法令也必须与公开审理原则互相平衡。《欧洲人权公约》（ECHR）第6（1）条规定："在限定公民的权利义务或提起刑事指控时，公民有权获得公开公正的审理。法律应组建公正、独立的法庭在合理的时限内作出公开判决……"（ECHR 1950）。

此外，《欧洲人权公约》第10条保障了言论自由权。禁止披露令也可能侵犯公民的言论自由权。所以，必须足够重大的权益才能抗辩公开审理的大原则。在2002年英国上议院审议史考特诉史考特案[26]时，针对隐匿信息、限制司法公开的议题，总理大臣哈尔丹说：

> 虽然公开审理是普遍适用的大原则，但它有明显的例外，比如我提到的就是例外。但是，这个例外本身是一个更为基本的原则性的结果，即法院的根本目标是确保司法公正。[27]

哈尔丹随后进一步解释了在特定程序中限制司法公开以保护诉讼标的物的必要性，他提道：

> 另一个涉及保密程序的情况是，公开审理很可能造成标

> process, where the effect of publicity would be to destroy the subject matter, illustrates a class which stands on a different footing. There it may well be that justice could not be done at all if it had to be done in public. As the paramount object must always be to do justice, the general rule as to publicity, after all only a means to an end, must accordingly yield.[28]

Marcus A. Wide v. First Caribbean International Bank[29] provides an example of extensive sealing and gagging relief (see box 2.3).

BOX 2.3 ***Marcus A. Wide v. FirstCaribbean International Bank*** [a]

Marcus A. Wide, insolvency representative of Tradex Ltd. (a company in liquidation), which had been involved in a widespread Ponzi scheme, instituted a long series of ex parte applications in The Bahamas; Belize; Dominica; Jamaica; Québec, Canada; Singapore; and the United States in an effort to recover assets of Tradex that had been misappropriated and concealed in various jurisdictions. The investigation of the affairs of Tradex required an extensive multijurisdictional investigation and court proceedings.

Mr. Wide was able to show that the results of the investigations were likely to be rendered worthless if the existence of the investigations and the proceedings was disclosed. (There was no countervailing interest on the part of Tradex to trump the necessity for the secrecy orders.) Wide obtained a series of disclosure orders accompanied by gag and seal orders at various stages of the proceedings, including an order that the court's file and record be sealed and all parties be prevented from disclosing either the fact of the application or the content of the pleadings, except as necessary to seek advice from legal counsel. The duration of these orders was then extended as necessary by the courts involved until Mr. Wide was in a position to freeze the assets found through the disclosure orders obtained and the investigations conducted. Thousands of bank, company formation, and other confidential records were accumulated over the course of two years of judicially sanctioned secret investigative activity. Millions of dollars of assets were discovered and frozen.

a. 2005/Com/bnk 21 (unreported).

Ex parte discovery provides access to information that the other party is not yet aware has been disclosed. It thus may provide significant strategic

的物被破坏，此时则面临两难。如果必须要将案件公开审理，则可能无法维护司法正义。司法必须以正义为首要目标，而公开作为一般原则始终只是维护正义的一种手段，所以需要后者让步。[28]

马克斯·韦德诉第一加勒比国际银行案[29]为禁止披露令提供了一个范例（见方框 2.3）。

方框 2.3　马克斯·韦德诉第一加勒比国际银行案[a]

Tradex 公司是一家被卷入大型庞氏骗局而被破产清算的公司。它的破产管理人马克斯·韦德在多国提出了单方申请，以追回在各地被转移和隐匿的 Tradex 公司的资产，包括巴哈马、伯利兹、多尼米加、牙买加、加拿大的魁北克省、新加坡和美国。追查这些资产需要进行大范围的跨国调查和跨国诉讼。

破产管理人能够证明，公开调查和诉讼极有可能会使调查结果变得毫无价值。（Tradex 公司也不存在捏造禁止披露令的必要。）韦德在诉讼的各个阶段都获得了一系列的禁止披露令，包括对判决等法院文件密封保存令，禁止所有诉讼当事方泄露案情或诉讼内容，除非特殊法律咨询的需要。相关法院还根据需要延长了该法令的期限直到破产管理人能够冻结所追查的资产为止。在为期两年的非公开司法调查中，大量银行和公司的机密文件被调查，价值数百万美元的资产被冻结。

a. 2005/Com/bnk 21 (unreported).

让一方获取另一方尚未察觉泄露的信息，可以抢先获得战略和战术上的巨大优势。一方获悉调查很容易打草惊蛇，这对申请调查的当

and tactical advantages. It is of the greatest benefit when knowledge by the opposing party that the discovery is being conducted could lead to evasive action, which would have a detrimental effect on the chances of the party seeking discovery to satisfy its claim.

In common law jurisdictions, a court may grant an ex parte disclosure order on the basis of common law or equitable principles. The jurisdiction exists separate from the rules for discovery prescribed by the applicable rules of court procedure or the civil procedure rules of the jurisdiction concerned.

Other Investigative Tools

Mareva Injunctions and Mareva by Letter in Common Law Jurisdictions

A number of common law jurisdictions provide for worldwide freezing orders called *Mareva* injunctions. These freezing orders originated in *Mareva Compania Naviera S.A. v. International Bulkcarriers S.A.*[30] and have been codified in section 37 of the U.K. Supreme Court Act 1981. These orders may be granted to prevent defendants from removing assets from a jurisdiction or otherwise disposing of them.

Mareva by letter notifies a third-party guardian or holder of assets, such as a bank, that those assets may be subject to a constructive trust. It informs the holder of the assets that their beneficial owner is not the account holder of record but rather a defrauded entity or government and advises them of their potential civil or criminal liability if it permits any transfer or disposal of those assets. *Mareva* by letter will generally dissuade a bank from transferring the funds until the case is resolved or until the funds are formally frozen following a court order. Informing a bank that it is being used for fraudulent activity and is therefore vulnerable to private or public legal action may cause it to prevent the funds' release or further misuse. The *Mareva* by letter procedure should be accompanied by criminal or civil

事方非常不利。非公开调查的最大好处就在于规避了此类风险。

在普通法国家，法院可以根据普通法或公平原则对一方授予披露令。该项制度区别于法院通常运用的披露程序，也区别于民事诉讼法中的披露原则。

其他调查工具

英美法国家的“玛瑞瓦禁令”和“玛瑞瓦信函”

许多英美法国家的法院可以签发全球冻结令，被称为“玛瑞瓦禁令”，这些冻结令源自玛瑞瓦诉国际散装货船公司案[30]，已被英国《1981年最高法院法》第37节收录。这项法令主要是为了防止被告转移资产或以其他方式处置资产。

玛瑞瓦通过信件的方式通知第三方监管人或资产保管人，如银行，并告知他们这些资产很可能以“推定信赖”的方式持有，实际所有权人并不是账户上登记的所有权人，而是被欺诈的政府或机构。同时也告知银行如果允许任何资产被转移或处置，银行很可能面临民事或刑事指控。在结案或依据法院正式签发资产冻结令之前，玛瑞瓦信函可劝阻银行不要转移资金，并告知资产很可能涉嫌贪腐、诈骗等非法活动，因此有很高的法律风险，进而阻止银行发放或滥用这些资金。玛瑞瓦信函的程序需要辅以受害人代表提起的民事诉讼或刑事诉讼。[31]

actions on behalf of the fraud victim.[31]

Freezing Orders in Civil Law Jurisdictions

Legal tools to seize or freeze assets are also available in civil law jurisdictions. In France, for example, the Code des Procédures Civiles d'Exécution (CPCEx) addresses potential civil remedies in asset recovery cases. In particular, article L.111-1 provides that any creditor is entitled to a provisional measure to ensure that his rights are respected. Similarly, article L.511-1 provides for temporary seizure of assets: a claimant may request, ex parte, a freeze on assets belonging to the defendant if the assets exist and are believed to be in danger of dissipation. The procedure is very informal; the claimant has to bring a request to a judge, who can grant a provisional order to seize the assets. A proprietary injunction covers the property or the traceable proceeds of the property (the proprietary assets) of the defendant and prohibits dealing in those assets. The claimant has to present a credible case and must demonstrate that it is just and convenient for the judge to grant the order. The risk of dissipation of the funds need not be proved separately because the defendant is holding the claimant's assets. An almost identical action called "embargo preventivo" is available under Argentina's Code of Civil and Commercial Procedure.

Discovery in Aid of Foreign Proceedings

Asset-related information is generally readily available in the United States. Section 1782 of the U.S. Code empowers courts to permit any interested party to obtain discovery for use in foreign proceedings from a person located in the judicial district, even if this evidence could not be accessed under the rules of the foreign proceeding.[32] When considering an application under section 1782, a U.S. district court may also consider: (1) whether the person from whom discovery is sought is a party to the foreign proceeding; (2) the nature of the foreign tribunal and the character of the foreign proceeding; (3) whether the request is an attempt to circumvent

大陆法国家的冻结令

大陆法国家的立法也提供了类似的扣押和冻结资产的法律工具。例如在法国，《民事诉讼执行法典》(CPCEx）就提供了这类民事救济措施。特别是该法典第L.111-1条规定：“任何债权人都有权采取临时措施以确保其合法权益得以维护。”同样，第L.511-1条对暂时扣押资产进行了规定：“如果资产存在提前处分的危险，申请人可以单方面要求冻结被告资产。”但这项程序并非正式程序，申请人需要向法官提出请求，法官再作出临时命令没收资产。这里的资产包括被告的财产以及可追溯的相关收益，都在禁止交易之列。申请人还必须提出可信的情形，并且证明法官批准该命令是正义且便捷的。由于被告实际占有申请人的资产，因此无须证明资产存在被不当处置的风险。在阿根廷《民事和商业程序法》中，有一个几乎一模一样的制度，被称为“预防性禁止转移”。

跨国司法协助下的证据开示

在美国，与资产相关的信息通常很容易获得。《美国法典》第1782条授权法院允许任何利害关系方从法院管辖区内获得外国案件所需要的证据，即便根据外国程序规则不能获取该项证据。[32]在考量如何适用第1782条时，法院也需要考量如下内容：(1）申请人是否是外国程序的当事人；(2）外国法院的性质以及外国程序的性质；(3）该请求是否试图绕过外国取证规则的限制；(4）要求本身是否需要承担过重的负担。[33]

evidence-gathering restrictions or policies in the foreign jurisdiction; and (4) whether the request is unduly intrusive or burdensome.[33]

For litigants outside the United States, section 1782 provides a quick, efficient, and relatively inexpensive method of obtaining evidence within the United States. Although most foreign countries provide for procedures enabling the gathering of evidence from foreign witnesses, or witnesses abroad, section 1782 is designed to provide foreign litigants the opportunity to obtain discovery of documents or tangible evidence located in the United States. Effectively, all the foreign litigant needs to establish is that, if the parties against whom discovery is sought were located within the foreign jurisdiction in which the underlying proceedings are taking place, the applicant could seek the same discovery relief they seek in the U.S. district court. The only reason the applicant comes for relief to the U.S. district court (as opposed to the foreign court) is that the evidence sought is not physically available to the applicant in the foreign jurisdiction.

Under section 1782, a court order for discovery may be made upon the application of any "interested person." Section 1782 does not require an interested person to first seek discovery from the foreign or international tribunal or that judicial proceedings be pending at the time assistance is sought. The fact that an interested person is contemplating bringing proceedings abroad is sufficient. Discovery under section 1782 is preaction discovery. The determination of whether to grant assistance under a section 1782 application hinges not on whether the proceeding is pending but on whether the requested discovery will likely be of use in a foreign judicial proceeding (or whether it will likely lead to the discovery of admissible evidence). Section 1782 provides a flexible procedure for the taking of depositions in aid of foreign proceedings. The section is supplemented by safeguards in the U.S. Federal Rules of Civil Procedure, particularly rules

对于美国境外的申请人，第 1782 条提供了一种快速、有效且便捷的在美国境内获取证据的方法。尽管大多数国家都规定了外国人取证的程序，但第 1782 条旨在方便外国申请人获取在美国境内的文件或其他有形证据。事实上，所有外国申请人都需要证明，如果需要该项证据的诉讼不在美国境内，他们也能在诉讼国提交和美国一样的取证申请。申请人向美国法院寻求救济的唯一原因是该项证据在地理意义上不属于本国的司法管辖范围。

根据第 1782 条，任何“利害关系人”都可向法院提出申请。该条不要求他们先向外国或国际法庭申请，在申请时也不需要已经启动外国程序，只需要利害关系人考虑将正在进行的诉讼延伸到国外这一客观事实就够了，所以第 1782 条可以适用于诉前取证。而法院是否决定根据第 1782 条批准提供司法协助，不取决于本国诉讼是否启动，而是取决于申请获取的证据对外国司法程序是否有用（包括用于发现其他证据）。第 1782 条为外国司法取证活动提供了灵活的程序。同时，《美国联邦民事诉讼规则》（特别是第 26 条至第 32 条）对该项程序补充了保障措施，防止该项程序被滥用。

26–32, which are designed to prevent misuse of the section.

The application is made to the U.S. district court in the location of the residence of the party from whom the evidence is sought. The application is based on an affidavit of the applicant, who must be an interested person, that is, a party to the anticipated foreign litigation. A person may not be compelled to give testimony or a statement or to produce documents or other items in violation of any legally applicable privilege. If an issue of discoverability is raised during the section 1782 application proceedings, the primary burden falls upon the applicant to make a showing that the information is discoverable under foreign law.[34]

Key Points from this Chapter

- Investigations may be conducted to develop information on the location of assets and the beneficial ownership of entities that are believed to have been used to move, conceal, or hold assets that were corruptly obtained.
- Information relevant to building a case is often available online or in virtual databases.
- Insolvency representatives are typically empowered to conduct examinations of witnesses who may have in their possession information likely to assist the representative in determining the state of affairs or assets of a debtor.
- Search and seizure orders may be available and particularly useful when an insolvency representative believes that relevant documents or property belonging to a debtor may be destroyed.
- Commonwealth courts have jurisdiction to grant prelitigation discovery orders known as Norwich Pharmacal orders, based on common law and equitable principles.
- Worldwide freezing orders (Mareva injunctions) inform asset holders (such as banks) that the beneficial owner of assets is not the account holder of record but a defrauded entity or government and advise them of their potential liability in the event of any transfer or disposal of the assets in question.

向证据所在地的美国地方法院提出申请的申请人须为预期参与诉讼的利害关系人。同时，不得强迫任何人违反任何法律的特殊保密规定提供证词、文件或其他证据。获取相关证据时，申请人必须证明该项证据也是外国法律允许获取的证据。[34]

本章要点

- 可以开展相关调查，获取涉案资产位置、资产实际所有人等相关信息。
- 相关信息通常可以从线上或电子数据库中获得。
- 破产管理人有权对证人开展调查，这些证人可能掌握着有助于确认债务人或其资产状态的信息。
- 当破产管理人认为债务人的相关文件或财产存在被销毁的风险时，搜查扣押令可在此时发挥作用。
- 英国联邦法院可以根据普通法和公平原则，批准第三方披露令。
- 全球冻结令（玛瑞瓦禁令）可以告知资产的当前持有人（如银行）其实际所有人并非账户登记的持有人，而是被欺诈的机构或政府，并告知任何转让或处置行为都可能使其面临法律风险。

Notes

1. See MF Global UK Ltd. (In Special Administration) [2015] EWHC 2319 (Ch) (July 31, 2015).

2. [1879] 12 ChD 77 (CA) 85.

3. [1968] 3 All ER 698, 700.

4. [1993] 178 CLR 408, 423–24.

5. [1976] Ch. 55 (CA).

6. [1992] 1 WLR 840.

7. [2006] 2 R.C.S.

8. See Directive 2004/48/EC of the European Parliament and of the Council of April 29, 2004, on the Enforcement of Intellectual Property Rights.

9. [1974] AC 133.

10. Ibid., § 175B-C (emphasis added).

11. In *Clarke v. Bank of Nova Scotia Jamaica Ltd.* (see box 2.2), the Supreme Court of Judicature in Jamaica disagreed with the proposition that *Norwich Pharmacal* jurisdiction does not apply when the target of discovery is itself a wrongdoer.

12. [1993] FSR 241.

13. [2013] EWCA Civ. 589.

14. [2012] EWHC 1737 (Admin) (June 26, 2012).

15. Ibid.

16. [2016] EWHC 317.

17. See Megaleasing UK Ltd. v. Barrett [1993] I.R.L.M. 497, 504 (Chief Justice Finlay) ("The remedy should be confined to cases where very clear proof of a wrongdoing exists and possibly, so far as it applies to an action for discovery alone prior to the institution of any other proceedings, to cases

注释

1. 参见 MF 国际（英国）有限公司（特别管辖）[2015] EWHC 2319 (Ch) (July 31, 2015)。

2. [1879] 12 ChD 77 (CA) 85.

3. [1968] 3 All ER 698, 700.

4. [1993] 178 CLR 408, 423–24.

5. [1976] Ch. 55 (CA).

6. [1992] 1 WLR 840.

7. [2006] 2 R.C.S.

8. 参见 2004 年 4 月 29 日欧洲议会和理事会第 2004/48/EC 关于知识产权保护的决议。

9. [1974] AC 133.

10. 同上，§ 175B–C (emphasis added)。

11. 在克拉克诉牙买加新斯科舍银行案中（见方框 2.2），关于不法行为人自身不能成为第三方披露令的对象这一规定，牙买加最高法院并不认同这样的主张。

12. [1993] FSR 241.

13. [2013] EWCA Civ. 589.

14. [2012] EWHC 1737 (Admin) (June 26, 2012).

15. 同上。

16. [2016] EWHC 317.

17. 详见英国大型租赁有限公司诉巴雷特案 [1993] I.R.L.M. 497, 504。主审法官芬莱认为：“该救济措施仅在具有非常清楚的证据表明不法行为时才得以使用，且如果是诉前行动，则披露范围只能是与不法行为人身份相关的信息，而不能针对具体的不法行为。”

where what is really sought is the names and identity of the wrongdoers rather than the factual information concerning the commission of the wrong.").

18. [2015] EWHC 2 (Ch) (January 12, 2015).

19. [1974] AC 133, 174.

20. [2014] EWHC 1447 (Ch) (March 6, 2014).

21. [2016] EWHC 361 (Comm) (February 26, 2016).

22. [2012] JMCA Civ. 8.

23. The *Bankers Trust* order comes from *Bankers Trust v. Shapira* [1980] 1WLR 1274.

24. [1964] AC 1254.

25. Ibid., 1301.

26. [1913] AC 417.

27. Ibid., 437.

28. Ibid.

29. 2005/Com/bnk 21 (unreported). See Peter Maynard and Colin Jupp. 2015. "Judicial Secrecy and Suspension of Adversarial Proceedings: Super-Injunctions, Sealing and Gagging as Effective Tools." https://www.ibanet.org/Article/NewDetail.aspx?ArticleUid=47185731-d747-4417-9c4b-d032df155b62.

30. [1975] 2 Lloyd's Rep. 509 (CA).

31. The fraud victim may obtain proprietary injunctions or the appointment of an insolvency representative at the same time as the *Mareva* by letter to prevent movement of the funds before the bank agrees to take steps to freeze the assets. The danger in not taking some form of injunctive relief at the same time as the *Mareva* by letter is that the defendant is on notice, but the bank has not been forced to act immediately. If the bank does not agree to take steps to prevent the movement of the funds, the defendant

18. [2015] EWHC 2 (Ch) (January 12, 2015).

19. [1974] AC 133, 174.

20. [2014] EWHC 1447 (Ch) (March 6, 2014).

21. [2016] EWHC 361 (Comm) (February 26, 2016).

22. [2012] JMCA Civ. 8.

23. “美国信孚银行令”源于信孚银行诉夏皮拉案 [1980] 1WLR 1274。

24. [1964] AC 1254.

25. 同上，1301。

26. [1913] AC 417.

27. 同上，437。

28. 同上。

29.2005/Com/bnk 21 (unreported). See Peter Maynard and Colin Jupp. 2015. “Judicial Secrecy and Suspension of Adversarial Proceedings: Super-Injunctions, Sealing and Gagging as Effective Tools.” https://www.ibanet.org/Article/NewDetail.aspx?ArticleUid=47185731-d747-4417-9c4b-d032df155b62.

30. [1975] 2 Lloyd’s Rep. 509 (CA).

31. 欺诈受害人可以在银行同意冻结资产之前，与申请“玛瑞瓦信函”同时，申请其他专属禁令或委任破产管理人，防止资金转移。如果不与“玛瑞瓦信函”同时采取某种禁令救济，则银行可能不同意阻止资金被转移。被告如果已经知情，则可能将资金转移到受害人无法触及的地方。

may transfer the money out of the reach of the victim.

32. 28 U.S.C. § 1782 (2019).

33. Intel Corp. v. Advanced Micro Devices, Inc., 542 U.S. 241 (2004).

34. In re Asta Medica S.A. 981 F.2d 1 (1st Cir. 1992).

Reference

ECHR (European Court of Human Rights). 1950. *European Convention on Human Rights.* Strasbourg: Council of Europe.

32. 28 U.S.C. § 1782 (2019).
33. 英特尔公司诉超微半导体公司案，542 U.S. 241 (2004)。
34. In re Asta Medica S.A. 981 F.2d 1 (1st Cir. 1992).

参考文献

ECHR (European Court of Human Rights). 1950. European Convention on Human Rights. Strasbourg: Council of Europe.

3. Identifying Insolvency and Receivership Targets and Other Liable Persons in Corruption Cases

Bribe Takers and Related Entities

The fight against corruption has gained momentum and is now a global initiative. Several jurisdictions have taken steps to strengthen their frameworks and mechanisms for the return of assets derived from corrupt activities by criminalizing and listing corruption as a predicate offense for money laundering.

In cases of bribing foreign officials and embezzling public funds in developing jurisdictions, however, there may be difficulties in any investigation seeking corruption proceeds. The proceeds are typically hidden abroad or laundered using overseas intermediary services provided by lawyers, accountants, or company formation agents. In the United Kingdom, for example, a recent Transparency International UK report found that as of 2016, 44,022 London land titles were owned by overseas companies; 91 percent of overseas companies owning London property did so through holding companies in offshore jurisdictions, known as "secrecy jurisdictions," that don't require beneficial ownership to be public; 986 land titles had links to politically exposed persons (PEPs)[1]; and over 75 percent of them were owned by companies based in the British Virgin Islands or Panama.[2] Over £180 million worth of property in the United Kingdom has been subject to criminal investigation as the suspected proceeds of

3. 确认腐败案件中破产对象及其他责任人

受贿人和相关实体

反腐败斗争势头强劲，已成为一项全球议题。一些国家已采取措施，将腐败作为洗钱的上游犯罪定罪量刑，以建立和巩固关于反腐败追查资产的法律框架和配套机制。

然而，在发展中国家，由于腐败收益和资产通常藏匿国外，或由律师、会计师、代理机构等提供海外服务进行洗钱活动，所以对贿赂外国公职人员或挪用公款等腐败行为的调查通常比较困难。例如，透明国际英国分部（Transparency International UK）的一份报告显示，截至 2016 年，44,022 个伦敦地产登记在海外公司名下。在伦敦拥有资产的海外公司中，91% 是离岸司法管辖区（或被称为“保密司法管辖区”）的控股公司。这些地区不需要公布实际所有权人就可以公开上市。报告披露，986 个地产与政治人物有关；[1] 其中超过 75% 的股份归英属维京群岛或巴拿马的公司所有。[2] 由于涉嫌国际腐败，英国超过 1.8 亿英镑的财产已经受到刑事调查。

international corruption.

Although the United Nations Convention Against Corruption (UNCAC) is explicit about the need to criminalize both bribe paying and receiving, many legislative provisions focus only on the bribe payer. For example, neither the U.K. Bribery Act nor the Foreign Corrupt Practices Act (FCPA) generally imposes liability on the public official who is the recipient of a bribe.[3] There are, however, many civil law jurisdictions that criminalize bribe taking.

Though most legislation focuses primarily on bribe payers, especially in common law countries, law enforcement has the ability to prosecute bribe takers. The lack of awareness by local law enforcement that such practices are occurring, and how they occur, contributes significantly to the relative impunity of bribe takers.

Official data on the enforcement efforts of the parties to the Anti-Bribery Convention were made public for the first time in the 2009 Annual Report of the Anti-Bribery Convention Working Group (OECD 2009). The Working Group has been collecting data from its members on investigations, proceedings, and sanctions, distinguishing sanctions upon conviction (or a similar finding of culpability for administrative and civil proceedings) from agreements to resolve proceedings without a conviction (or a similar finding of culpability for administrative and civil proceedings), with or without court approval. The data collected distinguish foreign bribery misconduct from other related offenses—in particular, accounting misconduct relating to the bribery of foreign public officials or attempts to conceal bribery—and, where relevant, track cases against individuals and entities separately.

The lack of any, or any effective, investigation to uncover the identity and activity of bribe takers is among the reasons for the relatively small number of cases in which bribe takers are punished or the proceeds of

尽管《联合国反腐败公约》(UNCAC)明确规定有必要将行贿和受贿都认定为刑事犯罪，但许多国家的立法只针对行贿行为。比如，英国《反贿赂法》、美国《反海外腐败法》(FCPA)一般都不对受贿的公职人员科以刑事处罚。[3]不过，许多大陆法系的国家是对受贿行为定罪的。

尽管大多数国家的立法主要针对行贿人，特别是英美法系国家，但执法部门其实有能力起诉受贿人。由于当地执法人员缺乏对受贿行为和腐败发生方式的认识，受贿人不受制裁的情形显著增加。

经合组织《反贿赂公约》工作组2009年的年度报告(OECD 2009)也首次公开了有关《反贿赂公约》缔约国执行工作的官方数据。工作组一直在搜集成员国的相关调查、诉讼和制裁的数据。将已结案件中的定罪裁决(或类似的行政或民事诉讼判决)与无论是否结案的未定罪的制裁(或类似的行政或民事诉讼判决)区别开来。还把涉外贿赂犯罪与其他犯罪区别开来，特别统计了贿赂公职人员罪和隐瞒贿赂罪，并将案件区分为个人犯罪和组织犯罪而分别追踪。

缺少关于受贿人身份的有效调查是受贿人逃脱制裁或立案较少的原因之一。跨国腐败案件的调查则更为困难，因为它涉及至少三个司法管辖区:(1)行贿人的司法管辖区;(2)受贿人的司法管辖区;

bribery are confiscated. Investigation of foreign bribery is even more difficult because it is likely to involve at least three jurisdictions: (1) the source jurisdiction of the bribe payer; (2) the destination jurisdiction of the bribe taker; and (3) any intermediary jurisdiction(s) used to launder the proceeds.

The main focus of multilateral conventions has been the pursuit of bribe payers. The fewer the bribe payers, the fewer the bribe takers. However, targeting the bribe takers should also be an integral part of any initiative to tackle corruption. Resources must be made available to investigate the demand side of the corruption equation, identifying those that take and those that assist the takers.

In an insolvency proceeding, bribe takers could be identified and targeted using the insolvency representative's powers to identify persons, natural and legal, who have received a benefit at a company's expense. In some common law jurisdictions, a company that is a bribe taker or recipient can be placed into insolvency to be wound up on just and equitable grounds because the company exists only to receive the bribe. The winding up is not a result of liabilities exceeding assets, but is a measure to remedy the wrong of corrupt activity. Corrupt actors use companies for various purposes, including as a conduit for tainted funds or as a repository. Directors of those companies may be nominees, and the truth may be further obscured by the use of companies or trusts standing in as shareholders. Companies have been wound up on just and equitable grounds on the basis of illegality of object and the failure of substratum (box 3.1).

A company that has been formed for an illegal purpose has no substratum. The only opportunity to trace and recover proceeds of corruption may be through gaining control of receiving companies. In Canada; Hong Kong SAR, China; Malaysia; and Singapore, as well as a

（3）洗钱行为地的司法管辖区。

多边公约一直将打击重点放在行贿人上，行贿人越少，则受贿人越少。但是，以受贿人为目标打击腐败也应成为所有反腐举措的重要组成部分，应竭力调动资源调查腐败链条的需求端，既要确定受贿人，也要确定受贿协助人。

在破产程序中，破产管理人有权对受贿人展开调查，进而确定其为自然人还是法人。在某些英美法国家中，可对受贿公司或为受贿服务的公司，以违反公平公正原则为由破产清算。清算虽然不是资不抵债的结果，但该公司存在只是为了收受贿赂或服务于受贿行为，对其破产清算是打击腐败、维护司法正义的表现。腐败分子通常利用公司作为获取腐败收益的渠道或金库，公司的董事大多只是受托人，将公司或者信托机构作为公司股东，掩盖非法目的，所以常以公平公正原则为由对其进行破产清算（方框 3.1）。

因非法目的而成立的公司没有实际的经营基础。追查腐败收益的唯一途径就是接管公司。在加拿大、中国香港特别行政区、马来西亚、新加坡，以及包括英属维京群岛、开曼群岛和根西岛在内的许多离岸司法管辖区，法院可以任命临时破产管理人开展破产调查而无需知会

BOX 3.1 Case Study on Just and Equitable Winding Up and the Appointment of an Insolvency Representative—*Montrow International Ltd.*[a]

Montrow International Ltd. (Montrow), a British Virgin Islands company, was owned by an offshore trust and corporate service provider, acting as trustee. Montrow owned the shares of another British Virgin Islands company, Likouala SA ("Likouala"). Likouala purportedly owned the rights to an oil field in the Democratic Republic of Congo. The rights to the oil field had been owned by the French oil company Total and transferred to the Democratic Republic of Congo for one franc. Total and the Democratic Republic of Congo were in dispute over the oil rights. The Democratic Republic of Congo purportedly sold the rights to the oil field to Likouala. Likouala had financed the purchase through a loan from a major bank. According to findings of the English High Court, the Democratic Republic of Congo had a history of defaulting on its debts and then seeking to disguise its assets behind trusts and company structures to prevent creditors from collecting what was owed to them. Some debts owed by the country to creditors were purchased by Kensington International Ltd., an investment fund (Kensington). Kensington alleged that the Montrow-Likouala structure was a sham, a method for the Democratic Republic of Congo to hide its assets. Kensington applied to have Montrow and Likouala wound up because of their inability to repay the loans. It was also alleged that the economic interest in the oil field still belonged to the Democratic Republic of Congo. The British Virgin Islands High Court granted the application that the companies be wound up on a just and equitable basis. It appointed a provisional insolvency representative over the companies who was able to discover information about the companies both within the British Virgin Islands and abroad.

a. Kensington International Ltd. v. Montrow International Ltd.

number of offshore jurisdictions including the British Virgin Islands, the Cayman Islands, and Guernsey, courts can appoint a provisional insolvency representative to conduct an investigation without notice to the real parties in interest. The English courts also have jurisdiction to appoint provisional insolvency representatives. Some jurisdictions specifically provide for the appointment of an insolvency representative for a foreign-domiciled company, depending upon where the company does business. For example,

方框 3.1 “公平公正”的清算与破产管理人的任命——基于蒙特罗国际有限公司案的分析[a]

蒙特罗国际有限公司是一家委托英属维京群岛信托公司持有的公司。该公司还持有利库阿拉公司的股份。据称，利库阿拉公司对刚果共和国的一处油田享有权利。该油田最初由法国的道达尔石油公司以 1 法郎的价格转让给了刚果共和国。但道达尔石油公司与刚果对油田的所有权产生了纠纷。据说刚果政府又将该油田转让给了利库阿拉公司，该公司为了收购油田申请了大额的银行贷款。而根据英国高等法院的调查，刚果素有拖欠债务的传统，并试图以信托公司的方式隐匿资产，拒绝对债权人进行清偿。肯辛顿投资基金购买了部分该国债券，并起诉蒙特罗、利库阿拉两家公司为诈骗公司，指控刚果通过它们隐匿资产。因刚果无法偿还贷款，所以肯辛顿投资基金向法院申请这两家公司破产，并主张油田的利益应归属于刚果共和国。英属维京群岛高等法院批准了基于“公平公正”原则的破产清算，并委任了临时破产管理人，调查他们在不限于英属维京群岛范围内的相关信息。

a. Kensington International Ltd. v. Montrow International Ltd.

利益相关人。英国法院也有类似的委任权。许多国家专门规定了外国公司的破产管理人的委任，主要取决于该公司在哪里开展业务。如果公司被认为与英国有“足够多的联系”，如在英国拥有资产，公司的负责人是英国居民或者公司通过伦敦的保险公司投保等，那么英国法院有权对其清算（麦克拉克兰和路易斯，2017）。

English courts have jurisdiction to wind up a company incorporated abroad if it has "sufficient connection" with the United Kingdom, such as that the company has assets in England, a director is resident there, or if company insurance policies have been placed through the London market (McLachlan and Loizou 2017).

The U.S. Federal Bureau of Investigation (FBI) has increased its efforts to tackle the demand side of foreign bribery—corruption and kleptocracy, in which state officials steal large sums of money from their country's coffers—a problem that has often been left to the foreign countries in which corrupt officials operate. The FBI and the U.S. Department of Justice's (DOJ) Asset Forfeiture and Money Laundering Section have been focusing on kleptocracy through the Kleptocracy Asset Recovery Initiative. In July 2016, the DOJ initiated the largest ever kleptocracy-related asset forfeiture action, in which $1 billion of assets were seized in Switzerland, the United Kingdom, and the United States.[4] The FBI has set up international corruption squads in Los Angeles, Miami, New York, and Washington, DC, to investigate violations of the FCPA, including acts of kleptocracy and money laundering. The squads will investigate both the supply and demand sides of international corruption.

Bribe Payers and Related Entities

Although bribe payers are specifically targeted by laws such as the U.K. Bribery Act and the FCPA, fines of any size are unlikely to be effective against an insolvent company that cannot pay. Bribers often pay bribes through intermediaries, which then disappear. Intermediaries that are convicted of bribery often have no resources to pay fines. Insolvency processes can prove useful in this scenario. An intermediary company that has been funded for the purpose of paying a bribe but

美国联邦调查局（FBI）已开始加大力度打击外国腐败犯罪的需求方，许多国家的腐败官员从本国侵吞大量资金，这个问题一般由其本国处理。而联邦调查局和美国司法部（DOJ）的“资产没收与洗钱犯罪调查科”一直在通过“反盗国贼行动计划”重点打击外国官员的贪腐问题。2016年7月，美国司法部发起了有史以来规模最大的有关外国腐败犯罪的资产没收行动。在英国、瑞士和美国共没收了近10亿美元的资产。[4]联邦调查局也在洛杉矶、迈阿密、纽约和华盛顿建立了反海外腐败小组，以调查违反《反海外腐败法》的贪腐和洗钱的行为，调查对象包括国际腐败行为的供需双方。

行贿人与相关人

尽管行贿人是英国《反贿赂法》和美国《反海外腐败法》主要针对的对象，但行贿人通过中间人行贿后便销声匿迹时，任何规模的罚款都无法奏效。被判贿赂罪的中间人通常无力支付巨额罚款。在这种情况下，破产程序能发挥作用。通过对为掩护腐败犯罪而成立的中介公司进行清算，破产管理人可对腐败交易的双方开展调查，确定实际的受益人并收回交易款项。

is subsequently rendered insolvent can be placed into liquidation; the insolvency representative can investigate the acts of corruption, identify the beneficiaries of the transaction on both the supply and demand sides, and recover monies paid.

These powers can also be used to investigate other intermediaries, which can lead to identification of the real parties in interest. Furthermore, such investigations can be conducted in secret to protect their integrity and ensure that those responsible and those who benefit cannot frustrate the process.

Agents and Other Facilitators

Agents and facilitators (such as lawyers, accountants, banks, and other intermediaries) can also be targeted through the insolvency process. In the United Kingdom and common law countries, an insolvency representative can discover the identity of agents or facilitators that have assisted an insolvent company in committing the act of corruption itself or in laundering the proceeds, either through statutory powers of investigation or by making application for a *Norwich Pharmacal* order to identify all known or unknown agents, facilitators, or other persons or entities who either knowingly colluded or were unknowingly used by the debtor.

Applications for *Norwich Pharmacal* orders can be made in any jurisdiction in which it is believed information on such facilitators may be located. If such powers are not available to an insolvency representative in a particular jurisdiction, recourse can be had to *Norwich Pharmacal* relief in common law jurisdictions where assets or defendants are located. (For a more detailed discussion of *Norwich Pharmacal* orders, see the section in chapter 2 titled *Norwich Pharmacal (or Disclosure) Orders in Common Law Jurisdictions*.)

这些方法也可以用于调查其他中间人，以确定真实的利益相关人和当事人。此外，为维护司法正义，防止相关责任人和受益人阻碍调查，允许此类调查秘密进行。

中间人和其他协助人

作为代理人的中间人或协助人，律师、会计师、银行和其他中间人都可以成为破产程序的调查对象。在英国等英美法系国家，破产管理人可通过法定调查权或第三方披露令确认已知或未知、无意或有意参与腐败的中间人、协助人等。

第三方披露令可在任何可能有相关信息的国家申请。如果该国并没有授予破产管理人此项权力，则破产管理人可向被告所在地或资产所在地的普通法司法管辖区申请。（关于该法令的更详细讨论，请参见第二章第三方披露令部分。）

Actions by an insolvency representative against a company's directors may extend to a director's corrupt acts, whether or not they benefit the company. Involving a company in criminal conduct or other wrongdoing is a breach of the duties of a director. Similar actions may be brought against others who facilitate the criminal conduct, such as auditors who fail to report or notice a pattern of criminal conduct.

A debtor company may not have the right, however, to bring an action against a third party accused of facilitating corporate wrongdoing. The in pari delicto (in equal fault) defense can sometimes preclude the insolvency representative from pursuing a cause of action against the facilitator on the company's behalf if it is alleged that the debtor company participated in the wrongdoing. In the United States, the debtor company may be charged with the acts of the officer implicated in the wrongdoing under the "corporate imputation" doctrine (known as the "corporate identification" doctrine in Canada and the United Kingdom).[5] Corrupt conduct might be argued to have been in the best interests of the company if it produced an advantageous result. Similar arguments have been made in U.S. bankruptcies with respect to claims against senior officers of a corporate debtor, and some courts take a short-sighted view of "benefit": even if the benefit is shortlived and harm ultimately ensues, it is nonetheless deemed to be a benefit (see box 3.2).

Commissions paid to agents or facilitators pursuant to an agreement to pay a bribe are recoverable by an insolvency representative because the agreements are illegal and therefore void. Again, however, such causes of action can be met with the defense of in pari delicto. The availability and application of this defense varies from jurisdiction to jurisdiction, and a fuller discussion of this evolving area of law is beyond the scope of this publication.

破产管理人针对公司董事采取的措施可以延伸到董事的腐败行为，无论该行为对公司有益与否。公司卷入犯罪行为或其他不法行为时，即可认定董事违反董事职责。对其他犯罪协助人，比如对未发现或未举报犯罪行为的审计人员，也可以采取相应的调查措施。

但是，公司作为债务人无权指控协助犯罪的第三方。在公司本身参与不法行为的情况下，允许“同等过失”（in pari delicto）的第三方协助人，以代表债务人行事为由，阻却破产管理人对其采取措施。在美国，公司的高级管理人员涉嫌腐败行为时，依据“公司归责”原则（在加拿大和英国被称为“公司确认”原则），由公司承担责任。[5]如果腐败行为的最终结果为公司带来实际收益，可能会将其认定为符合公司利益。在美国破产案件中，针对公司高管的指控也有类似的争论，一些法院采取了短视的观点，认为即便是短期收益，并且最终会造成损害，但仍应该认为其是有益于公司的（见方框 3.2）。

根据协议，用于支付代理人的贿赂款或协助人的佣金，可以被破产管理人追回。由于协议本身非法，可被认定为无效。同样地，这次认定也可能遭遇“同等过失”原则的抗辩。抗辩的适用与否和适用方式因国家而异。该项制度不断更新发展，本书不作更多讨论。

BOX 3.2 ***Kirschner v. KPMG LLP and Teachers' Retirement System of Louisiana v. PricewaterhouseCoopers, LLP*** [a]

These cases, decided together by the Court of Appeals of New York, arose from certified questions from the U.S. Court of Appeals for the Second Circuit and the Supreme Court of Delaware regarding the application of the in pari delicto doctrine and the adverse interest exception under New York law.

In *Kirschner*, the CEO of the corporate debtor Refco created a falsely positive picture of Refco's financial condition, which had short-term benefits but ultimately resulted in Refco's filing for bankruptcy under chapter 11. Refco's subsequently formed litigation trust brought suit against Refco's auditors, law firm, and the investment banks involved in Refco's leveraged buy-out and initial public offering for failing to detect the fraud. The district court dismissed the claims against these third-party professionals, holding that they were barred by the in pari delicto doctrine under New York law because the fraudulent acts of Refco's president and CEO were imputable to the corporation.[b]

In *Teachers' Retirement System*, a derivative (shareholder) action was brought in the Delaware Court of Chancery on behalf of AIG alleging that AIG's senior officers fraudulently inflated AIG's financial performance to deceive investors, and that AIG's auditor, Pricewaterhouse Coopers was negligent in failing to detect the fraud.The court of chancery concluded that the claims were barred under NewYork law because the actions of AIG's senior officers were imputable to AIG and, by extension, the derivative plaintiffs.[c]

The New York Court of Appeals held that self-interest does not trigger the adverse interest exception because the wrongdoing in these cases provided short-term benefits to the debtors before the fraud was exposed. Those benefits consisted of, among other things, enabling the raising of funds, attracting customers, or completing acquisitions. The court defended its reasoning thus: "To allow a corporation to avoid the consequences of corporate acts simply because an employee performed them with his personal profit in mind would enable the corporation to disclaim, at its convenience, virtually every act its officers undertake."[d]

a. Kirschner v. KPMG LLP, 15 N.Y.3d 446, 938 N.E.2d 941 (2010).

b. Kirschner v. Grant Thornton LLP, 2009 WL 1286326 (S.D.N.Y. April 14, 2009).

c. In re American International Group Inc., 965 A.2d 763 (Del. Ch. 2009).

d. Kirschner v. KPMG LLP, 15 N.Y.3d 446, 938 N.E.2d 941.

方框 3.2 科施纳诉毕马威会计师事务所案（以下简称科施纳案）和路易斯安那州教师退休计划诉普华永道会计师案（以下简称教师退休计划案）[a]

这两起案件由纽约州上诉法院共同裁决。美国第二巡回上诉法院和特拉华州最高法院，就该如何适用纽约州法律中的“互有过失”原则和“不利利益例外”原则的问题申请批复。

在科施纳案中，瑞富公司（Refco）的首席执行官对公司的财务状况做了虚假陈述，尽管能带来短期收益，但根据相关规定，最终会导致瑞富公司破产。瑞富公司随后成立诉讼信托基金以未发现欺诈行为为由起诉了未尽到监管义务的审计师、法律顾问和其他参与瑞富公司杠杆收购和首次公开募股的投资银行等。地方法院驳回了针对上述第三方的诉讼，法院认为根据纽约州法律的“互有过失”原则，瑞富公司首席执行官欺诈行为的法律责任应由公司承担。[b]

在教师退休计划案中，美国国际集团（AIG）的股东向特拉华州法院提起一项派生诉讼，起诉该集团的高管故意夸大了集团的财务状况欺骗投资者，而集团的审计团队普华永道会计师事务所因为疏忽未能发现欺诈行为。法院认为，公司高管的行为应归责于该公司甚至是股东自己，依据纽约州法律裁定驳回起诉。[c]

纽约上诉法院认为，利于公司自身的行为并不会触发“不利利益例外”的原则。因为在这些案件中，行为人的欺诈行为在被揭露前，确实为公司提供了短期利益，有助于筹集资金、吸引客户以及完成收购等。因此，法院认为，“如果仅仅因为员工的个人行为就免除公司的法律责任，会导致公司在任何必要之时，否认员工的任何一项行动”。[d]

a. Kirschner v. KPMG LLP, 15 N.Y.3d 446, 938 N.E.2d 941 (2010).

b. Kirschner v. Grant Thornton LLP, 2009 WL 1286326 (S.D.N.Y. April 14, 2009).

c. In re American International Group Inc., 965 A.2d 763 (Del. Ch. 2009).

d. Kirschner v. KPMG LLP, 15 N.Y.3d 446, 938 N.E.2d 941.

Strategic and Tactical Considerations

Actions against bribe takers, agents, or facilitators, and investigations to identify such persons, can be costly. A lack of funds may severely restrict an insolvency representative's options for pursuing recovery. Some creditors may be willing to fund litigation or take assignment of claims. An insolvency representative may also be able to procure external funding, such as third-party litigation funding, if permitted by the legal system in which the insolvency is supervised. The ability to fund investigations or actions against suspected facilitators is significant and intertwined with the degree of likelihood of success and the ability to recover. Insolvency representatives may need to address, among other things: (1) the choice of insolvency forum when more than one is available; (2) the choice of forum for independent actions for either discovery in respect of, or relief against, facilitators or recipients; (3) the availability of defenses to claims against facilitators in a particular jurisdiction; and (4) the availability and location of assets against which to enforce any judgments against facilitators or recipients.

A chain of intermediaries may each have received some benefit. The cost of pursuing individuals must be weighed against the benefit to be achieved. Very often, the middlemen have few resources, and they may be more useful as sources of information than as sources of asset recovery. Depending upon the size and geographical reach of the acts of corruption, their willingness to divulge valuable information may be tempered by a fear of reprisals. Insolvency representatives must also be aware of the risk that investigations may be sabotaged, may lead down intentionally false paths, or may be met with threats of retaliation. When the stakes are high, as they are in large corruption schemes, corrupt actors may be willing to go

战略和战术考虑

对受贿人、贿赂代理人或协助人的调查往往花费不菲。资金短缺可能会严重限制破产管理人的策略选择。一些债权人愿意为诉讼提供资金或者转让债权。如果当地的破产制度允许，破产管理人也可以向其他第三方获取诉讼资金。获取资金的能力与能否成功追回资产息息相关。其中，破产管理人需要解决以下问题:（1）多个破产法院均有管辖权时，择一诉讼;（2）应选择允许采取独立行动，以便分别为针对受贿人和协助人的单独调查确认相关法院;（3）在特定司法管辖区，对贿赂协助人的指控是否有抗辩的可能;（4）涉案资产所在地以及执行可能性。

有时，一连串的中间人各自均获得了好处。衡量追查成本时也要考虑获取的收益。中间商通常掌握资源较少，将其作为信息源比对其进行资产追讨更为有效。依据腐败规模和影响范围的不同，中间商可能会因担心被打击报复而减少提供信息的意愿。破产管理人还必须意识到其他可能会面临的风险，比如，调查遭到蓄意阻挠，由此引起调查策略选择的误判、恐吓或者遭到报复等。当涉及巨额利益，或是牵扯到庞大关系网时，犯罪分子会因竭力自保而不惜动用绑架、勒索或死亡威胁的手段。

to great lengths to protect their interests, sometimes including kidnappings, extortion, and death threats.

Claims against Corporate Officers, Agents and Third-Party Facilitators

In *Official Receiver v. Wadge Rapps & Hunt*,[6] the House of Lords referred to the dual purpose of a winding up—not just settlement of liabilities and distribution of surplus but also the holding to account of persons responsible for the company's demise. Lord Walker of Gestingthorpe explained that:

> winding up has and has had almost throughout the history of company law, a dual purpose. One purpose is the orderly settlement of a company's liabilities and the distribution of any surplus funds, prior to the company being dissolved. The other is the investigation and the imposition of criminal and civil sanctions in respect of misconduct on the part of persons (especially directors of an insolvent company in compulsory liquidation) who may be shown to have abused the privilege of incorporation with limited liability. The first function is primarily a concern of a company's creditors and shareholders; the second function serves a wider public interest.[7]

The primary objective of an insolvency representative is to maximize the value of a debtor's estate for the benefit of its creditors. Maximizing value in winding-up cases entails not only the management and sale of tangible assets but also the monetization of intangibles, including potential claims for damages against persons who have diminished or enabled harm to the debtor's estate. These claims are considered "property" and belong to the estate because they represent wrongs against the estate that caused, facilitated, or prolonged the damages to the creditors and victims of the fraud. Such causes of action may lie against directors and other officers,

针对公司员工、代理中介和第三方协助者的诉讼

在破产管理人诉瓦奇·拉普斯与亨特案[6]中，上议院提到，破产清算的双重目的，除了盘点债务和分配盈余，还包括追究导致公司破产人员的责任。沃克大法官对此解释道：

> 清算制度贯穿公司法的历史，其具有双重目的：一是在公司解散之前，有序地偿还公司的债务，并分配盈余资金。二是对公司人员滥用职权的不当行为（特别是导致公司破产的不当行为）开展调查并实施相应的刑事或民事的制裁。[7]前者主要涉及公司的债权人和股东所关心的问题，后者则服务于更广泛的公众利益。

为了维护债权人的权益，将债务人财产价值最大化是破产管理人的主要目标。在破产案件中，财产价值最大化不仅需要管理和出售有形资产，还需要将无形资产兑现，包括对已经损害或可能损害债务人资产的责任人提起赔偿。“赔偿”被认为是债权人的“财产”，属于破产财产，因为它们代表了相关责任人的不当行为，这些不当行为会造成或推动造成债权人的损害，也会使债权人所受损害被放大。赔偿可以针对公司董事、职员、代理人或协助人，如银行、律所、会计或审计事务所以及其他代理公司。

agents, and those who have facilitated wrongs against the debtor such as banks, law firms, accounting or auditing firms, and company formation agents.

Substantial value can be recovered from damages claims directed against third-party facilitators and agents who have enabled the public corruption or the secondary costs of laundering or concealing its proceeds. This value can exceed what may be recovered in traditional assets (such as bank deposits, real estate, or investment securities) from primary targets such as state officials or bribe payers. The use of insolvency proceedings to facilitate the development and prosecution of tertiary damages claims against enablers of corruption or of the laundering of its proceeds can substantially expand the potential recovery for a state that has suffered damages caused by corruption.

For example, in the United States, following the discovery of two of the largest Ponzi schemes in history, the DOJ was able to recover almost $2 billion in bank fines in the New York–based Madoff scheme and may recover several million dollars from Swiss banks in the Houston-based Stanford Financial Group scheme, all of which are to be paid to victims of the respective frauds. Similarly, the U.S. receiver and the Antiguan foreign joint insolvency representatives in the Stanford scheme have reached multimillion-dollar settlements against some law firms and other third parties and continue to litigate significant claims against banks, law firms, and others.

Insolvency law can be used by a victim state to step into the shoes of intermediary companies used by corrupt officials or businessmen, enabling an insolvency representative to take charge of causes of action vested in a company whose assets have been stripped from it by its "controlling minds" with the assistance of banks, lawyers, accountants, or directors who served

如果第三方协助人、中介代理实施了助长腐败的行为，如造成公共利益二次损害的洗钱、隐瞒资产等，此类赔偿诉讼的标的往往可观，甚至可能超过从主要目标（国家官员或腐败犯罪分子）处获得的传统资产（如银行存款、房地产或证券投资）的价值。利用破产程序将诉讼范围扩展到助长腐败、协助洗钱的第三方，可以大大提高受害国的追偿能力。

例如，在美国，历史上两个最大的庞氏骗局被发现之后，司法部追回了“纽约马多夫计划”（New York-based Madoff scheme）近 20 亿美元的银行罚款，从瑞士银行手中追回了“休斯顿斯坦福金融集团计划”（Houston-based Stanford Financial Group scheme）的数百万美元。这些资产都将作为两个骗局受害者的赔偿金。同样地，美方破产管理人和安提瓜破产管理人也与部分律所等第三方机构达成数百万美元的和解。同时，也持续对其他相关机构提起诉讼。

受害国可以利用破产法介入腐败交易的中间公司，了解幕后实际的“主脑”（controlling minds）利用中间公司转移资产的真正原因，以及过程中参与协助的银行、律师、会计师或者其他持有公司账户的董事（见方框 3.3）。

the company and who may be held to account (see box 3.3).

BOX 3.3 Case Study on the Principle of the "Controlling Mind"[a]

Federal Republic of Brazil and Municipality of São Paulo v. Durant International Ltd. and Kildare Finance Ltd.

The facts of this case can be found in box I.1. Brazil and São Paulo had to prove that Durant International Ltd. (Durant) and Kildare Finance Ltd. (Kildare) knowingly received the proceeds of the fraud, or dishonestly assisted in the fraud, or both, to hold them legally responsible. "Knowing receipt" means that the company had knowledge of the fraud. "Dishonest assistance" means that the companies themselves were dishonest in their assistance. A corporation is a legal entity, separate from the people who run it, and therefore it is considered to have its own "mind." The court in Jersey had to decide who was the controlling mind of the companies. A company usually acts through its board of directors and the officers and management who carry out the day-to-day activities. Paulo Maluf had never been a director of the companies. The directors included, among others, a Swiss investment manager and, for a time, Maluf's son Flavio. The court did not, however, look only at the board of directors. It sought to determine who was the company's controlling mind and decided it was Paulo Maluf. The companies had been established on his instruction and for his benefit. He was in control. The knowledge of shadow directors and the people who truly control a company can be attributed to the company, and the company can be held liable on the basis of their actions, in this case, the actions of Paulo Maluf.

a. [2015] UKPC 35.

The Duties of Directors and Managers of Companies

Statutory causes of action vary from jurisdiction to jurisdiction. Many are simply codifications of preexisting law. In the majority of jurisdictions, directors and managers of corporate entities owe duties of care and loyalty to the entity that they manage. Although the specific duties and how they may be enforced vary, the duty of care generally requires that directors and managers exercise the degree of care that ordinarily careful and prudent people would use in similar circumstances. The duty of loyalty requires directors and managers to act in good faith in the best interests

方框 3.3 “主脑”原则的案例分析

巴西联邦政府和圣保罗市诉杜兰特国际有限公司和基尔代尔金融有限公司案[a]

案情提要详见方框 I.1。巴西和圣保罗市必须证明杜兰特有限公司（Durant）与基尔代尔有限公司（Kildare）在知情的情况下参与欺诈、获取欺诈收益或两者兼而有之，才能追究其法律责任。“知情”，表示公司明确知悉欺诈行为。“不诚实地协助欺诈”，是指公司违背忠实义务参与欺诈活动。公司是独立于其经营者的法人，因而被认为具有独立的“思想”。泽西岛法院必须确定谁是公司的实际控制人。一般而言，公司通过董事会和公司职员行事。保罗 · 马洛夫从未担任过公司董事，而董事曾包括某瑞士投资经理以及马洛夫的儿子弗拉维奥。但是，法院并没有仅依据董事会成员就确定公司的“主脑”，而是最终锁定了保罗 · 马洛夫。法院发现公司依据他的指示行事，也是因其而成立，他掌握了公司的实际控制权。由于公司实际控制人以及影子董事的主张也应归责于公司，所以公司需要为保罗 · 马洛夫的行为承担责任。

a. [2015] UKPC 35.

公司董事和经理的职责

法定的诉由因国家而异，许多国家还停留在立法草案阶段。在大多数国家，公司的董事和经理应对公司负有谨慎和忠实的义务。虽然具体的职责和履行方式不同，但一般而言，对董事和管理人员谨慎程度的要求，达到在类似情况下一般人普遍会采取的谨慎程度即可。忠实义务要求公司的董事和管理人员应代表公司和股东的最大利益，不可从事可能损害公司或利用职务之便谋取私利的活动，如禁止秘密收取佣金等。忠实义务还包括禁止自我交易以及篡夺公司控制权等。大多数国家的立法都认为董事负有一定的信赖义务，源自董事必须为公

of the corporation and its shareholders and to refrain from engaging in activities that might damage the corporation or enable them to receive an improper personal benefit arising from their relationship with it. This would include, for example, a duty not to receive secret commissions. The duty of loyalty also encompasses a prohibition on self-dealing and the usurpation of corporate opportunities by directors. Most, if not all, jurisdictions acknowledge that directors have some form of fiduciary duty, derived from the principle that directors are required to act in the best interests of the corporation and its shareholders.

In cases involving public corruption, companies are almost inevitably used as intermediaries to launder and retain the proceeds of bribery or misappropriation of state assets. The directors and officers (as well as the individuals who control the company, directly or indirectly, or who are de facto directors) of such companies may be sued by an insolvency representative for breaches of their fiduciary duties if such companies are placed into insolvency, and, for example, those individuals are found to have participated in a scheme to use the companies as vehicles to launder or conceal stolen state assets.

Directors must be able to make business decisions without the fear of being held to account, however, if those decisions ultimately cause damage to the company. Therefore, many jurisdictions permit an element of leeway or discretion. In the United States, for example, under the "business judgment rule," the directors of a corporation are presumed to have acted on an informed basis, in good faith, and in the honest belief that the action taken was in the best interests of the company. Any party challenging the decision in question bears the burden of establishing facts that rebut this presumption. Equivalents or variants of the business judgment rule exist in most jurisdictions. However, the parameters and application of such rules

司及股东的最大利益行事的原则。

公共腐败：指不可避免地将公司作为中介，用以洗钱、挪用公款或获取腐败收益的非法行为。在该类案件中，如果公司被置于破产状态，破产管理人可以以违反信赖义务为由起诉公司董事及相关管理人员（包括直接或间接控制公司的个人、实际董事等），如将公司作为洗钱工具，隐匿、侵吞国家资产等。

公司管理层必须能够在无需顾忌事后追责的前提下作出商业决策，即便这些决策最终可能有损公司利益。许多国家立法对此留有酌情处理的空间。比如，美国根据“商业判断规则”，推定公司董事在知情并善意的基础上履行义务，并诚实地认为行事符合公司的最大利益。任何质疑这一推定的当事方，都应承担相应的举证责任。大多数国家都有类似的立法，但在具体细节和适用层面相差很大。试图指控公司董事或高管的破产管理人，可以主张公司破产本身就代表了公司董事违反了商业判断的规则，但法院仍然会酌情考虑商业判断规则或相类似的立法。不同国家对该规则的认定和适用也不相同。[8]

vary considerably. An insolvency representative who seeks to challenge the actions or decisions of an officer or director may argue that insolvency is itself proof of the violation of the business judgment rule. Nonetheless, the business judgment rule or its equivalent in the jurisdiction concerned must be addressed. The deference afforded to the rule or presumption varies considerably from jurisdiction to jurisdiction.[8]

In all jurisdictions and in all situations—including insolvency—the duty of directors is to manage the affairs of the corporation to maximize its value for the benefit of its stakeholders. When a corporation is solvent, those stakeholders are the corporation's shareholders. When the corporation is insolvent, the creditors take the place of the shareholders as the residual beneficiaries of any increase in its value. The insolvency representative, who replaces the directors of the company, is thus under a duty to maximize the assets of the corporation for the benefit of its creditors.[9]

In considering a cause of action against the directors or officers of a corporation, an insolvency representative would address both the mechanics of such an action and the likelihood of recovery. Even a strong cause of action is meaningless if the defendant has no assets against which to execute judgment. An insolvency representative will pursue only those claims for which investigation shows there are assets available to satisfy them. In other cases, an insolvency representative may consider pursuing other actors who facilitated breaches of duty or who may have received benefits. Banks, accounting, or audit firms that may have failed to discover fraud or dishonesty on the part of the directors of a company will likely have more assets than a director or officer who has fled the jurisdiction or who is insolvent. In some instances, directors' and officers' liability insurance may provide a recovery if a director has committed misconduct.

Corporate officers and directors are not permitted to use their position

在所有国家的部门法（包括破产法）中，董事负责管理公司事务，最大程度地提升公司价值，为相关利益人服务。正常情况下，利益相关人就是公司的股东。但当公司破产时，债权人取代股东成为公司的权益人，而破产管理人取代董事，负有使公司利益最大化的义务，从而维护债权人的权益。[9]

在起诉公司董事时，破产管理人既要考虑诉讼的机制，也要考虑追偿的可能性。如果被告没有资产可被执行，那么再有力的诉由也没有意义。破产管理人应该只追讨那些在调查中证实可被执行的资产。在某些情况下，破产管理人也可起诉其他协助违反职权或获取不法利益的行为人。他们可能是相关的银行、会计或审计公司，因为未能及时发现公司董事的欺诈行为而成为被告。相关协助人的资产可能比潜逃的公司董事或破产公司的更多。在某些情况下，还可用公司董事和高管的不法行为责任险进行赔偿。

公司董事和高管不得利用职务之便获取信任，为个人谋利。公司

of trust and confidence to further their private interests. Any secret commissions received are recoverable by the company or, in the case of insolvency, by the insolvency representative. If a director had a personal financial interest in a transaction or received a benefit over and above that which flows to the corporation or all stockholders generally, that benefit is recoverable and the business judgment rule will not protect the decision to engage in it.

An insolvency representative must consider the applicable law in the jurisdiction of domicile of the corporation in determining whether to pursue an action against a director. Both procedural and substantive laws must be addressed, including laws on how to prove bad faith or on the presumption that operates in favor of the director. The fiduciary duties of directors in the jurisdiction must be analyzed as well as the liability standard for breaching them. An insolvency representative will need to ascertain whether a country's corporate governance jurisprudence prohibits directors from selfdealing and permits insolvency representatives to pursue actions to hold directors accountable for breaches of their fiduciary duties.

The World Bank Principles set out best practices for directors' obligations as well as possible liability and remedies for breach. When insolvency systems impose specific duties on directors, and they are regularly held accountable in practice, directors' incentives for malfeasance are reduced. In some jurisdictions, a bribe taker can be held accountable if he had a fiduciary duty, which can be relevant in the context of stolen asset cases. Box 3.4 sets out the World Bank Principle that addresses directors' obligation prior to insolvency.

可追讨其收取的任何秘密佣金。公司一旦破产，由破产管理人负责追偿。如果董事在公司交易中谋取个人利益或个人利益超过了公司和全体股东的利益，该利益也应被收回，并且该行为不受“商业判断规则”的保护。

破产管理人在起诉公司董事时，必须考虑公司所在地的适用法律，包括如何证明董事并非“诚实善意”，有哪些有利于公司董事的推定规则等程序性或实体性的内容，该国法律中董事信托责任成立及违背的标准是如何规定的，以及该国的公司法是否禁止董事自我交易，是否允许破产管理人对违反信赖义务的董事提起诉讼，等等，都需要破产管理人确定和厘清。

世界银行《关于有效破产及债权人债务人制度的准则》提供了董事的义务标准、违规责任和相应的救济措施。只有破产制度对董事职责及监督方法予以明确规定，才能有效减少其渎职的诱因。在一些国家，结合资产流失的具体情况，受贿的信赖责任人也会面临追责和制裁。方框 3.4 阐明了世界银行“临近破产期间的董事义务”的准则。

BOX 3.4 World Bank Principle B2—Directors' Obligations in the Period Approaching Insolvency

Laws governing directors' obligations in the period approaching insolvency should promote responsible corporate behavior while fostering reasonable risk taking and encouraging business reorganization. The law should provide appropriate remedies for breach of directors' obligations, which may be enforced after insolvency proceedings have commenced.

B2.1 The obligation. The law should require that when they know or reasonably ought to know that insolvency of the enterprise is imminent or unavoidable, directors should have due regard to the interests of creditors and other stakeholders, and should take reasonable steps to either avoid insolvency, or where insolvency is unavoidable, minimize its extent.

B2.2 Persons owing the obligation. The law should specify the persons owing the obligation, which may include any person formally appointed as a director and any other person exercising factual control and performing the functions of a director.

B2.3 Liability and remedies. Where creditors suffer loss or damage due to a director's breach of their obligations, the law should impose liability subject to possible defenses (including that the director took reasonable steps to avoid or minimize the extent of insolvency). The extent of any liability should not exceed the loss or damage suffered by creditors as a result of the breach. The law should specify that the remedies for liability found by the court to arise from a breach of the obligations should include payment in full to the insolvency estate of any damages assessed by the court. The insolvency representative should have primary standing to pursue a cause of action for breach.

B2.4 Funding of actions. The law should provide for the costs of an action against a director to be paid as administrative expenses.

Personal Liability Actions against Directors

In jurisdictions with well-developed insolvency frameworks, directors of insolvent companies may be held personally responsible, without any limitation of liability, for any or all of the debts or other liabilities of the company if they knowingly participated in the fraudulent operation of the businesses. These claims generally arise under "wrongful trading" or

方框 3.4　世界银行准则 B2：临近破产期间的董事义务

临近破产期间公司董事义务的相关立法应倡导“负责任公司行为”，鼓励合理的风险承担，促进公司业务重整。法律也应该提供违反董事义务的救济措施，在破产程序开始后，破产管理人可据此获得救济。

B2.1 义务：法律应规定，董事在知道或应该知道公司即将破产或不可避免破产时，应充分考虑债权人等的权益，并采取合理的措施避免破产或在无法避免破产的情况下将损失减至最小。

B2.2 责任人：法律应明确规定，承担责任的主体可能包括正式任命的董事，也包括行使实际控制权、履行董事职责的其他人。

B2.3 违规责任与救济：如果债权人因董事违规而遭受损失，法律应规定相应的赔偿责任（包括为避免或减轻损失，董事应采取的合理措施）。责任范围不应超过债权人的实际损害。法院应对资产损害进行评估，由责任人足额赔偿。破产管理人在追偿诉讼中应占主导地位。

B2.4 诉讼费用：法律应规定对董事的诉讼费用作为破产过程中的行政开支。

针对董事个人责任的诉讼

在破产制度完善的国家，知情并参与了欺诈性经营的公司董事，对公司的相关债务承担个人无限责任。这由“不当交易”“通知义务”的条款发展而来。在董事知情且债权人不存在任何知情可能的情况下，公司因不当经营而产生的债务，应由董事个人承担。

"duty to file" provisions when the company continues to operate and incur debts with, to the knowledge of the directors, no reasonable prospect of the creditors being paid. Directors can be personally liable for such debts.

Insolvency representatives have to demonstrate fault, damages, and causation as in typical tort cases. In some countries, it is sufficient to show that the action of the directors "contributed to the bankruptcy" to obtain compensation for the insufficiency of assets. In addition to fraud and criminal offenses, fault can include obvious managerial mistakes or dishonest actions, including risky investments, conduct of operations outside the company's purpose, lack of supervision, continuation of operations in spite of deficits, recourse to ruinous means to finance operations, or pursuit of activity in a personal interest.

In some countries, such as Belgium and France, the law allows actions against both legal and de facto directors who had the power to make managerial decisions. Directors or managers include those serving as of the commencement of insolvency proceedings and former directors. Former directors are liable only if the insufficiency of assets existed at the date of their resignation or removal and if the insufficiency was the result of their fraudulent activities. They may be obligated to pay compensation only for the increase in the shortfall of assets between the date on which they committed a fault and the final balance. In such countries, actions are generally time limited.[10]

Proceedings for Fraudulent or Wrongful Trading

Insolvency representatives who suspect wrongdoing on the part of directors may consider whether to pursue actions for fraudulent or wrongful trading—fraudulent trades can be used to justify payments to third parties or receive or conceal corrupt assets. The distinction between wrongful and fraudulent trading derives from the intent of the director. Wrongful

和一般侵权案件一样，破产管理人必须证明过错、损害结果，以及二者之间的因果关系。在一些国家，依据上述要素足以认定公司董事“导致了破产”的，董事需要为损害承担赔偿责任。除了欺诈性经营和刑事犯罪外，“过错”还包括明显的管理过失或欺诈性行为，即冒险性投资、违背公司宗旨的经营、监督不善、持续性的负债经营、谋取个人私利和破坏性的财务运作等。

在一些国家，如比利时和法国，法律允许对法定董事和实际董事提起诉讼。这里的董事包括在破产程序开始时在任的董事及前任董事。前任董事只对卸任前因欺诈经营而产生的债务承担损害赔偿责任，从不当经营开始之日到清算终结之日为计算期间。在这些国家和地区，诉讼也往往有时效的限制。[10]

欺诈性交易或不当交易的诉讼程序

当破产管理人怀疑董事存在违规操作时，可以考虑提起以欺诈性交易或不当交易为由的诉讼。诉讼也可以针对第三方的交易、接收、隐匿腐败资产等行为。应依据董事的动机区分不当交易和欺诈性交易。不当交易主要指管理不善，如未能及时纳税、未申报退税等违规操作。而欺诈性交易则指存在故意欺诈的企图而进行交易的行为。例如，董

trading involves mismanagement and might include, for example, failing to pay company tax liabilities or to file statutory returns. Fraudulent trading involves a deliberate attempt to defraud—dishonest intent can be inferred when, for example, a company continues trading even though the directors know that the company can no longer satisfy its current liabilities or when the directors cause the company to incur additional debt when they knew that there is no reasonable prospect of that debt being paid. In the United Kingdom, fraudulent and wrongful trading claims can now be assigned to third parties. Unsecured creditors, either individually or as a group, may pursue claims against directors.

The burden of proving fraudulent intent is high, which means that in practice the claim is rarely brought. One of the benefits of a fraudulent trading action in the United Kingdom, however, is that section 213 of the Insolvency Act 1986 has extraterritorial effect.[11] Section 213(2) provides:

> The court, on the application of the insolvency representative may declare that any persons who were knowingly parties to the carrying on of the business in the manner abovementioned are to be liable to make such contributions (if any) to the company's assets as the court thinks proper.[12]

In the United Kingdom, an insolvency representative bringing a claim for wrongful trading need not show that the directors had knowledge or ought to have concluded that there was no reasonable prospect that the company would avoid insolvent liquidation at a specific time, only that they knew or ought to have known that the company had no reasonable prospect of avoiding liquidation at some time before the winding up. Once it has been established that a director knew or ought to have known that there was no reasonable prospect of the company avoiding liquidation, the onus of establishing a defense under section 214(3) of the Insolvency Act 1986 falls

事明知公司已经资不抵债，或明知无法支付但仍继续交易的行为。在英国，欺诈性交易和不当交易都可以针对第三方提起诉讼。无担保的债权人，无论个人或集体，均可对董事提起诉讼。

由于“具有欺诈意图”的举证责任标准很高，所以实践中索赔成功的案例很少。在英国，欺诈性交易诉讼的优点之一是《1986 年破产法》第 213 条具有域外效力。[11] 第 213（2）条规定：

> 法院可应破产管理人的要求，裁定从事上述交易的任何当事人都应就公司资产受损部分，承担法院认为合理的赔偿。[12]

在英国，提起不当交易诉讼的破产管理人，不需要证明在某个具体的时间点，董事已知或应知公司无避免破产的合理可能。只需要证明在清算之前的一段时间，董事已知或应知公司无避免破产的合理可能即可。一旦确定了这一点，根据《1986 年破产法》第 214（3）条，在已知或应知破产的情况下，董事必须证明已尽最大努力使债权人的潜在损失降至最低。[13]

on the director. Directors must show that they made every effort to minimize the potential loss to the company's creditors.[13]

Section 213 of the Insolvency Act 1986 provides that if, during a company's winding up, it appears that any business has been carried on with intent of defrauding the company's creditors or the creditors of any other person, or for any fraudulent purpose, the court may, on the insolvency representative's application, declare that anyone who knowingly carried on the business is liable to make such contributions (if any) to the company's assets as the court thinks proper. Under section 214 of the Insolvency Act 1986, directors of a company in liquidation can be ordered by the court to contribute personally to the assets in the liquidation if they are found to have been guilty of wrongful trading. Claims for wrongful trading cannot be brought against nondirectors.

Preferences and Transactions at Undervalue

The ability to assign claims also applies to preferences[14] and transactions at undervalue. Preferential payments to a particular creditor, or the sale assets below their fair market value, are both likely to be investigated if a company becomes insolvent. Undervalued transactions in particular can be a way to shift "value" from one company to another—a method of laundering assets—which can be used by corrupt officials hiding funds.

An insolvency representative has a duty to investigate preferential payments and transactions at undervalue and can apply to the court to set them aside. In the United Kingdom, transactions at undervalue and preferences can be set aside pursuant to sections 238 and 239 of the Insolvency Act 1986, respectively. Similar provisions are found in most, if not all, jurisdictions with a codified insolvency framework. They differ with respect to the timeframe during which the transactions are subject to being set aside. In the United Kingdom, for example, transactions at undervalue

英国《1986年破产法》第213条规定，在公司清算过程中，对任何涉嫌故意欺诈债权人及其他权益人的行为，法院可应破产管理人的申请，要求相关责任人以法院认为适当的方式，承担赔偿责任。根据《1986年破产法》第214条，在清算过程中，若公司董事有任何不当交易的行为，法院可令其对损失承担个人责任。但此条不适用于公司董事以外的人员。

优先清偿和低价交易

破产管理人也可对优先清偿[14]和低价交易提起诉讼。公司一旦破产，向特定债权人的优先清偿或者以低于市场一般价格出售资产都可能面临调查。这种低价出售资产的行为，实际上是一种将资产价值转移的洗钱方法，腐败官员利用这种方法隐匿腐败资金。

破产管理人有责任调查任何涉嫌优先清偿和低价交易的交易，并向法院申请将其暂时搁置。在英国，根据1986年《破产法》第238条和第239条的规定，涉嫌低价交易和优先清偿的交易可以被暂时搁置。大多数国家的破产制度存在类似的条款，只是交易被搁置的时间范围有所不同。以英国为例，破产前两年内涉嫌低价交易的，可以被搁置。涉嫌优先清偿的，破产管理人可以对两年前的相关方，或六个月前非相关方的潜在优先清偿开展调查。各国对“破产开始”的认定也有所不同。一般来说，以起诉当天或相关文件签发当天作为破产程序的起算日。

within two years prior to the onset of insolvency are likely to be set aside. An insolvency representative may investigate potential preferences to a connected party going back two years and to a nonconnected party going back six months. There may also be differences between jurisdictions on the meaning of "onset of insolvency." The onset of insolvency is generally considered to be the date on which a petition or other document is filed initiating the process.

Other Breaches of Duty

Directors may be also held to account for other breaches of duty, such as, in the United Kingdom for example, the duty to avoid conflicts of interest; the duty to exercise reasonable care, skill, and diligence; the duty to act within lawful authority; the duty not to accept benefits from third parties; and the duty to declare one's interest in proposed transactions or arrangements.

Directors are also subject to other statutory requirements, such as the duty to keep proper books and records, and restrictions on entering into certain transactions with, or accepting loans from, the company. Breach of these duties and requirements can result not only in directors being disqualified from their positions but can also expose them to personal liability. The insolvency representative may bring such claims, and in some cases the directors may also be held criminally liable.

If property of the company has been misapplied or improperly retained, creditors, shareholders, or in the case of insolvency, the insolvency representative, can pursue claims against officers or others concerned in its management. Such claims can also be brought against facilitators. Potential causes of action that can be brought against officers or facilitators outside the statutory setting include actions for monies had and received, for unjust enrichment, and for knowing assistance or knowing receipt.

其他违规操作

公司董事还负有其他义务。在英国，其他义务包括避免利益冲突、必要程度的谨慎、专业且勤勉、在合法权限内行事、不收取第三方利益以及申报特定交易相关人的利益。

董事还受到其他法定要求的约束，例如，保留必要的财务记录，禁止与公司自交易或向公司贷款等。违反上述职责不仅会被取消董事资格，还可能承担相应的个人责任，由破产管理人索赔。在某些情况下，还需要承担刑事责任。

如果公司财产被不当使用或不当扣留，债权人、股东以及破产管理人都可以向董事、高管或其他协助人提起诉讼。除了法定的诉由外，还可包括不当得利或任何虽知情但仍提供协助的行为。

Actions commenced prior to insolvency by creditors or shareholders are often transferred to, and thereafter prosecuted by, the insolvency representative. If there are insufficient funds with which to pursue these actions (either by the insolvency representative or private parties), some jurisdictions permit their assignment to others who are financially able to prosecute them. Assignment provides an insolvency representative with funds that can be used either to pay creditors or to fund or partially fund other projects designed to maximize value for the estate. In the United Kingdom and the United States, the insolvency representative can also assign statutory causes of action. Fraudulent and wrongful trading claims can also be assigned to third parties, as can claims regarding preferences and transactions at undervalue. Assignment is not universally available, and, in common law jurisdictions, the laws of maintenance and champerty[15] may bar assignment or render it a nullity. Not all jurisdictions have repealed, or introduced the requisite exceptions to, the rules prohibiting the assignment or funding of certain causes of action.

In many civil law countries, insolvency laws contemplate a duty, mainly but not only on the part of management, to file for insolvency within a specified time after a director knows or should have known that the company would be unable to repay its debts. For example, Germany's insolvency statute (*Insolvenzordnung*) requires filing for insolvency within 21 days after a director acquires or should have acquired such knowledge. This has inspired many other similar laws, for example in the Balkans, that replicate or approximate the 21-day timeframe. In such jurisdictions, directors that do not file for insolvency within the specified period may be held liable.

Derivative Actions

What can be done if directors remain in charge of a company and they

在破产程序开始后，债权人或股东在破产开始前的行动一般由破产管理人继任，并代为提起诉讼。若破产管理人或其他当事方缺乏诉讼资金，一些国家的破产制度允许通过诉讼融资的方式募集资金，所募资金既可用来偿还债权人，也可投资其他可将破产资产价值最大化的项目。英国和美国允许破产管理人转让债权。针对欺诈和不当交易的诉讼请求权，以及优先清偿、低价交易的赔偿请求权都可以转让给第三方。债权转让并不是普遍可用的，在一些普通法国家，仍存在唆讼罪和帮讼罪以禁止诉讼融资。[15] 并非所有国家都废除了禁止诉讼融资的条款，部分立法也规定了必要的例外情况。

在许多大陆法系国家，破产法详细规定了公司董事（包括但不限于）在已知或应知公司破产的情况下，于一定期间内申请破产的义务。例如，德国的破产法要求董事在已知或应知上述情况后的 21 天内申请破产。这被许多国家效仿，如巴尔干半岛也参考了 21 天的期限。未在指定期限内申请破产的，应承担相应责任。

派生诉讼

如果所有董事仍然负责公司事务并且他们集体同意保持现状，那

all agree to preserve the status quo? There is no prospect of an action being brought against delinquent officers. Assume that a shareholder, or group of shareholders, discovers that the company has been involved in a long-running corruption scheme, through which the directors have been receiving substantial kickbacks. The company is not insolvent, but the shareholders fear for the company's future.

Derivative actions, actions brought by shareholders, not to enforce their own rights, but to enforce the rights and liabilities of the company, are an especially useful tool when a company is controlled by "wrongdoers." A successful public prosecution does not guarantee recompense to shareholders who suffer financial loss; imposition of fines against the company may result in depleting the company's value even further. Private derivative actions enable shareholders to hold company management accountable for misconduct. Derivative actions can also be brought against advisers, such as auditing companies, who turned a blind eye to or actively facilitated corruption or mismanagement. In *WGI Emerging Markets Fund, LLC v. Petróleo Brasileiro S.A.*,[16] a derivative claim was filed in a federal court in New York against Petróleo Brasileiro S.A. (Petrobras) and PricewaterhouseCoopers (PwC) Auditores Independentes, accusing Petrobras of a "pervasive bribery and money laundering scheme," ignored by auditor PwC, that overstated the value of the company's assets and profitability by at least $17 billion. The case is still pending.

Piercing the Corporate Veil

Insolvency representatives may be faced with complex corporate structures in their attempt to recover value for an estate. A bankrupt or insolvent company may have transferred assets to a corporate entity in an attempt to evade liability or to frustrate the insolvency representative's efforts to recover or maximize value. Because a corporation has an

该怎么办？这种情况下，无法对违规董事提起诉讼。假设股东们发现公司长期参与了一项腐败交易并因此获取了可观的回扣，也许该公司并没有出现资不抵债的财务危机，但股东们对公司的未来仍然感到担忧。

当公司被“不法之徒”控制时，股东可依据公司的权利而非自身的权利发起派生诉讼这一有效的救济手段。公诉程序并不能保证股东所受的经济损失获得赔偿，对公司处以罚金又会进一步削弱公司的价值。由股东私人发起的派生诉讼则能使公司的管理层为其不当行为负责，还可以对诸如审计、公司顾问等采取同样措施，使其为忽视腐败交易及不当管理从而助长腐败的后果承担相应责任。在 WGI 新兴市场基金有限公司诉巴西石油股份有限公司案[16]中，纽约联邦法院对巴西石油公司和普华永道会计师事务所提起了派生诉讼，指控巴西石油公司涉嫌“大规模的受贿和洗钱”，而普华永道会计师事务所作为公司审计却忽略了这一项腐败行为，这导致该公司的资产和盈利虚报了至少 170 亿美元。此案仍在审理中。*

揭开公司面纱

破产管理人在追回资产时可能会面临复杂的公司结构。无力偿债的公司可能已将资产转移，以逃避责任或阻碍破产管理人收回资产。由于公司具有独立法人的身份，所以通常很难接触到幕后的实际控制

* 经查实，该案已审结。——译者注

independent identity, it can be difficult to reach the individuals behind the façade. By "piercing the corporate veil," the rights and duties of a corporation are considered to be the rights and liabilities of its shareholders. The English judiciary and others take a cautious approach to treating a company and its owners as the same legal entity, as shown in the recent decision of the English Supreme Court in *Prest v. Petrodel Resources Ltd.*[17] In *Prest*, a divorcing husband disputed his wife's right to share in properties owned in the name of corporations through which he had the right to transfer property. The Supreme Court upheld the principle set out in *Salomon v. Salomon*,[18] holding that the "corporate veil" should be pierced only in very limited circumstances. Lord Sumption, delivering the leading speech, referred to the limited exceptions as the "concealment principle" and the "evasion principle"[19] and emphasized the importance of the concept of separate corporate personality: "The separate personality and property of a company is sometimes described as a fiction, and in a sense, it is, but the fiction forms the whole foundation to English company and insolvency law."[20]

The courts will come to the aid of insolvency representatives or others, however, on a showing of evidence of deceit or an intention to evade legal obligation. In *Prest*, the Supreme Court did not leave the wife without remedy, holding instead that her husband held the property in the form of a resulting trust and that she was entitled to a portion of those properties (see box 3.5).

Following *Prest*, the corporate veil can be pierced only if a person seeks deliberately to evade a legal obligation, liability, or restriction by interposing a company under his control. In *Prest,* Lord Sumption limited the circumstances in which the separate corporate personality may be ignored to those involving evasion. In those circumstances, the Court may

人。“揭开公司面纱”，就是将公司的权利义务视为其股东的权利和义务。从英国最高法院最近对普雷斯诉彼得罗资源有限公司案（以下简称普雷斯案）[17]的裁决可以看出，英国法院和其他司法部门对“揭开公司面纱”采取非常谨慎的态度。在一起正离婚的案件中，丈夫对妻子有权分得其公司名下的财产提出异议，而他有权通过这些公司转移财产。英国最高法院在所罗门诉所罗门案[18]中认为，只有在非常有限的情况下才可“揭开公司面纱”。桑普敦大法官在开篇提到，“有限”的情况也有例外，这里的例外包括“隐蔽原则”和“规避原则”[19]，并重申了公司独立人格的重要性：“公司拥有独立人格和财产常被认为是拟制的，在某种意义上的确如此，但这种拟制的形式构成了英国公司法和破产法的基础。”[20]

但在有证据表明存在欺诈意图或企图逃避法律义务的情况时，法院可以为破产管理人提供必要的援助。在普雷斯案中，最高法院并没有弃妻子于不顾，而是认定公司只是受托人，而丈夫是这些财产的实际持有人，所以妻子有权获得一部分财产（见方框 3.5）。

普雷斯案表明，只有当个人故意通过操控公司的方式逃避法律责任时，才能“揭开公司面纱”。在该案中，桑普敦大法官限制了这一原则的应用。法院可以违背“公司的法人身份应独立于其所有人的身份”这一基本原则，揭开公司面纱，但仅限于公司或其实际控制人试图利用二者的独立人格获取不当利益的情形。桑普敦大法官对此提到

BOX 3.5 ***Prest v. Petrodel Resources Ltd.***[a]

Prest had set up and funded a number of companies to purchase real estate. In divorce proceedings in the United Kingdom, Justice Moylan ordered the transfer of seven U.K. properties, legally owned by British companies that Prest controlled, to Prest's ex-wife in partial satisfaction of a lump sum order on the grounds that Prest had effective control of the companies and was in the same position as if he had been the beneficiary of a bare trust or if the companies were his nominees.[b] The companies that owned the properties had existed for a number of years and, in some cases, had owned the properties before Prest's marriage. There was no suggestion that the companies had been set up to avoid legal obligations or that the companies were being run dishonestly. The companies appealed and won, and Prest's ex-wife appealed to the Supreme Court.

In the Supreme Court, Lord Sumption refused to pierce the corporate veil because the companies did not represent an attempt to hide assets. There was no evidence that the companies were deliberately set up to evade an obligation or frustrate the operation of law, in his view, the occasions when the veil should be pierced. Lord Sumption decided, however, that the properties owned by the companies were owned beneficially by Prest by means of a resulting trust, rather than by piercing the corporate veil. Under certain circumstances a transfer may not be deemed final and, despite the transferee's apparent ownership of the asset, the ownership "springs back" to the transferor. Vice Chancellor Megarry stated, in *Re Sick and Funeral Society of St John's Sunday School, Golcar*,[c] that a "resulting trust is essentially a property concept; any property that a man does not effectually dispose of remains his own."

a. [2013] UK SC 34.
b. Ibid., 39.
c. [1972] 2 All ER 439.

depart from the fundamental principle that a company is a legal personality separate from that of its owners and pierce the corporate veil, but only for the purpose of depriving the company or its controller of the advantage they would have obtained through the company's separate legal status. Lord Sumption referred to two principles:

> They can conveniently be called the concealment principle

方框 3.5 普雷斯诉彼得罗资源有限公司案[a]

普雷斯成立并投资了许多公司，以购买不动产。在这起英国的离婚诉讼中，莫兰法官判处，将普雷斯名下公司所持有的 7 处英国资产一次性全部转归其妻子所有，因为他是这些公司的实际控制人、收益人或者委托人。[b] 但这些公司已经成立多年，有些属于普雷斯的婚前财产。同时，没有迹象表明公司成立是为了不法经营或逃避法律责任。于是这些公司提起上诉并胜诉，而普雷斯的前妻又向最高法院提起上诉。

在最高法院，桑普敦大法官拒绝“揭开公司面纱”，认为这些公司没有隐藏资产的企图，也没有证据表明这几家公司是为了逃避法律责任而成立的，不属于“揭开公司面纱”的情形。但他认为尽管并非基于“揭开公司面纱”，但是基于委托，这些公司财产仍然属于普雷斯个人。在有些情况下，财产被转让给一方并非最终的状态，尽管此时公司作为表面上的受让人持有财产，但这些财产还可以“原路返回”给原转让人。梅加里法官在戈卡尔圣约翰主日学校病患与殡葬协会破产一案的判决[c]中写道，“由此产生的信赖利益，本质上仍然是一个财产概念，个体未进行有效处分的财产仍归其所有”。

a. [2013] UK SC 34.
b. 同上，39。
c. [1972] 2 All ER 439.

了两个原则：

为了方便，称其“隐蔽原则”和“规避原则”。隐蔽原

> and the evasion principle. The concealment principle... does not involve piercing the corporate veil at all... . In these cases the court is not disregarding the "façade," but only looking behind it to discover the facts which the corporate structure is concealing...
>
> The evasion principle is different. It is that the court may disregard the corporate veil if there is a legal right against the person in control of it which exists independently of the company's involvement, and a company is interposed so that the separate legal personality of the company will defeat the right or frustrate its enforcement.[21]

In *Wood v. Baker*, a court was willing to pierce the corporate veil in a bankruptcy.[22] The English High Court was willing to grant an injunction to the bankruptcy trustees and to pierce the corporate veil of companies that were operated by a bankrupt person as his agents and nominees and that held assets on his behalf (see box 3.6).

The theory of piercing the corporate veil can be applied in civil law jurisdictions. Judges may apply the legal concept of "confusion of estates" to refuse to differentiate between what belongs to a shareholder or director of a company and what belongs to the corporate person. Judges may apply the same concept to companies whose equity is held by a parent company. As a result, a parent company, shareholders, or directors can be held liable for the debt of the insolvent entity. Boxes 3.7, 3.8, and 3.9 illustrate how this approach is applied in Brazil.

则……完全不涉及揭开公司面纱。在这些案件中，法院并非无视“面纱”，而是透过公司确定背后隐藏的东西……

规避原则则不同。当某项独立于公司运营而存在的合法权利与其控制人相冲突，且该控制人试图利用公司的独立法人人格对抗该项权利时，法院可以揭开公司面纱。[21]

在伍德诉贝克案中，法院支持“揭开公司面纱”。[22] 英国高等法院授权破产管理人“揭开公司面纱”，包括实际控制人和委托人名下的所有公司（见方框 3.6）。

“揭开公司面纱”理论也适用于大陆法系国家。法官可运用“资产混合”的法律概念拒绝将公司股东、董事的财产和公司法人的财产做区分。所以，母公司、股东或董事可以承担无力偿债的子公司的债务。方框 3.7、方框 3.8 和方框 3.9 说明了巴西如何适用这种方法。

BOX 3.6 ***Wood v. Baker***[a]

Baker was declared bankrupt in 2005. He had been convicted and sentenced on multiple charges, including passport and invoice fraud and attempts to pervert the course of justice. His assets were held by third parties, including companies and other businesses. He had failed to cooperate with the trustees in bankruptcy, and his discharge from bankruptcy was suspended indefinitely.

Upon bankruptcy, all assets beneficially owned by a debtor vest in the trustees in bankruptcy pursuant to section 306 of the Insolvency Act 1986. Under section 307, if the bankrupt acquires other property during his bankruptcy (after-acquired property), the trustees can serve a written notice claiming the after-acquired property for the bankrupt's estate. Pursuant to section 307(3), ownership of such property is deemed to have vested in the trustees as of the date the debtor acquired his interest in it.

Following investigations into Baker's affairs, the trustees discovered that substantial sums of money were being paid through accounts held by certain companies. The trustees made an urgent application for an injunction to preserve the funds in those companies' bank accounts and sought declarations that the business and assets of the companies were held in trust for Baker and constituted after-acquired property.

The court granted the injunction against the companies, finding that there was evidence that Baker was effectively behind the various companies that were being used to shelter money, business, and assets that belonged to him and that the assets were subject to section 307(3).

a. [2015] EWHC 2536 (Ch).

BOX 3.7 ***Bankruptcy Estate of Petroforte v. Securinvest Holdings S.A.***

In *Bankruptcy Estate of Petroforte v. Securinvest Holdings S.A.*, the trustee of Petroforte filed a request in civil court to pierce the corporate veil and to extend the bankruptcy to another economic group (Securinvest Group), arguing that both economic groups acted as one in order to divert assets from Petroforte, in prejudice of the creditors of the Petroforte Bankruptcy Estate. The debts of the Petroforte Bankruptcy Estate were estimated to be approximately $400 million.

The final ruling on the merits was issued by Minister Nancy Andrighi of the Superior Court of Justice, the highest Brazilian federal court, affirming the piercing of the corporate veil and the extension of the bankruptcy to approximately $300 million

方框 3.6　伍德诉贝克案[a]

贝克于 2005 年宣告破产，曾被指控伪造护照、虚开发票和妨碍司法公正等多项罪名。其名下资产由第三方公司持有，但并未委托破产管理人，所以针对他个人的破产程序被无限期中止。

破产后，依据英国 1986 年《破产法》第 306 条，债务人实际拥有的所有财产都由破产管理人处分。根据第 307 条，债务人在破产期间获得其他财产（事后获得）的，破产管理人可以以书面通知的形式要求获取后续财产。根据第 307（3）条，自债务人获得财产之日起，该财产视为被破产管理人所有。

对贝克进行调查之后，破产管理人发现大量资金从公司的特定账户转出，于是紧急申请禁令冻结该资金，并申请宣告公司的资产和业务实际是受贝克委托管理，因此属于破产事后财产。

法院也发现贝克利用上述公司隐匿资产，批准了禁令，因而这些资产属于第 307（3）条的约束范围。

a. [2015] EWHC 2536 (Ch).

方框 3.7　彼得罗夫破产管理人诉证券投资控股有限公司案

在彼得罗夫破产管理人诉证券投资控股有限公司案（以下简称彼得罗夫案）中，彼得罗夫的破产管理人向民事法院申请“揭开公司面纱”，并将破产范围扩大至另一个证券投资集团，主张这两家公司实际上隶属一个集团。公司成立完全是为了转移彼得罗夫的资产，损害债权人的权益。据估计，彼得罗夫的破产债务约 4 亿美元。

这起案件由巴西最高法院高级法官南希 · 安德里希作出最终裁决，裁决支持“揭开公司面纱”并将破产范围扩大到该集团。它名下拥有约 3 亿美元的资产，包括酒精工厂、农场、房地产、酒店等。彼得罗夫案开创了

continued

of assets owned by Securinvest Group, including an ethanol plant, farms, real estate, a hotel, and other assets. *Petroforte* set the national precedent for piercing the corporate veil and establishing a preponderance of the evidence as the standard of proof. The case shows that economic crimes, which are always evolving, require contemporary and innovative solutions, including disregarding the legal entity when the entity has no real independence from parent companies or stakeholders.

BOX 3.8 ***Bankruptcy Estate of Mabe Brasil v. Mabe/General Electric/ Penteado Family*** [a]

BSH Continental (BSH) was a major appliance manufacturer with headquarters in São Paulo State. In 2009, BSH was acquired by the Mexican group Mabe, and renamed Mabe Brasil.The Penteado family and General Electric (GE) also invested in Mabe Brasil, acquiring part of its stock. Shortly after their investment, the Penteados and GE filed for judicial reorganization of Mabe Brasil and, in February 2016, Mabe Brasil was declared bankrupt. More than 2,000 employees were unpaid and left unemployed. Data collection and forensic work performed by the bankruptcy trustee showed that the controllers of Mabe Brasil drained its assets, leading to the insolvency.

Based on the findings of fraud, the trustee applied to pierce the corporate veil, requesting an ex parte freeze order against Mabe Brasil's former controllers. The State Court noted that even before the company entered judicial reorganization, Mabe Brasil, with the knowledge and participation of the Penteado Family, the GE Group, and Mabe México, conducted improper and predatory actions that depleted the company's assets and ultimately led to its insolvency.

The State Court argued that the right invoked by the plaintiff was plausible and the grant of a preliminary freeze order was justified, not only because the respondents were freely able to travel abroad, but because the shifts in shareholder control of the respondent companies might prevent the identification of their beneficial owners and the whereabouts of their assets.

An ex parte order was issued, freezing US$266 million in the respondents' accounts. The judge, taking into account the need for secrecy, ordered that the freeze be kept under seal during this process, enhancing its effectiveness. The seal would be lifted after the orders were carried out.

续表

“揭开公司面纱”的先例，案中的大量证据被确立为此类案件的标准证据。该案表明，应对不断演变的经济犯罪，需要采取更加先进、创新的解决方案，包括当公司与其母公司或股东并非真正独立时，拒绝将其视为独立法人的情形。

方框 3.8　马贝巴西的破产管理人诉马贝集团 / 通用电气集团 / 蓬特亚多家族案[a]

BSH 公司是一家大型电器制造商，总部位于巴西圣保罗州。2009 年，该公司被墨西哥马贝集团收购，并更名为马贝巴西。蓬特亚多家族和通用电气（GE）也投资了马贝巴西并持有部分股份。随后，马贝进行了破产重整并于 2016 年宣告破产，因此造成 2000 多名员工失业并被欠薪。破产管理人调查后发现，马贝巴西的实际控制人掏空了资产，才导致公司破产。

基于调查，破产管理人申请“揭开公司面纱”，要求对马贝巴西的前任控制人执行单方面的冻结令。州法院认为，早在公司进入破产重整之前，蓬特亚多家族、通用集团甚至最早的马贝墨西哥集团都对马贝巴西进行了非法性掠夺，掏空了公司资产并最终导致其破产。

由于被告可以自由出境，并且股东控制权的流转可能会影响原告追查实际所有人及相关资产的下落，所以州法院认为原告主张的权利合理，并签发了预先冻结令。

于是被告账户中 2.66 亿美元被冻结。为了保障冻结令的效果，法官也要求冻结行动全程保密直到结束。封条将在命令执行后解除。

continued

GE was the first respondent to file an interlocutory appeal, requesting a suspension of the order. After the São Paulo Court of Appeal denied the motion for a suspension, GE filed a writ of mandamus, which was terminated by Court of Appeal Judge Cesar Ciampolini with the following remark: "Extreme situations deserve from the judiciary, once it is provoked, proportional and reasonable measures, which can be drastic, in order to preserve the right of individuals in good faith, preserving the useful result of legal actions tackling fraud."[b]

a. State of Sáo Paulo, No. 1000641-02.2019.8.26.0229, Mabe Brasil Eletrodomésticos LTDA, General Electric International (Benelux) B.V.

b. Ibid.

BOX 3.9 ***MMX Sudeste under reorganization v. Batista***[a]

MMX Sudeste, based in Belo Horizonte, State of Minas Gerais, Brazil, is directly owned by EBX Economic Group, and ultimately owned by Eike Fuhrken Batista da Silva. Batista has in the past been listed as one of the richest men in the world. MMX Sudeste's core business is extraction and trade of iron and minerals, and it holds extraction rights for mines in the middle eastern section of Brazil. It filed for judicial reorganization on October 16, 2014.

The judicial administrator appointed by the court suspected that MMX Sudeste became insolvent due to fraud, including fraudulent accounting that misled investors and the market. An investigation was authorized by the court to determine whether the shareholders and the controlling minds of MMX Sudeste should be held liable for its debts. Data collection showed that Batista, using MMX Sudeste, lured investors worldwide, advertising results that he knew the company was unable to produce, using a modus operandi similar to that perpetrated by other companies of EBX Economic Group.

Based on findings of fraud, an order was issued in 2017 to pierce the corporate veil to reach the controllers of MMX Sudeste. The order created an important precedent in Brazil because it was issued even though a plan of payments was approved by the creditors. For the Brazilian court, the creditors' approval of the plan of payments was not an impediment to recovering the money.

Data collected in an auxiliary insolvency proceeding in the United States showed a flow of money from MMX Sudeste to several other offshore entities and to Batista's older son, who had acted as Batista's strawman, incorporating entities, hiring lawyers, and paying bills. A second order was issued in Brazil in March 2019 by Honorable Judge

续表

通用电气公司是第一个提起非正式上诉、申请中止冻结令的被告。圣保罗上诉法院驳回上诉并批复道："一旦极端状况发生，就应采取严格、相称、合理的措施，以维护个人正当权利和打击行动的成果。"[b]

a. State of Sáo Paulo, No. 1000641-02.2019.8.26.0229, Mabe Brasil Eletrodomésticos LTDA, General Electric International (Benelux) B.V.

b. 同上。

方框 3.9 MMX 公司（重组中）诉巴蒂斯塔案[a]

MMX 公司，总部位于巴西的米纳斯吉拉斯州，隶属 EBX 经济集团，实际所有人是曾被评为世界级富豪之一的巴蒂斯塔。该公司的核心业务为铁矿开采，并拥有巴西在中东矿山的开采权，于 2014 年 10 月 16 日申请破产重组。

法院任命的司法行政官认为，MMX 破产涉嫌财务造假、误导投资人和市场等欺诈行为。法院授权进行调查，已确定 MMX 公司的股东和实际控制人需要承担相应的债务。而调查显示，巴蒂斯塔利用 MMX 吸引全球投资者，虚假宣传了公司的实际产值，这与他操作 EBX 经济集团的手法如出一辙。

基于调查结果，法院在 2017 年批准了"揭开公司面纱"的裁决以确定该公司背后的实际控制人。该法令在巴西开创了重要的先例，即使一项交易付款的完成获得了债权人的批准，裁决仍然生效。对巴西法院而言，债权人批准的已付款交易并不妨碍相关款项被撤回。

美国一项辅助破产程序收集的证据显示，资金是从 MMX 公司流向其他几个离岸公司和巴蒂斯塔的大儿子的，后者作为他的"稻草人"协助成立公司，雇佣律师并负责各项开支。荣誉法官克劳迪娅·海伦娜·巴蒂斯塔（尽管也姓巴蒂斯塔，但无关），于 2019 年 3 月在巴西签发了第二份"揭开公

continued

Claudia Helena Batista (no relation), piercing the corporate veil to reach the offshore entities and Batista's son and to hold them liable for MMX Sudeste's debts.

a. State of Minas Gerais, No. 19.006.144-0, MMX Sudeste under Reorganization v. Batista.

Key Points from this Chapter

- Although the UNCAC is explicit about the need to criminalize both bribe payers and receivers, many legislative provisions focus on the bribe payer.
- Insolvency proceedings can be useful for prosecuting bribe payers, particularly when intermediaries are involved and can be placed into liquidation. Pursuing bribe takers through insolvency proceedings is challenging but possible in certain jurisdictions.
- Agents or facilitators (such as lawyers, accountants, banks, or other intermediaries) whose identity can be discovered, either through an insolvency representative's statutory powers of investigation or through an application for a *Norwich Pharmacal* order, can also be targeted in insolvency proceedings.
- Maximizing value in winding-up cases can entail the monetization of intangibles, including potential claims for damages against persons who have diminished or enabled harm against the debtor's estate.
- Substantial value can potentially be recovered from damages claims directed against third-party facilitators and agents who have enabled the perpetration of acts of public corruption.
- The "duty of care" generally requires that directors and managers exercise the degree of care that ordinarily careful and prudent people would use under the circumstances.
- In some jurisdictions, a director may be held personally responsible for all debts or liabilities of an insolvent company if he was knowingly a party to fraud.
- Insolvency representatives may pursue actions for preferences, transactions at undervalue, breach of duty, or fraudulent or wrongful trading.
- Derivative actions (brought by shareholders to enforce the rights of the company) are a useful tool if a company is controlled by "wrongdoers."
- Piercing the corporate veil is the legal decision to treat the rights and duties of a corporation as the rights and liabilities of its shareholders.

续表

司面纱”令，用以追究离岸公司和巴蒂斯塔的儿子对 MMX 公司债务应承担的责任。 a. State of Minas Gerais, No. 19.006.144–0, MMX Sudeste under Reorganization v. Batista.

本章要点

- 尽管《联合国反腐败公约》明确指出有必要将受贿人和行贿人一并定罪量刑，但许多国家立法仍然偏重于制裁行贿人。
- 破产程序对起诉行贿人成效显著，特别是有中间人参与的情况下，可对其清算。通过破产程序追究受贿人的责任有一定难度，但在一些国家是可行的。
- 通过破产管理人的法定调查权或通过申请第三方披露令确认相关代理人或贿赂协助人，如律师、会计师或银行等作为破产程序的目标。
- 破产清算中，为了使破产资产的价值最大化，需要兑现其中的无形资产，包括对已损失或可能损失资产的债务人提起损害赔偿。
- 针对腐败行为的第三方（如协助人、代理人等）行为提起诉讼，可能获得更可观的赔偿。
- “谨慎义务”通常要求董事和经理谨慎行事的程度为：在相同情况下，一般人会采取的谨慎程度。
- 在某些国家，董事明知一方欺诈，应对破产公司的相关负债承担个人责任。
- 破产管理人可以针对优先清偿、低价交易、违背职责、欺诈性交易和不当交易等行为采取法律行动。
- 如果公司已被“不法之徒”控制，则股东可以提起派生诉讼主张公司权利。这也是一个行之有效的策略。
- “揭开公司面纱”是将公司的权利和义务视为股东的权利和义务。

Notes

1. In financial regulation, PEP describes someone who has been entrusted with a prominent public function. PEPs generally present a higher risk for potential involvement in bribery and corruption by virtue of their position and influence.

2. Transparency International UK, "London Property: Top Destination for Money Launderers" (December 1, 2016), https://www.transparency.org.uk/publications/london-property-tr-ti-uk/.

3. The United Kingdom makes an exception to this rule when the bribe taker has committed offenses under section 2 of the Bribery Act and if there are territorial links under section 12.

4. The assets were tied to 1Malaysia Development Berhad, which was established as a strategic development company under the Malaysia Ministry of Finance.

5. A full discussion of what constitutes a divergent and often confusing body of law in this area and across jurisdictions is beyond the scope of this publication.

6. [2003] UKHL 49.

7. Ibid., para. 77.

8. In Germany, for example, courts accord a lesser degree of deference to corporate decision makers in exercising their business judgment than would the courts of Delaware in the United States. There is no explicit statutory business judgment rule in French corporate law. French courts are unlikely, however, to second guess business decisions as long as the corporation remains solvent and the actions are within the limits defined by the laws and the stated purpose of the company. Within the EU, Croatia, Germany, Greece, Portugal, Romania, and Spain have codified a version of

注释

1. 在金融监管体系中，政治人物一般指担任了重要公共职务的人，凭借其地位和影响力，通常具有较高的贿赂犯罪和腐败的潜在风险。

2. 英国透明国际协会，《伦敦：洗钱者的首选目的地》（2016 年 12 月 1 日），https://www.transparency.org.uk/publications /london-property-tr-ti-uk/。

3. 当受贿人犯有《贿赂法》第 2 条所规定的罪行，并且依据第 12 条有属地管辖权的关联时，则适用该条的例外规则。

4. 这些资产与马来西亚财政部下属的战略发展公司贝哈德马来西亚发展有限公司有关。

5. 对该领域各个地区之间富有分歧且混乱的法律规定的完整讨论，超出了本书的范围。

6. [2003] UKHL 49.

7. 同上，para. 77。

8. 在德国商事判决中，法院对公司决策的尊重程度不如美国特拉华州。法国《公司法》没有明确规定商事判决规则，但只要公司仍具有偿付能力并且在法定范围内行事，法院就很难对公司的决策进行干预。在欧盟内部，克罗地亚、德国、希腊、葡萄牙、罗马尼亚和西班牙，已经编纂了一部商业裁判规则法典。奥地利、比利时、保加利亚、塞浦路斯、丹麦、芬兰、匈牙利、意大利、立陶宛、卢森堡、斯洛文尼亚、瑞典和英国虽然没有明文规定，但实际上为董事作出业务决策提供了一定酌情处理的空间。捷克、爱沙尼亚、法国、爱尔兰、拉脱

the business judgment rule. Austria, Belgium, Bulgaria, Cyprus, Denmark, Finland, Hungary, Italy, Lithuania, Luxembourg, Slovenia, Sweden, and the United Kingdom have no express rule but in practice afford some margin of discretion for directors in making business decisions. The Czech Republic, Estonia, France, Ireland, Latvia, Malta, Poland, and the Slovak Republic have neither an express nor implied business judgment rule. (Gerner-Beuerle et al. 2013).

9. In some jurisdictions, the debtor remains "in possession" after initiation of the insolvency process, either administering the assets itself (as in the United States, for example) or co-administering them under the supervision of the insolvency representative. In these cases, the debtor would owe a fiduciary duty to the residual beneficiaries, the creditors.

10. In France, an action must be instituted in the commercial court within three years after the liquidation judgment. The action is usually initiated by the insolvency representative, but article L651-3 of the Commercial Code also authorizes the public prosecutor to do so.

11. Jetivia SA *v.* Bilta (UK) Ltd. [2015] UKSC 23. In this case, which was brought by a liquidator, the defendant argued that the company itself was a wrongdoer and therefore could not sue directors for breach of fiduciary duty under the doctrine of illegality. The argument was rejected.

12. Insolvency Act 1986, § 213(2).

13. See Brooks and Willetts v. Armstrong and Walker [2015] EWHC 2289 (CH).

14. A preference is any transaction that puts a creditor, or any surety or guarantor of the company's liabilities, in a position better than that they would have upon liquidation or administration.

15. Maintenance and champerty, often considered antiquated, are doctrines in common law jurisdictions to preclude frivolous litigation.

维亚、马耳他、波兰和斯洛伐克则没有明示或默示的商业裁判准则。（Gerner–Beuerle et al. 2013）

9. 在某些国家，债务人在破产程序启动后，仍然“占有”公司财产，或者自行管理资产（例如美国），抑或在破产管理人的监督下共同管理资产。在这些情况下，债务人将对破产财产的受益人即债权人承担受托义务。

10. 在法国，必须在清算判决后的三年内向商事法院提起诉讼，诉讼一般由破产管理人提出，但《商业法》第 L651–3 条也可以授权检察官提起诉讼。

11. 瑞士捷蒂维亚（Jetivia) 诉英国比尔塔（Bilta）有限公司案 [2015] UKSC 23。此案由清算人提起，被告辩称公司才是不法行为人，不能根据公司的违法行为起诉董事违反受托义务，但被法院驳回。

12. 英国 1986 年《破产法》，第 213(2) 条。
13. 参见威利兹诉阿姆斯特朗和沃克案 [2015] EWHC 2289 (CH)。

14. 优先权是指债权人或者债务担保人获得优于原本清算中所处序位的清偿。

15. “唆讼”和“帮讼”现今被认为是比较陈旧和过时的概念，是普通法为防止轻率诉讼而订立的概念。非利益相关方挑唆一方提起诉

"Maintenance" occurs when a disinterested party encourages the bringing of a lawsuit. "Champerty" is the financial support of a party to a lawsuit in return for a share of the recovery. Champerty, where legal, is now commonly known as litigation financing, and the agreements are most often made with third-party funders.

16. WGI Emerging Markets Fund, LLC v. Petróleo Brasileiro S.A. (Petrobras) (In re Petrobras Securities Universities Superannuation Scheme Ltd.), Docket No. 16-1914-cv (2d Cir. July 7, 2017).

17. [2013] UKSC 34.

18. [1897] AC 22.

19. [2013] UKSC 34, 28.

20. Ibid., 8.

21. Prest v. Petrodel Resources Ltd. [2013] UKSC 34.

22. [2015] EWHC 2536 (Ch).

References

Gerner-Beuerle, Carsten, Philipp Paech, and Edmund Philipp Schuster. 2013. *Study on Directors' Duties and Liability*. London: LSE Enterprise.

McLachlan, Tom, and Dafni Loizou. 2017. "Jurisdiction of the English Court to Wind Up Foreign Companies in the Public Interest." Charles Russell Speechlys. https://www.charlesrussellspeechlys.com/en/news-and-insights/insights/litigation--dispute-resolution/2017/jurisdiction-of-the-english-court-to-wind-up-foreign-companies-in-the-public-interest/.

OECD (Organisation for Economic Co-operation and Development). 2009. *Working Group on Bribery Annual Report*. Paris: OECD.

讼时，为“唆讼”。“帮讼”是为诉讼一方提供经济支持以换取部分赔偿的收益。合法的“帮讼”现在通常被称为诉讼融资，由诉讼一方与第三方出资人签订融资协议。

16. WGI 新兴市场基金有限公司诉巴西石油股份有限公司（巴西石油证券大学退休金项目公司）案卷号：16–1914–cv (2d Cir. July 7, 2017)。

17. [2013] UKSC 34.

18. [1897] AC 22.

19. [2013] UKSC 34, 28.

20. 同上，8。

21. 普雷斯诉彼得罗资源有限公司案 [2013] UKSC. 34。

22. [2015] EWHC 2536 (Ch).

参考文献

Gerner-Beuerle, Carsten, Philipp Paech, and Edmund Philipp Schuster. 2013. *Study on Directors' Duties and Liability*. London: LSE Enterprise.

McLachlan, Tom, and Dafni Loizou. 2017. "Jurisdiction of the English Court to Wind Up Foreign Companies in the Public Interest." Charles Russell Speechlys. https://www.charlesrussellspeechlys.com/en/news-and-insights/insights/litigation--dispute-resolution/2017/jurisdiction-of-the-english-court-to-wind-up-foreign-companies-in-the-public-interest/.

OECD (Organisation for Economic Co-operation and Development). 2009. *Working Group on Bribery Annual Report*. Paris: OECD.

4. Privilege

Clients who consult lawyers are entitled to the protection of legal professional or attorney-client privilege: their communications are confidential and unavailable to third parties. The usefulness of these communications to an insolvency representative seeking targets and sources of information raises the question of when the privilege applies. The ability of an insolvency representative to access privileged material can change the course of a case of corruption or asset tracing. In *Federal Republic of Brazil and Municipality of São Paulo v. Durant International Ltd. and Kildare Finance Ltd.*,[1] discussed in box I.1, the first documents obtained by the court-appointed insolvency representatives of the defendant companies came from the lawyers who had acted for the companies at trial— documents that were covered by privilege. Because the insolvency representatives were appointed to control the companies, however, they were entitled to documents in the company's possession. The information proved to be tremendously helpful.

This chapter provides an overview of the core principles of privilege in the common law jurisdictions of the United Kingdom and the United States and the civil law jurisdiction of France, including the extent of the privilege and who has the right to assert it. The chapter considers how the normal rules of privilege can be modified for different insolvency processes and, in particular, whether privilege belongs to the insolvent body or individual or to the insolvency representative, and how the answer to this question—

4. 特权规则

聘请了律师的当事人有权获得法律专业人士或律师与客户专属特权的保护，确保他们的沟通内容是保密的，任何第三人不得获取或利用。但对负责追查信息的破产管理人而言，在特权生效时，如何从中获取有用的信息就成了问题。破产管理人获取的机密信息直接决定了追查腐败资产的进程。在方框 I.1 讨论的巴西联邦政府和圣保罗市诉杜兰特国际有限公司和基尔代尔金融有限公司案[1]中，法院指定的破产管理人所获取的第一批保密文件就来自公司的代理律师。破产管理人受托接管公司因而有权获取此类文件。事实证明，这些文件对于案件的审理起到了至关重要的作用。

本章概述了在英国和美国等英美法国家以及大陆法系的法国，特权的核心原则、特权范围和特权的申请主体等内容。本章讨论了如何依据不同的破产程序修改一般的特权规则。当特权分属破产公司、个人或是破产管理人，依据不同破产程序的类型，可能会有不同的答案。这也直接影响到破产管理人剥夺特权进行取证的能力。例如，在资产追查的过程中，如果认为保密材料归原告所有，那么原告则可查阅之前公司和律师所共享的信息。

which can vary according to the type of insolvency procedure—may affect the representative's ability to waive privilege and access probative evidence. In asset recovery proceedings, for example, the claimant may be able to gain access to information previously shared with the corrupt entity's lawyer if ownership of the privileged material is deemed to vest in the claimant.

Privilege in England

Forms of Privilege at Common Law

Privilege is a fundamental legal right. It allows parties to litigation, arbitration, and investigations to resist disclosure of confidential and sensitive material. This section discusses two types of privilege under U.K. law—legal advice privilege and litigation privilege. The English rules on privilege have generally been adopted in other Commonwealth jurisdictions, including Guernsey, the Isle of Man, and Jersey.

Legal Advice Privilege

Legal advice privilege protects confidential communications, whether written or oral, between lawyers and clients, made for the purpose of giving or receiving legal advice.

The privilege protects the communications of both lawyers and clients. The privilege ensures that, in the interests of justice, parties can seek advice openly from lawyers, without fear that what is said may be repeated to another party or stated in court. It enables clients to be fully transparent in discussing their affairs with legal advisers. The privilege extends even to lawyers' preparatory materials that are not communicated to clients. Although communications between lawyers and clients must be confidential, not all confidential and sensitive material is privileged. Privilege applies only to documents that are both confidential and not publicly available. It covers advice given in a legal context, but would not, for example, cover

英国法中的特权

英美法中特权的形式

特权是一项基本的法律权利。诉讼、仲裁和调查涉及的相关方有权拒绝披露机密和敏感的材料。本节讨论英国立法中的两种特权类型——法律咨询特权和诉讼特权。英国的特权规则也被根西岛、马恩岛和泽西岛等其他英联邦司法管辖区所采用。

法律咨询特权

法律咨询特权保护律师与客户之间以提供或接受法律咨询服务为目的而进行的私密联络，既包括书面沟通也包括口头沟通。

该特权保护的是律师和客户之间的交流，确保在出于正义目的的前提下，当事方可以坦然地征求律师意见而不必担心谈话内容被复述、呈现在法庭上，客户可以开诚布公与法律顾问讨论事务。特权保护范围还包括律师正在准备的尚未传达给客户的资料。尽管律师与客户之间的沟通必须是保密的，但并非所有机密和敏感的材料都受特权保护。特权仅适用于既保密又不能从公开途径获得的文档，包括法律建议，但不适用于律师为履行公司管理或执行专门业务的情形。这主要是针对内部律师，他们除了自身的法律业务外，也会涉及其他公司业务。

situations in which lawyers act in a business, executive, or administrative capacity. This caveat predominantly affects inhouse lawyers who may perform general business functions in addition to their legal roles.

The term "lawyer" encompasses a foreign qualified lawyer, a barrister or solicitor, a paralegal or trainee (provided they are supervised by a qualified lawyer) and, generally, an in-house lawyer. It does not, however, extend to other professions, such as accountants, even when they provide advice on, for example, tax law. The European Court of Justice has also held that communications between a company and its in-house lawyers during a competition investigation are not protected by legal advice privilege because in-house lawyers, unlike outside counsel, are not considered sufficiently independent. The definition of client has been restricted under recent English case law[2] to refer, for a corporate entity, only to those individuals who have been instructed to obtain legal advice on a matter rather than to all employees.

Litigation Privilege

Litigation privilege protects a wider category of documents—those between clients or lawyers and third parties—but only when they are created (1) after proceedings have been commenced or contemplated, and (2) for the dominant purpose of seeking or giving advice in such proceedings.

Because litigation privilege can potentially protect a wide class of documents, the courts carefully analyze whether the two criteria have been met. Litigation privilege applies only when litigation or arbitration has already begun or is genuinely contemplated. If a communication has more than one purpose, a court will assess its purpose objectively, taking into account all the relevant circumstances. Recent case law has sought to limit the scope of the litigation privilege, suggesting that documents created to obtain advice about how to avoid anticipated litigation are not privileged

“律师”一词包括外国具有执业资格的律师、本国的出庭律师、事务律师、律师助理、实习生（一般受训于取得执业资格的律师）以及一般意义上的内部律师。但律师不包括如会计师等其他行业，尽管他们也提供有关税法的建议。欧洲法院还认定，在纠纷调查期间，公司与其内部律师之间的信息沟通不受法律咨询特权的保护。这是因为内部律师与外部律师不同，法律上不将其视为独立于公司的人员。根据（作者成文时）最近的英国判例法[2]，“客户”的定义受到限制，对公司来说，它仅指被委派而征询法律建议的个人，而非所有公司职员。

诉讼特权

诉讼特权将文件的保护范围扩大到客户、律师以及第三方之间的文件，但需要满足以下两个条件：（1）在诉讼程序启动之后；（2）以咨询法律建议为目的。

由于诉讼特权可以为各种文件提供潜在的保护，因此法律会仔细甄别其是否符合上述两个条件。此外，诉讼特权也只在诉讼或仲裁开始后才能适用。如果相关文件有多个目的，法律会依据情况客观评估目的是否符合条件。最近的判例法试图限制诉讼特权的适用范围，认为获取如何避免诉讼的建议不应纳入特权保护范围，并强调，以调查是否存在不法行为为目的的文件不享有特权。[3]

and reasserting that documents whose primary purpose is to investigate whether wrongdoing has occurred are not privileged.[3]

Common Interest Privilege

Clients with joint or common interests may share privilege of communications; each party will be entitled to assert the privilege against third parties. This right will remain after any breakdown of their relationship, such as the case of a divorcing couple.

Which Law Applies?

Notwithstanding that privilege is generally considered a substantive right,[4] English courts apply the law of the forum for the purpose of privilege, that is, English law in any dispute in an English court, irrespective of the law that governs the substantive dispute.

What is the result when the question of whether documents are privileged is governed by, for example, Luxembourg law, but the insolvency proceeding is being heard in England? *Re Hellas Telecommunications (Luxembourg)* II *SCA*[5] provides the answer. The insolvency representative argued that the issue of which law applies was governed by the European Commission Regulation on Insolvency Proceedings 1346/2000 (the precursor to European Union (EU) Regulation 2015/848). England has substantive jurisdiction over all liquidations taking place in its courts.

The respondent argued that the insolvency representative's right to receive the information and documentation was governed by Luxembourg law. The English court should not exercise its discretionary powers under section 236 of the Insolvency Act 1986 (Insolvency Act) to order the inspection of documents because the disclosure would breach Luxembourg's laws of professional secrecy.

The court ruled that the applicable law was English. Insolvency proceedings are governed by the law of the Member State in which they

共同利益特权

具有联合利益或共同利益的客户，可以共享信息的特权。各方均有权对第三方主张该特权，即使在双方关系破裂或终结后，如离婚夫妻，仍保有这项权利。

适用什么法?

尽管特权通常被认为是一项实质性权利，[4] 但英国法院会为了特权的目的而适用法院所在地的法律。也就是说，在英国法院提起的诉讼就适用英国法，与解决实质争议的法律无关。

比如，如果文件是否享有特权的问题受卢森堡法律的约束，但是破产程序是在英国审理的，那么结果会如何？希腊电信（卢森堡）控股有限公司破产一案 [5] 提供了答案。破产管理人认为，法律适用的问题受《关于破产程序的欧洲理事会第 1346/2000 号条例》（欧盟理事会《破产程序条例》的前身）约束，英国法院对所有在英国起诉的破产清算具有实质性的管辖权。

被告则辩称，破产管理人获取信息的权利受卢森堡法律管辖。英国法院不应根据 1986 年《破产法》第 236 条授权破产管理人调查相关文件，造成的信息披露违反了卢森堡有关职业保密的法律。

法院裁定适用英国法律。[6] 理由是在英国已经启动“主要破产程序”[7]，同时案件并未在其他国家启动次要程序，因此适用英国法律。

were commenced.[6] "Main insolvency proceedings"[7] had been opened in England, and there were no secondary proceedings elsewhere; therefore English law applied.

Luxembourg law, under which the legal advice had been sought, would be relevant to the exercise of the English court's discretion. Any order made by the English court could be recognized by a Luxembourg court under article 25 of the Regulation, and that court could decide whether the English order violated the public policy of Luxembourg under article 26 of the Regulation.

Waiver

Privilege is an absolute right, and courts do not engage in a balancing test to determine whether a legitimate claim to privilege can be denied. The person to whom the privilege belongs may choose to waive it. A litigant in possession of a favorable legal opinion with respect to its claim may choose to show it to the other side to facilitate settlement.

Insolvency

It is important in an insolvency to determine to whom privilege belongs. Can an insolvent entity assert privilege over legal advice provided prior to the insolvency, or does the privilege vest in the insolvency representative, who can choose to waive it? The answer to the question can affect an insolvency representative's ability to use his ancillary powers, discussed in chapter 2, such as voiding transactions at undervalue or transactions defrauding creditors.

Insolvent entities often take legal advice on ways to keep assets out of creditors' reach; uncovering such advice can help determine whether assets were legally or fraudulently transferred. English law varies according to whether the insolvent is an individual or a corporate entity.

英国法院裁定时也可能以法律意见的形式参考卢森堡法律。英国法院作出的任何裁定都可以由卢森堡法院根据《欧盟理事会条例》第25条予以承认，也可以依据第26条裁定英国法令是否违反了卢森堡的公共政策。

放弃

特权是一项绝对权，法院不会采用平衡原则决定是否拒绝特权申请。特权所属人可以选择放弃特权。诉讼当事人如果掌握了对其有利的法律意见，也可以选择主动将其出示给另一方，以协助纠纷的解决。

破产程序

在破产案件中，确定特权主体非常重要。法律意见特权应归属于破产公司，还是享有放弃权的破产管理人？问题的答案会影响破产管理人对是否采用其他辅助权力的选择，如针对低价交易或欺诈性交易的撤销权。这在第二章中进行了讨论。

破产公司通常会就如何将资产置于债权人无法控制的范围内寻求法律意见。这类意见的披露有助于确定资产是否被欺诈性的不法行为转移。对此，英国法律依据破产主体是公司还是个人有不同的规定。

Individual Bankruptcy

An individual's ability to assert privilege in an insolvency has been clarified in two recent cases. In *Avonwick Holdings Ltd. v. Shlosberg*,[8] the Court of Appeal held that the privilege attaching to information and documents of a bankrupt person was not property that vested in the trustees under the Insolvency Act.

Shlosberg was a Russian businessman based in England. Shlosberg failed to pay a substantial judgment awarded to Avonwick and was bankrupted on Avonwick's petition. Avonwick was represented in the proceedings against Shlosberg by solicitors who were then appointed to act for Shlosberg's trustees in bankruptcy, a relatively common scenario. The trustees exercised their powers under section 311(1) of the Insolvency Act to obtain privileged and confidential documents held by Shlosberg's former solicitors. The trustees provided those documents to the solicitors who acted both for them and for Avonwick. Avonwick subsequently issued proceedings against Shlosberg for conspiracy, based in part on the privileged documents.

The trustees argued that the privilege was theirs and could be waived by them. They argued that they were entitled, as trustees, to take possession of the documents that contained the privileged information, and that the Insolvency Act provides that trustees can exercise any powers with respect to a bankrupt's property that the bankrupt himself could have exercised. They also cited case law that a trustee who obtains title to specific property of the bankrupt also obtains ancillary rights of privilege with respect to that property.

The Court of Appeal, however, held that privilege in English law is a fundamental right. Curtailing the right of privilege by statute requires express words or necessary implication. The court rejected the argument that rights of privilege constitute property within the meaning of the Insolvency

个人破产

最近的两个案例表明，个人有权在破产程序中主张特权。在艾文威客控股有限公司诉罗斯博案[8]中，上诉法院认为，破产人相关文件信息上所附有的特权并不属于《破产法》中规定的破产管理人享有的“财产”。

罗斯博是一个在英国的俄罗斯商人，因无法支付对艾文威客控股有限公司的败诉赔偿，而被该公司起诉破产。在对罗斯博的诉讼中，艾文威客控股有限公司的代理律师被任命为破产管理人，这是一种比较常见的情形。破产管理人依据《破产法》第311（1）条的权利，获取了艾文威客控股有限公司与前律师的相关机密文件以及其上附有的特权，并将这些提供给了艾文威客控股有限公司的其他律师。随后，该公司利用这些文件以串谋为由起诉罗斯博。

管理人认为，因为特权归属于自己，所以自己有权放弃，他们作为破产管理人有权获取特权保护的文件和信息。他们还认为《破产法》规定受托人可以对本属于破产人的财产行使任何权利。同时，他们引用了判例法，认为管理人不仅获得了破产人特定财产所有权，也获得了其上的附加特权。

但是，上诉法院认为，英国法律中的特权是一项基本权利，放弃或剥夺该项权利必须具备明示或必要的默示要件。法院驳回了《破产法》意义上特权构成财产的论点。受托人援引了《破产法》第311（1）条的规定，即特权并不意味着破产者有权拒绝向受托人提供与其财产

Act. The trustees had also suggested that an abrogation of privilege was implicit in section 311(1) of the Insolvency Act. Section 311(1) provides that privilege does not entitle a bankrupt to refuse to supply documents relating to his estate to the trustee. The court held, however, that, although a trustee could use such documents in the bankruptcy, he had to preserve their privilege in doing so.

The Court of Appeal also held that, even if Shlosberg's privilege in the documents had been lost, providing the documents to an individual creditor to aid its litigation against the bankrupt person is not a purpose of bankruptcy.

The Court of Appeal left open the question whether a trustee in bankruptcy who takes possession of specific property to which legal advice relates inherits privilege with respect to that property. *Crescent Farm (Sidcup) Sports Ltd. v. Sterling Officers Ltd.*,[9] a decision of first instance, suggested that the benefit of the privilege would pass with the property, which became known as the *Crescent Farm* principle.

In a later bankruptcy proceeding, the High Court decided this question in favor of the bankrupt. In *Leeds v. Lemos*,[10] the trustee sought to give a creditor access to the bankrupt's privileged documents to enable the creditor to bring an action to set aside certain transactions entered into prior to the bankruptcy. The trustee relied on the *Crescent Farm* principle. The court ruled, however, that there should be no distinction between documents relating to bankruptcy assets and those relating to liabilities when considering the effect of the bankruptcy on privilege. *Crescent Farm* was distinguishable because that case did not involve bankruptcy. Privilege was a fundamental common law right, and the court had no authority to direct a bankrupt person to waive it under the Insolvency Act or otherwise. The court added that even if the *Crescent Farm* principle applied to the automatic

有关的文件，认为这条规定隐含了特权可以被废除的意思。但是，法院认为，尽管受托人可以在破产程序中使用此类文件，但他在这么做时仍必须保留相关的特权。

上诉法院还认为，即使罗斯博作为破产人丧失了文件附加的特权，但将文件提供给针对破产人的债权人用于破产诉讼，也不是破产制度的目的。

但上诉法院并没有解决这个问题，破产管理人占有法律意见涉及的财产，是否也应该继承该财产上的特权呢？新月农场体育有限公司诉斯特林军官有限公司案[9]（以下简称新月农场案）是赞同特权将随着所依附的财产本身一起流转的第一起案件。因此该原则被称为“新月农场原则”。

在之后的破产案件中，高等法院的判决都支持破产人。在利兹诉莱莫斯案[10]中，破产管理人依据“新月农场原则”申请代表债权人获取破产人的特权文件便于债权人提起诉讼，撤销破产人在破产前的部分交易。但法院认为，在考虑破产程序中的特权效力时，破产资产相关的文件和破产债务相关的文件不应该区别对待。新月农场案之所以与众不同，是因为该案不涉及破产。特权是普通法中的一项基本权利，法院无权要求破产人根据《破产法》或其他方式放弃特权。即使“新月农场原则”支持特权自动归属破产管理人的财产，但从撤销破产前的交易中收回的任何财产都不构成《破产法》意义上的“财产”。

vesting of property in a trustee in bankruptcy, any property recovered under a claim challenging transactions that predated the bankruptcy would not constitute "property" for the purposes of the Insolvency Act.

The two judgments together provide that there is no distinction between the privileges relating to asset and liability documents—a trustee has the right to see privileged information when necessary for the performance of his statutory function. There is, however, no authority in the Insolvency Act that allows a court to compel a bankrupt person to waive privilege.

Care should be taken when dealing with privileged documents. Although a trustee has the right to see privileged documents, which may prove helpful in carrying out his statutory function, and to use them in proceedings against the bankrupt person, the trustee can neither waive privilege without the bankrupt's consent, nor compel waiver by court order. In practice, a bankrupt person is unlikely to agree to waive privilege. Trustees should instruct solicitors different from those used by major creditors or, when one law firm acts for both, instruct a different group within the firm and establish a firewall.

Corporate Insolvency

Unlike in an individual bankruptcy, the property of a corporate bankrupt is not transferred to the trustee. Instead the insolvency representative takes control of the company, its assets and liabilities, and the benefit of any privileged legal advice the company has received.[11] The insolvency representative or administrator acts as an agent of the company and can waive the company's privilege.

This approach favors insolvency representatives and creditors. Public policy may also play a role—individuals have more rights than companies. Moreover, a company may not exist after insolvency. Nevertheless, allowing a trustee in bankruptcy to see privileged documents, but not to use them,

两项判决共同表明，与资产相关的文件和与负债相关的文件这二者的特权之间没有区别。破产管理人有权视需要查看特权保护的信息，但《破产法》并没有规定法院可以强制破产人放弃特权。

在处理特权文件时应格外小心，尽管破产管理人有权查看，也有权在对破产人的诉讼中使用这些特权文件，但他既不能在未经破产人同意的情况下放弃特权，也不能通过法令强制破产人放弃特权。事实上，破产人不太可能同意放弃特权，所以破产管理人此时指示的必须是除主要债权人的律师以外的律师。当一家律所同时都是双方代理时，也应该指示该律所的不同团队，并建立相关的“防火墙”机制。

企业破产

与个人破产不同，公司破产的财产不会转让给破产管理人。相反，破产管理人控制和管理公司、资产、负债以及任何公司法律意见所附有的特权。[11] 破产管理人作为公司的代理人，有权放弃公司的特权。

这项规定有利于破产管理人和债权人。公共政策也能发挥作用——让个人比公司拥有更多的权利。此外，公司破产后可能不复存在。尽管如此，允许破产管理人不使用查阅特权，即使是个人破产，实践中都很难实现。本章其余部分介绍了美国和法国的特权规则。

even against the bankrupt individual, raises practical difficulties. The rules on privilege in the United States and France are described in the remainder of this chapter.

Privilege in the United States

U.S. laws on privilege broadly mirror the English rules. The purpose of privilege is to "encourage full and frank communication between attorneys and their clients and thereby promote broader public interests in the observance of law and administration of justice."[12]

To establish the privilege, a party must demonstrate that a communication between client and counsel (1) was intended to be and was kept confidential, and (2) was made for the purpose of obtaining or providing legal advice. The work product doctrine is similar to the English concept of litigation privilege.

Corporate Insolvency

In *Commodity Futures Trading Commission v. Weintraub*,[13] the U.S. Supreme Court held that, because the attorney-client privilege is controlled outside of bankruptcy by a corporation's management, the person or body whose duties most closely resemble those of management should control the privilege within bankruptcy.

In a corporate bankruptcy, the right to exercise attorney-client privilege passes to the trustee, including a liquidation trustee, provided the trustee has been vested with control over the debtor's bankrupt estate or the particular claims to which the privilege applies.

Personal Insolvency

The control of privilege in a consumer bankruptcy is more complex. As is true in English law, the rights of an individual differ significantly from those of a corporation. The Fifth Amendment's protection against

美国的特权规则

美国关于特权的规定大致借鉴了英国的立法。特权的目的是“鼓励律师与其委托人之间进行充分而坦诚的沟通，从而在法律的调整和规范下促进更广泛的公共利益”。[12]

为了符合特权构成的条件，当事人必须证明委托人和律师之间的信息符合以下要求:（1）是需要保密的;（2）目的是征询法律意见。美国的“工作成果豁免权”类似于英国“诉讼特权”的概念。

企业破产

在商品期货交易委员会诉温特劳布案[13]中，美国最高法院裁定，由于“律师—客户”特权不属于公司破产事务，所以应由与这一管理职责最接近的个人或部门在破产程序中行使该权利。

在企业破产程序中，只要破产管理人控制了破产财产，“律师—客户”特权就移交给破产管理人，包括清算管理人。

个人破产

消费者破产程序中的特权规定更加复杂。例如，在英国法中，个人权利与公司权利有很大的区别。美国宪法第五修正案禁止自证其罪的内容就不适用于公司。个人破产程序中关于“律师—客户”特权的

self-incrimination is not available to a corporation. The case law governing the control of attorney-client privilege in individual bankruptcies varies between, and within, federal circuits.

In a liquidation under chapter 7 of the Bankruptcy Code, the trustee, rather than the individual debtor, controls the assets of the bankrupt estate. Which of them controls attorney-client privilege? Case law falls into three categories: (1) those that allow the trustee to control attorney-client privilege in individual bankruptcies; (2) those that give the individual debtor exclusive control over attorney-client privilege; and (3) those that balance the facts and circumstances to determine whether the individual debtor or the chapter 7 trustee controls the privilege. The most common approach is the balancing test.

Prospective claimants should determine which test the relevant jurisdiction follows if attorney-client privilege is likely to be an issue in a bankruptcy proceeding.

The law is now clear in the United Kingdom that bankrupt individuals have greater rights to preserve their privileged documents than insolvent corporations. This mirrors the U.S. position and may have its origins in the rights individuals have that corporations do not. Whatever party one represents, whether a corporation, individual, or trustee, a lawyer must carefully consider issues of privilege and their potential effects on the client.

Professional Secrecy in France

French law does not define legal privilege. The relationship between a lawyer and a client is protected, however, by the *secret professionnel* (professional secrecy).

The general principle is established in article 226-13 of the French Criminal Code. It applies to any professional in a position to receive

判例在联邦巡回法院之间和之内也都有不同的判决。

在《破产法》第七章的清算程序中，破产管理人取代破产债务人控制破产财产，但谁来行使“律师—客户”特权呢？判例法分了三种情况：（1）在个人破产程序中，破产管理人享有“律师—客户”特权；（2）个人债务人享有“律师—客户”特权；（3）依据当时的情形权衡确定由个人债务人还是破产管理人享有该特权。权衡比照是最常用的情形。

如果破产程序中产生了“律师—客户”特权的争议，则原告应决定选用上述哪一项方法解决争议。

如今，英国法律明确规定在获得特权文件方面，个人破产比公司破产享有更多权利。这也反映了美国的立场，这些都源于许多个人享有而公司不享有的权利。无论哪一方，无论是公司、个人还是破产管理人、律师，都必须仔细考虑特权问题及其对客户的潜在影响。

法国的职业保密规则

法国法律并没有法律特权的概念。但是，律师和客户之间的关系受到“职业保密”规则的保护。

《法国刑法》第 226-13 条规定了一般原则。它适用于任何能够接触秘密信息的专业人员，包括法院任命的破产管理人，也可通过职业

confidential information, including administrators appointed by courts, and may also be imposed upon individuals by their professional codes.

Professional secrecy as applied to attorneys is established by article 2 of the *Code de Déontologie*, the attorneys' code of ethics. An attorney is a confidant of his client and therefore the information they exchange is protected by professional secrecy.

Scope and Application of the Professional Secret

The obligation of professional secrecy imposed on attorneys is general, absolute, and unlimited in time; it applies to all professional information and documents exchanged between clients and their attorneys during their professional relationship. Information given to attorneys through a personal relationship, however, is not protected.[14]

Professional secrecy covers not only information given to attorneys by clients, but also information relating to clients or their cases provided to attorneys by third parties, as well as any conclusion drawn by attorneys on the basis of the information received.

Sanctions for Violation of Professional Secrecy by an Attorney

Violations of professional secrecy can include giving protected information to a third party, such as a judge, another party to the litigation, the media, or a former client. Under article 226-13 of the French Criminal Code, a violation can subject an attorney to one year of imprisonment and a fine of up to €15,000.

An attorney who violates professional secrecy can also be sanctioned by the disciplinary board that regulates the legal profession.

Issues Relating to Corporate Insolvency and Bankruptcy Proceedings

In a corporate insolvency, the court will determine whether the insolvency representative will have access to documents and information held by the company's attorney or whether the attorney will be able to

守则予以规定。

《律师道德守则》第 2 条规定了律师的职业保密义务。律师作为客户的同盟，他们之间的通信应受职业秘密的保护。

职业秘密的适用范围

律师负有的职业保密义务具有普遍、绝对、无期限的特点，适用于客户与律师在职业关系存续期间往来的所有职业信息与文件，通过个人关系获取的信息除外。[14]

职业保密的范围不仅涵盖客户提供给律师的信息，还包括第三方提供给客户的信息以及律师根据所知信息得出的任何结论。

律师违反职业保密义务的法律责任

违反职业保密义务，是指将保密信息提供给第三方，如法官、诉讼另一方、媒体或前客户等。根据《法国刑法》第 226–13 条，违反义务可被判处监禁一年并处以最高 15,000 欧元的罚款。

违反职业保密义务的律师还可能受到律师行业纪律委员会的制裁。

与企业破产和破产程序相关的议题

在公司破产程序中，法院确定破产管理人是否有权查阅公司法务和律师所持有的文件和信息，或律师能否在职业保密义务的约束下隐瞒信息。其他受职业保密义务约束的专业人士，如银行从业人员、特

withhold the information under professional secrecy. The same issue arises with respect to information held by other professionals bound by professional secrecy such as banks, chartered accountants, and auditors.

The insolvency representative temporarily represents the company and takes over its management, which provides him with access to all information and documents, including information that would otherwise be subject to professional secrecy. The company's attorney will not be entitled to withhold that information.

Professionals who receive confidential information, such as company auditors, cannot invoke professional secrecy to withhold information from a bankruptcy judge or an insolvency representative. Professional secrecy does not apply even though the insolvency representative is a third party.

Although insolvency representatives have access to information and documents protected by professional secrecy, creditors of insolvent companies do not have access to documents protected by professional secrecy.

Issues Relating to Individual Insolvency

In individual insolvency proceedings, an insolvency representative's rights are limited to actions relating to the individual's professional activities. Under article L622-3 of the Commercial Code, the individual retains the right to manage his personal estate and make personal decisions.

There is no law on professional secrecy in individual insolvency proceedings or any law that entitles insolvency representatives to personal information that is subject to professional secrecy. An individual's lawyer may be able to invoke professional secrecy against an insolvency representative with respect to personal information given to him by the individual.

By analogy, a company attorney who has privileged and personal

许会计师和审计师等，也面临同样的情形。

破产管理人临时代理并接管公司，被授权查阅所有信息和文件，包括本属于职业保密范围内的信息。公司的律师无权扣留该信息文件。

掌握机密信息的专业人士，如公司的审计师，不能援引职业秘密原则拒绝向法官或破产管理人披露信息。即使破产管理人为第三方，职业保密原则也不适用。

尽管破产管理人有权访问受保护的文件，但破产公司的债权人无权访问此类机密文件。

个人破产的相关议题

在个人破产程序中，破产管理人的权力仅限于与破产个人相关的职务活动。根据《商业法》第 L622–3 条，破产个人仍保有财产处分和其他事项的决定权。

在个人破产程序中，还没有职业保密的相关立法，无法赋予破产管理人获取受职业保密原则保护的信息。律师获得破产人的相关信息时，可能援引职业保密原则对抗破产管理人。

以此类推，握有公司董事、高管信息的公司律师可以依据职业保

information about a director or officer of the company should be able to invoke professional secrecy against an insolvency representative with respect to matters that do not concern or prejudice the company; this, however, is only a hypothesis.

Conclusion

In France, an insolvent or bankrupt company has the right to invoke professional secrecy in dealing with third parties. Neither the company nor the attorney, however, will be able to invoke professional secrecy against an insolvency representative with respect to documents exchanged by the attorney and the company. The insolvency representative will be entitled to use these documents in litigation or asset recovery. Personal, nonprofessional information relating to a director or an officer may be entitled to confidentiality, although there is no case law on the issue.

Key Points from this Chapter

- In cases of corruption and asset tracing, the ability of insolvency representatives to access privileged material can change the course of a case.
- In English and Commonwealth systems, legal advice privilege protects confidential communications between a lawyer and her client for the purpose of giving or receiving legal advice. Litigation privilege protects a wider category of documents—those between a client or lawyer and a third party.
- In the U.S. and U.K. systems, a party claiming privilege must demonstrate that a communication between client and counsel was intended to be confidential and was made to obtain or provide legal advice.
- Bankrupt individuals have greater rights to preserve their privileged communications than insolvent corporations in the United Kingdom and the United States.
- In France, neither the company nor the attorney can invoke professional secrecy against an insolvency representative.

密原则，在不损害公司利益的情况下对抗破产管理人。但这只是一个设想。

结论

在法国，破产公司有权对第三方援引职业保密原则。但无论是公司还是律师，都不能对破产管理人援引该原则而拒绝披露相关文件。破产管理人有权在诉讼或资产追查过程中使用这些文件。虽然没有判例，但对公司董事、高管的非业务相关的个人信息可以保密。

本章要点

- 在腐败资产追查的案件中，破产管理人获取机密材料的能力会影响案件的进程。
- 在英国和英联邦立法体系中，法律意见特权可以保护律师和客户以征询法律意见为目的的机密通信。诉讼特权可以保护更大范围的文件和信息，包括客户、律师及第三方。
- 在美国和英国，申请特权保护的一方必须证明委托人和律师之间的通信是保密的并且其目的在于征询法律意见。
- 在英国和美国，破产个人比起破产公司在通信保密方面享有更大的特权。
- 在法国，公司和律师均不得针对破产管理人援引职业保密原则。

Notes

1. [2015] UKPC 35.

2. Three Rivers (No. 5) [2004] EWCA Civ. 218; the RBS Rights Issue Litigation [2016] EWCH 3161 (Ch).

3. [2017] EWHC 1017 (QB).

4. The RBS Rights Issue Litigation [2016] EWCH 3161 (Ch).

5. [2013] B.P.I.R. 756.

6. European Commission Regulation on Insolvency Proceedings 1346/2000, art. 4.

7. Ibid., art. 3.

8. [2016] EWCA Civ. 1138.

9. [1971] 3 All ER 1192.

10. [2017] EWHC 1825 (Ch).

11. Re Brook Martin [1993] BCLC 328.

12. Upjohn Co. v. United States, 449 U.S. 383 (1981).

13. 471 U.S. 343 (1985).

14. Cass. crim., 2 mars 2010, n 09-88.453.

注释

1. [2015] UKPC 35.

2. Three Rivers (No. 5) [2004] EWCA Civ. 218；苏格兰皇家银行供股诉讼案 [2016] EWCH 3161 (Ch)。

3. [2017] EWHC 1017 (QB).

4. 苏格兰皇家银行供股诉讼案 [2016] EWCH 3161 (Ch)。

5. [2013] B.P.I.R. 756.

6. 欧盟委员会破产程序规则 1346/2000, art. 4。

7. 同上，art. 3。

8. [2016] EWCA Civ. 1138.

9. [1971] 3 All ER 1192.

10. [2017] EWHC 1825 (Ch).

11. Re Brook Martin [1993] BCLC 328.

12. Upjohn 公司诉美国案，449 U.S. 383 (1981)。

13. 471 U.S. 343 (1985).

14. Cass. crim., 2 mars 2010, n 09-88.453.

5. Further Issues on the Use of Insolvency for Asset Recovery

Major Challenges for Asset Recovery in Developing Jurisdictions

Global insolvency systems vary around the world. In many developing countries, outdated insolvency laws remain on the books and there may be limited or no local experience in conducting insolvency cases. These jurisdictions may face challenges in using insolvency as a tool for cross-border asset recovery. This section discusses some of the challenges that may frustrate the efficient recovery of assets through insolvency proceedings in developing countries. Many of these challenges can be overcome; it is important, however, to be aware of them and to address them with a local lawyer experienced in insolvency proceedings. Some of the challenges discussed in this section apply to varying degrees in developed jurisdictions.

Jurisdiction matters significantly—in law and in practice—for both standard insolvency processes and the recovery of assets. If the matter is a corporate insolvency case filed against a company incorporated in an offshore jurisdiction, for example, the offshore law and jurisdiction would most likely apply. However, if a bribe-taking company is incorporated in a developing country, that country's law and jurisdiction would most likely apply.[1] Therefore, a claimant seeking asset recovery must be ready to face the challenges highlighted in this section of the guidebook.

5. 利用破产追回资产的其他议题

发展中国家资产返回面临的主要挑战

全球破产制度在世界各地不尽相同。许多发展中国家仍然沿用过时的破产法，办理破产案件的经验也比较缺失。这些国家通过破产策略追查腐败资产面临着不小的挑战。本章讨论了部分发展中国家利用破产策略工具追查腐败资产中可能遇到的阻碍。其中很多阻碍都可以被成功克服，但重要的是认清阻碍本身以及与本土经验丰富的破产律师共同协作。本章讨论的部分挑战也被发达国家不同程度地借鉴与适用。

无论是在立法还是实践中，司法管辖权对于标准的破产程序和资产追查都至关重要。例如，如果破产程序针对的是某个在海外离岸地区注册的公司，那么离岸地区的法律或本国法都可能是适用的。但如果在发展中国家注册以收受贿赂为目的的公司，则该国具有管辖权的同时也适用该国法律。[1] 因此，追查时必须做好充分准备，应对本章内容中的挑战。

Commencement Obstacles

Insolvency proceedings can be commenced if a debtor is unable to pay debts as they come due or if the debtor's balance sheet shows that liabilities exceed assets. Many developing jurisdictions, especially those using civil law systems, do not provide for the commencement of insolvency proceedings on just and equitable grounds, as do some common law jurisdictions. This presents a significant obstacle for asset recovery if the bribe-taking debtor is solvent.

Further, because of unclear legislation or lack of expertise, many developing countries do not have well-defined criteria for the commencement of insolvency cases. Even if the grounds for commencement would typically be sufficient elsewhere, a claimant (in this guidebook likely the state pursuing the recovery of assets) may have difficulty bringing a case in a developing jurisdiction.

Unregulated or Insufficiently Regulated Insolvency Representatives

Many of the suggestions in this guidebook presume that a jurisdiction has an established concept of "insolvency representative". Some developing countries, however, provide little or no guidance or regulation for insolvency representatives. Some countries specify categories of professionals (such as lawyers and accountants) that can be appointed as insolvency representatives without necessarily requiring that the individuals appointed have any specialized knowledge of insolvency. Others have regulations for insolvency representatives but lack a regulatory body to monitor them or respond to complaints. Others have remuneration systems with potentially skewed incentives: for example, the longer a case takes, the more the representative is paid. In many jurisdictions, creditors do not have a say in the appointment of the insolvency representative, and courts may be legally obligated to appoint, for example, a randomly selected individual;

启动障碍

如果债务人到期无法偿还债务或者债务人的资产负债表显示其负债已超过资产价值，则可以启动破产程序。许多发展中国家，特别是适用大陆法系的发展中国家，并不像普通法系国家一样，允许基于“公平公正”原则启动破产程序。如果受贿的债务人此时具有偿付能力，将成为资产追回的重大障碍。

此外，由于立法不完善或者缺乏专业知识，许多发展中国家并没有明确的启动破产程序标准。即使在其他国家有充分的启动理由，赔偿申请人（很多时候是资产追查国）也可能难以将案件提交发展中国家管辖。

监管缺失的破产管理人

本指南中的许多建议都假定一个国家已经确立了“破产管理人”的概念。但许多发展中国家关于破产管理人的指导规范可以说几乎没有或是相当欠缺。有的国家虽然指定了破产管理人的专业资格，如律师或会计师，但并不要求他们具备破产相关知识。有的国家对破产管理人有一定的规范，但缺乏相应的监督机制履行监督职能或回应投诉；还有些国家的薪酬制度存在不合理的激励措施，例如，案件审理时间越长，破产管理人的薪资就越高。在许多国家，债权人对于破产管理人的任命并没有发言权，法院可能随机挑选破产管理人。根据普遍的破产管理人的经验和知识，这种方法可能根本无法解决案件中的核心问题。还有些国家，破产管理人甚至和债务人、前高管以及其他相关方串通损害债权人的利益。在方框 1.4 中讨论的欧洲复兴开发银行《破产管理人守则》，与各国的破产管理人监管制度相比，更能识别各国司法系统中的弱点并提供解决方法。

depending on the appointee's experience and knowledge, this approach might leave important features of a case unaddressed. In some jurisdictions, insolvency representatives have colluded with debtors, past management, or other parties. Comparing a jurisdiction's regulatory framework for insolvency representatives with the European Bank for Reconstruction and Development's Insolvency Office Holder Principles discussed in box 1.4 provides a basis for identifying the weaknesses in a jurisdiction's system.

Ineffective or Nonexistent Anti-Avoidance System

As discussed in the sections in chapter 3 titled *Proceedings for Fraudulent or Wrongful Trading* and *Preferences and Transactions at Undervalue*, in leading practice jurisdictions, voidable transactions and the look-back period enable insolvency representatives to cancel transactions that are improper or prejudicial. In other jurisdictions, however, (1) there may be no legal provision allowing the insolvency representative to cancel transactions (a small minority of countries, because avoidance actions have become standard); (2) laws that permit avoidance are unclear or incomplete; (3) look-back periods are too short; and (4) laws have procedural or design problems, such as the failure to specify that creditors can pursue avoidance actions if the insolvency representative fails to do so.

If a jurisdiction does not enable an insolvency representative to avoid improper transactions, or if the law is not sufficiently clear, fraudulent proceeds may be recoverable using the criminal law or other breach of duty regulations, such as the civil law "actio pauliana" (action to avoid fraud, analogous to recovering a fraudulent conveyance under common law).

Slow, Unresponsive, or Inexperienced Judicial Systems and Lawyers

Insolvency proceedings used for the recovery of stolen assets benefit from proceeding quickly. The longer a proceeding takes, the greater the risk that assets will be transferred, documents will disappear, or witnesses will

无效或缺失的撤销系统

如第三章中优先清偿和低价交易等欺诈性交易或不当交易等内容所讨论的，在某些先进国家立法中，无效交易和回溯期的规定使破产管理人有权撤销不当或显失公平的交易。但是，某些国家的立法：（1）可能没有相关立法允许破产管理人撤销交易（少数国家，毕竟撤销权已普遍存在）；（2）规范撤销交易的法律不明确或不完善；（3）回溯期过短；（4）法律存在程序或设计上的漏洞，例如，未能明确在破产管理人不行使撤销权时债权人是否可以撤销交易。

如果某个国家没有破产管理人撤销权的相关立法，也可以以违反刑法或其他法律法规为由，如利用民法中的“避免欺诈行为”（类似于普通法下追回转移的欺诈性资产）条款，追回相关资产。

反应迟钝、欠缺经验的律师和司法系统

通过破产程序追回腐败资产对程序的时效性要求较高。诉讼程序耗时越长，资产转移或文件灭失、证人难以作证的风险就越大。

move out of reach.

The World Bank's *Doing Business Report 2019* (2018) indicates that, in Latin America and the Caribbean and in Sub-Saharan Africa, almost three years pass, on average, between a company's default and the payment of some or all of the money owed to a creditor. The process takes a little over half that time in countries in the Organisation for Economic Co-operation and Development.[2] In some jurisdictions, recalcitrant debtors have many tactics at their disposal to delay proceedings. In jurisdictions where little or no action can take place until an appeal has been heard (especially appeals of interlocutory decisions), multiple appeals are often filed. The appellate process can take years to complete. In many countries there is no limit on the number of extensions of time or adjournments that can be granted.

Many developing countries have general courts that handle a wide range of issues from criminal to family to corporate law, making it difficult for judges to master complex and technical areas of law such as insolvency. This can slow down proceedings or lead to incorrect decisions. Only 101 of the 190 countries measured by the World Bank's *Doing Business Report 2019* (2018, 56) have specialized commercial courts, and only 31 have bankruptcy courts for insolvency cases. Specialized commercial or insolvency jurisdiction can result in shorter resolution times (World Bank 2018, 56). Training judges on insolvency is critical.

In some jurisdictions, the ability to bring cases in dedicated commercial courts or before dedicated insolvency judges may enable claimants to avoid these delays.

Ineffective or Nonexistent Collateral Registry Systems

A modern collateral registry system—centralized, notice-based, and accessible online—is another valuable component of the insolvency

世界银行《2019 年经商环境报告》指出，在拉丁美洲和加勒比地区以及撒哈拉以南的非洲，从公司违约到部分或全部清偿债务平均需要 3 年时间。即便在经济合作与发展组织（OECD）的成员国，这个过程也至少需要一年半的时间。[2] 在某些国家，强硬的债务人还会采用许多手段拖延诉讼。在许多国家的立法中，提起上诉之前（特别是中间裁决的上诉）几乎没有任何救济手段，而上诉往往会进行多次，过程需要经历数年才能完成。在许多国家，诉讼期限延长的范围和次数都没有限制。

许多发展中国家的普通法院需要处理从刑法到家庭法再到公司法的各种案件，这使得法官很难掌握破产等复杂的技术性领域的法律知识，很可能造成拖慢案件进程或作出错误裁决的后果。世界银行《2019 年经商环境报告》评估的 190 个国家中，只有 101 个设有商事法庭，31 个设有破产法庭。专门的商事或破产法庭可以有效缩短案件的进程（世界银行，2018，56）。同时，法官培训也至关重要。

在某些国家，案件提交专门的商事法庭或由专门的破产法官审理能有效避免破产进程的延误。

无效或缺失的抵押登记系统

现代抵押登记系统囊括了集成性、通知式、可在线访问等诸多优点，是破产追查的重要组成部分。注册管理机构允许债权人在无实物

framework for asset recovery. Registries allow a lender to take a security interest in an asset without the requirement of physical custody. The debtor retains title and possession. Without registration of these transactions, there is no transparent guarantee for the lender and no assurance that the lender is the only one claiming an asset. When a debt is originated, collateral registries enable potential creditors or buyers to discover any existing liens on a property and allow them to register their own security interest, establishing priority over other creditors in case of the debtor's default. Collateral registries also enable insolvency representatives to quickly identify which assets are owned free and clear by the company and which have been used as collateral for lending. In asset recovery cases, the registry enables insolvency representatives to trace company assets and determine whether they are subject to liens. Insolvency representatives can also confirm which encumbered assets are subject to the collateral guarantee.

Many developing countries, however, do not have modern collateral registries. As of 2015, only 18 of 189 countries had a modern registry system. Only 25 countries had a notice-based registry, and 28 had an online registry (World Bank 2014, 67). The lack of an established registry can make it difficult for insolvency representatives to identify assets for recovery.

Impediments to Enforcement

In asset recovery cases, insolvency representatives may need to conduct enforcement actions to recover assets from a company's debtors. These actions may be filed directly with the bankruptcy court or in other civil or commercial courts of the jurisdiction.

Effective debt enforcement requires that the legal, tax, and regulatory elements of the framework are mutually reinforcing and work together for a timely, efficient, and costeffective resolution. Moreover, effective

保管的情况下获得资产的担保权，债务人保留所有权和资产实体。未经注册的交易，则无法为债权人提供透明的担保，也无法保证债权人单独享有担保权。抵押登记处让债权人能够在债务产生后确认资产上的任何抵押权益，允许他们注册自己的担保权益，并可在债务人败诉的情况下，设立优先权高于其他债权人的担保权。在抵押登记处破产管理人还能够快速追查公司资产并确定其抵押担保的状态。

但是，许多发展中国家没有现代化的抵押登记系统。截至 2015 年，189 个国家中只有 18 个国家拥有现代化的注册系统，只有 25 个国家或地区拥有通知型登记制度，28 个国家拥有在线注册中心（世界银行，2014，67）。缺乏固定的登记系统会使破产管理人难以识别和追踪目标资产。

执法障碍

在资产追查案件中，破产管理人需要采取相关执行措施，从公司债务人手中追回资产。这些行动可直接向破产法院或管辖区内的其他民商事法院申请。

有效的债务执行需要法律、税收和监管等制度通力协作，才能及时、高效、低成本地实现目标。此外，有效的债务执行还取决于完善的司法制度、独立而专业的司法机构以及透明、公开、统一的执法。

debt enforcement depends on a strong institutional infrastructure, with an independent and competent judiciary that applies the law in a transparent, predictable, and consistent manner.

Other institutional elements also play a significant role. In jurisdictions where bailiffs oversee enforcement, they must be adequately trained, supervised, and paid. If bailiffs are paid in advance, adequate incentives must ensure that they perform their function.

Transparency and Accountability of Legal Insolvency Frameworks

The bedrock of any legal process is transparency of decision making and accountability of all participants. Many developing countries do not publish lower court decisions, and in some jurisdictions, appellate court decisions are published only selectively or sporadically; both have consequences for the recovery of assets through the insolvency process. First, parties will have little recourse in the event of a questionable decision by a judge. Second, the inability to consult precedent makes it difficult for litigants to predict how a court might rule and deprives judges of the means of developing consistent rulings on similar issues.

The level of accountability in the court system can be an issue in developing countries. Inefficiencies and delays can result when judges are not accountable to a chief justice who can monitor progress on cases and set time standards. A lack of accountability also affects the functioning of judicial officers, such as registrars and bailiffs, who may play an important role in litigation in many developing jurisdictions.

Recognition and Use of Laws and Proceedings in Cross-Border Insolvency

Many large corporations and individuals have international operations or customers and suppliers throughout the world. Corruption and asset

其他体制因素也从中发挥重要作用，如对执法人员进行充分的培训、监督和薪酬激励等。预支薪酬的，还需要采取足够的激励措施确保执法人员严格执法。

破产法制度下的透明度和问责制

任何法律的基础都包括决策的透明度和参与人的问责制。许多发展中国家不公开地方基层法院的判决，有些国家对上诉法院的判决部分公开或不定期公开，都会对破产程序追回资产造成影响。首先，如果法官裁决有误，当事双方几乎无法采取任何救济措施；其次，由于无法参考先例，当事人很难预测法院将如何裁决，也造成实践中法院就类似案件难以形成统一的裁决标准。

在发展中国家，法院系统中的责任划分和逐级问责是个重要问题。大法官负责监督法官和案件的进展和时限，当法官无法对大法官负责时，就会造成审理效率低下、案件延误等问题。缺乏问责制还极大影响了司法主管、执行官等司法人员的职能，他们也在发展中国家的司法体系中发挥着重要的作用。

跨境破产中法律与程序的承认与适用

许多大型企业及个人在全球范围内开展业务，拥有许多国外的客户或供应商。反腐败资产追查通常涉及这些资产、个人和企业。他们

recovery cases often involve assets, individuals, or entities located in a jurisdiction different from the jurisdiction in which the insolvency litigation was begun. This section provides an overview of the legal tools that enable the use or enforcement of insolvency legislation and orders in cross-border cases.

The UNCITRAL Model Law on Cross-Border Insolvency

Many countries have adopted or enacted legislation to ensure transnational consistency in the application and enforcement of cross-border insolvency laws. In 1997, the United Nations Commission on International Trade Law (UNCITRAL) adopted the Model Law on Cross-Border Insolvency (Model Law), to provide "effective mechanisms for dealing with cases of cross-border insolvency" (UNCITRAL 2014, 3). The Model Law promotes, among other things, "cooperation between the courts and other competent authorities of [the adopting] State and foreign States involved in cases of cross-border insolvency" (UNCITRAL 2014, 3). In 2013, UNCITRAL added the Guide to Enactment and Interpretation, which provides commentary on the provisions of the Model Law (UNCITRAL 2014).

As of 2019, the Model Law has been adopted in 44 states in 46 jurisdictions, including Australia, the British Virgin Islands, Canada, Colombia, Gibraltar, Japan, Kenya, Mexico, New Zealand, the Republic of Korea, Singapore, South Africa, the United Kingdom, the U.S. Virgin Islands, and the United States.[3] Many of the signatories have adopted individual variations that are beyond the scope of this chapter.

The Model Law includes provisions that are intended to facilitate the orderly administration of cross-border insolvency estates. The first is access—giving foreign representatives and creditors of the insolvent person or entity access to the courts of the enacting jurisdiction to seek relief in the

往往位于与破产程序启动地不同的司法管辖区。本节概述了在跨境案件中可以使用的相关破产法律工具。

联合国国际贸易法委员会《跨国界破产示范法》

许多国家已经通过或颁布了相关立法以确保跨国界破产法的适用和执行。1997年，联合国国际贸易法委员会（UNCITRAL）通过了《跨国界破产示范法》（以下简称《示范法》），以提供“处理跨国界破产案件的有效机制”（UNCITRAL，2014，3）。除此以外，《示范法》还“促进了采用示范法各国之间的法院或主管当局在跨境破产案件上的合作”（UNCITRAL，2014，3）。2013年，联合国国际贸易法委员会还补充了该法的颁布与解释指南，对《示范法》的规定做了更详细的说明（UNCITRAL，2014）。

截至2019年，《示范法》已在46个司法管辖区中的44个司法管辖区施行，包括澳大利亚、英属维京群岛、加拿大、哥伦比亚、直布罗陀、日本、肯尼亚、墨西哥、新西兰、韩国、新加坡、南非、美属维京群岛和美国。[3] 许多成员国在本国颁布了修订版，本章暂不讨论。

《示范法》旨在促进跨境破产资产的有序管理。主要内容包括：（1）“准入”：破产公司或破产个人的外国破产管理人能够在外国司法管辖区获得当地法院的救济。（2）“承认”：快速经济地对外国程序及破产管理人予以资格认定及法律许可。为此，《示范法》还引入了

local and other jurisdictions. The second is recognition—a speedy and cost-effective method of qualifying and legitimizing both the foreign proceeding and the representative of that proceeding. To facilitate recognition, the Model Law introduces the "center of main interest" (COMI), from which the debtor conducts the administration of its business on a regular basis. The third is specifically delineated relief, both on an interim basis and upon recognition, to identify the applicable law and governing jurisdiction and reduce the risk and cost of litigating the impact of foreign law on the recognition procedure. The fourth is cooperation—to empower local and foreign courts to communicate and jointly address issues raised in the administration of cross-border insolvencies. (In July 2018, the UNCITRAL adopted a Model Law on Recognition and Enforcement of Insolvency-Related Judgments.)

The Model Law has not yet been adopted by many European nations. Regulation (EU) 2015/848 of the European Parliament and of the Council of May 20, 2015, on Insolvency Proceedings (EU Regulation), provides a framework of common rules on cross-border insolvency proceedings applicable to European Union (EU) Member States.

The Model Law was, however, codified in the United States as chapter 15 of the U.S. Bankruptcy Code, enacted in 2005.[4] Under chapter 15, recognition requires the filing of a petition by a judicial administrator, insolvency representative, or similar representative appointed by a foreign court or body.[5] A certified copy of the order commencing the proceedings and appointing the foreign representative must be included with the filing. (Other more detailed procedural steps are beyond the scope of this chapter.) The petition must allege a foreign judicial proceeding for the restructuring or liquidation of debts and assets in a foreign court and that the affairs of the debtor are subject to the supervision of a foreign court. The petition

"主要权益中心"（COMI）的概念，指债务人日常业务经营的主要地点。（3）在过渡或确认期间内的特别临时救济，以确认和识别应适用的法律和相关管辖权，并降低对外国法律承认的成本和风险。（4）合作：加强本地法院与外国法院沟通的能力，合作解决跨境破产管理中的问题。（2018 年 7 月，联合国国际贸易法委员会《关于承认和执行与破产判决的示范法》）

《示范法》尚未被一些欧洲国家采用，2015 年 5 月 20 日，欧洲议会与理事会第 2015/848 号条例，对《破产程序条例》（EU 条例）进行了修订，为欧盟成员国提供了跨境破产的法律框架。

但在美国，《示范法》被纳入 2005 年颁布的《美国破产法》第十五章。[4]《美国破产法》第十五章规定，承认外国破产程序，应由司法人员、破产管理人或外国法院任命的其他代理人提出申请，[5]有关外国破产程序和破产管理人委任的证明文件也应一并提交。（其他更详细的程序步骤不在本章范围内）申请书应写明外国破产程序为破产重组还是破产清算。同时，债务人、破产资产等相关事项应受到外国法院的监督。申请书还必须标明，外国程序是主要程序还是非主要程序，并且申请承认的外国破产管理人视为"个人"，"个人"既包括个人也包括其他法律实体。[6]通常满足以上条件，就允许承认外国程序，但也有例外，法院认为"明显违反美国公共政策"的将不予确认。[7]

must also allege that the foreign proceeding is a foreign main or nonmain proceeding and that the foreign representative applying for recognition is a person, defined as including both individuals and juridical entities.[6] If the requirements are met, there is a strong presumption that the foreign proceeding will be granted recognition. Courts may, nevertheless, deny recognition that would be "manifestly contrary to the public policy of the United States."[7]

The remainder of this section describes the Model Law as adopted in the United Kingdom and the United States, which use similar legal and procedural methods for obtaining cross-border recognition and maintaining open communication between courts.

Foreign Main Recognition

A debtor's COMI determines whether a foreign proceeding will be granted "foreign main" or "foreign nonmain" recognition, which are accompanied by greater or lesser rights, respectively. Foreign main recognition is granted to a "collective judicial proceeding under a law relating to insolvency or adjustment of debts" that is "pending in the country where the debtor has the center of [its] main interests or establishment."[8] Section 1516 of the U.S. Bankruptcy Code further provides that, in the absence of evidence to the contrary, the bankruptcy court may presume that the bankrupt debtor's COMI is the location of its registered office, if an entity, or the habitual residence of a person.[9] The Bankruptcy Code does not define "habitual residence" but the term is understood to imply "an element of permanence and stability and is comparable to domicile; it connotes a meaningful connection to a jurisdiction, a home base where an individual lives, raises a family, works, and has ties to the community."[10] "Habitual residence" has also been defined as the place where a person resides with the intent to remain indefinitely. In determining a debtor's COMI, courts have

本章其余内容介绍了《示范法》在英国和美国被采用的情况，他们都采用了相似的法律程序申请跨国承认并在法院之间保持交流。

外国主要承认程序

债务人的“主要权益中心”决定了授权“外国主要承认”程序还是“外国非主要承认”程序，不同程序分别享有不同的权利。外国主要承认程序承认的是“与破产法或债务调整有关的综合司法程序”，它们是“在债务人主要营业国的待决程序”。[8]《美国破产法》第1516条进一步规定，在没有相抗证据的情况下，破产法院可以推定破产债务人的主要权益中心为公司注册地或破产个人的常住地。[9]《美国破产法》没有定义“常住地”，但应认为是具有“永久性、稳定性的特征，与永久居住地等同。它意味着与个人、家庭、社区及司法管辖区存在一定联系的基地”。[10]“常住地”还可以被定义为保有无限期居住意图的场所。在确定债务人的主要权益中心时，法院需要考虑诸多因素，如债务人的移民身份、债务人主要资产所在地、债务人的多数债权人所在地等，都会对该案以及该案归属哪个司法管辖区产生影响。[11]

considered factors such as the debtor's immigration status, "the location of a debtor's primary assets; the location of the majority of the debtor's creditors or [where] a majority of creditors would be affected by the case; and the jurisdiction whose law would apply to most disputes."[11]

Foreign Nonmain Recognition

A foreign nonmain proceeding is one that is pending in a jurisdiction where the debtor has an establishment, but which is not its COMI.[12] An establishment is "any place of operations where the debtor carries out a nontransitory economic activity."[13] A "place of operations" is a place from which the debtor conducts economic activities, whether the activities are commercial, industrial, or professional.[14] To determine the establishment of an individual debtor, courts have looked to the legislative history of the European Union Convention on Insolvency Proceedings on which the drafters of the Model Law relied: if a claim of primary place of business abroad is rejected, a secondary place of business or a secondary residence constitutes an establishment.

Public Policy Exception to Recognition

A bankruptcy court may refuse to recognize a foreign proceeding if it believes doing so would be "manifestly contrary to public policy of the United States."[15] This provision, included in the Model Law, enables bankruptcy courts not to follow chapter 15 if doing so would contradict fundamental principles of U.S. law, particularly statutory and constitutional guarantees.[16]

By its use of the term "manifestly," the U.S. Congress intended that this provision be interpreted restrictively and "invoked only under exceptional circumstances concerning matters of fundamental importance to the United States."[17] Courts should consider "(1) whether the foreign proceeding was procedurally unfair; and (2) whether the application of foreign law or the

外国非主要承认程序

外国非主要承认程序，是指在债务人的营业场所但非主要权益中心（COMI）的代决程序。[12]营业场所，是指“债务人进行非暂时性经济活动的任何营业地点”。[13]“营业地点”就是债务人进行经济活动的地方，经济活动包括商业活动、产业活动和专业活动。[14]为了确定债务人的营业地，法院参考了欧盟《破产程序条例》（《示范法》草案也以其为蓝本）的制定过程，并认为当法院拒绝认定外国主要权益中心时，次要营业地或者次要住所可以被认定为营业场所。

承认程序的“公共政策”例外

当破产法院认为某外国程序“明显违背美国的公共政策”时，可以拒绝承认该程序。[15]《示范法》规定破产法院在明显违背美国法律的基本原则，特别是违宪时，不必遵循《美国破产法》第十五章的规定。[16]

通过“明显”一词可以看出，美国国会试图对此条进行严格的限制性解释，“仅在出现违反美国根本性利益的极端情况下援引”。[17]法院应考虑：“（1）外国程序的公平性；（2）根据《美国破产法》第十五章适用外国法律或承认外国主要程序是否会‘严重影响’美国法特别是美国宪法规定下的权利价值，以至于会‘严重阻碍美国破产法院’

recognition of foreign main proceeding under Chapter 15 would 'severely impinge the value and import' of a U.S. statutory or constitutional right such that granting comity would 'severely hinder United States bankruptcy courts' abilities to carry out … the most fundamental policies and purposes of these rights."[18] Another court concluded: "Significantly, the fact that application of foreign law leads to a different result than application of U.S. law is, without more, insufficient to support §1506 protection, … [as] the whole purpose of Chapter 15 would be defeated if local or parochial interests routinely trumped the foreign law of the main proceeding."[19] The cases in which U.S. courts have found that recognition is unavailable on the basis of public policy concerns had facts in which affirmative violations of law had been committed or were being asked for.[20]

Relief Under Chapter 15 Upon Recognition

The recognition of a foreign main proceeding confers on the foreign representative immediate remedies and powers,[21] including the automatic stay provided for under the Bankruptcy Code of all proceedings against the debtor or the property of the debtor and the ability of the foreign representative to operate the debtor's business. The automatic stay prohibits creditors from pursuing actions against the debtor or its assets to satisfy debts owed to them, and, absent exigent circumstances, the stay remains in effect until the close of the foreign main proceeding.[22] The automatic stay has four main purposes: (1) to stop collection efforts, which gives the debtor time to devise a plan to resolve the financial situation that caused the insolvency; (2) to permit the foreign representative to collect the debtor's assets and liquidate them for the benefit of all creditors; (3) to give assurance to all creditors that other creditors are not pursuing independent remedies (either judicial or nonjudicial) to drain the debtor's assets; and to harmonize the interests of the creditors and the debtor.

的运作能力……”[18]另一家法院认为:“显然，适用外国法律所产生的结果与适用美国法律不同，这一结果不符合第1506条的保护初衷。如果他国利益能经常性地突破外国主要承认程序，第十五章的立法本意就被完全消解了。”[19]美国法院基于“公共政策”而拒绝承认的，必须符合确实存在既定的或正在发生的违法事实的条件。[20]

承认程序的救济手段

外国主要承认程序授权外国破产管理人立即采取措施，[21]包括《美国破产法》规定的中止所有对债务人或其财产的司法程序，以及赋予外国破产管理人接管债务人业务的权力。自动中止使债权人无权对债务人或其资产采取清偿行动。中止效力直到外国主要程序结束为止，有紧急情况的除外。[22]自动中止主要有四个目的:（1）停止清偿工作，使债务人有时间制订计划修正财务状况;（2）授权外国破产管理人为了债权人的权益接管债务人的资产并清算;（3）向全体债权人确保任何债权人不得为了获取债务人的资产采取独立的救济措施（无论司法还是非司法的手段）;（4）协调债权人和债务人的权益。

Upon a main or nonmain recognition, the court, at its discretion, may also (1) grant a stay of proceedings and execution of judgment against the debtor that might otherwise fall outside the scope of the automatic stay; (2) provide for the right to request documentation and oral testimony "concerning the debtor's assets, affairs, rights, obligations or liabilities"; and (3) authorize the foreign representative to administer the asset of the debtor within the United States.[23] The ability to obtain discovery in a chapter 15 proceeding[24] is national in scope and so broad it has been described by several courts as a court-sanctioned fishing expedition.[25]

Remedies not Available Under the U.S. Bankruptcy Code

The U.S. Bankruptcy Code and the insolvency laws of most countries provide for "avoidance actions," pursuant to which preferential transfers, transfers for insufficient value, and certain other unauthorized transfers may be cancelled and the transferred assets or their value recovered for the benefit of creditors.[26] Upon the avoidance of a transfer, either the property transferred or its value must be returned to the bankruptcy estate.[27] In a chapter 15 proceeding, a foreign representative may initiate an avoidance action only if it is based on state or foreign law (as opposed to federal bankruptcy law).[28]

Section 1509 (comparable to the right of direct access under article 9 of the Model Law) places restrictions on a foreign representative's access to local courts. Although section 1509(a) permits a foreign representative to file a petition for recognition "directly with the court," section 1509(d) states that, if recognition is denied under chapter 15, the court may issue "any appropriate order necessary to prevent the foreign representative from obtaining comity or cooperation from courts in the United States." Section 1509(f) further states that, although a foreign representative *need not* proceed under chapter 15 to have standing to sue in the United States, a

经过主要或非主要承认程序后，法院还可以视情况决定：（1）延长对债务人的中止或执行判决，否则可能超出自动中止的时限；（2）要求提供“与债务人资产、事务、权利、义务或负债相关的”文件或证明；（3）授权外国破产管理人在美国境内管理债务人的资产。[23]《美国破产法》第十五章[24]中提到的取证能力，是指国家层面的。因其太过宽泛，许多法院已将其明确为法院授权的审前调查。[25]

《美国破产法》不可用的救济手段

《美国破产法》和大多数国家的破产法规定了“撤销交易”的权力，可以撤销优先清偿、低价交易或其他未经授权的财产转移，并为债权人的利益收回已经转移的资产或收益。[26]撤销交易后，必须将先前交易或转移的资产退回。[27]在《美国破产法》第十五章的程序中，破产管理人只能基于与该州法律或与联邦破产法相当的外国法律才能启动撤销交易的行动。[28]

《美国破产法》第1509条（相当于《示范法》第9条规定的直接申请权）限制了外国破产管理人直接向法院提出申请。尽管第1509（a）条允许外国管理人“直接向法院”申请承认程序，但第1509（d）条指出：如果法院依据第十五章拒绝承认外国破产程序，则有权发布“任何必要且适当的命令，防止外国破产管理人从任何美国法院获取协助”。第1509（f）条进一步指出，如果出现外国管理人未依据第十五章的要求在美国提起诉讼而遭到法院驳回的情况，法院驳回外国管理人其他协助申请的风险也会增加。

denial of recognition under chapter 15 carries the risk that later attempts to seek comity and cooperation from U.S. courts will be barred.

United Kingdom Cross-Border Insolvency Regulations 2006

The United Kingdom adopted the Model Law in 2006 as the Cross-Border Insolvency Regulations 2006 (2006 Regulations). The 2006 Regulations are intended to supplement rather than replace the EU Regulation, to which, as of mid-2019, the United Kingdom remained subject. In the event of a conflict between the 2006 Regulations and the EU Regulation, the EU Regulation controls. The effect of Brexit on this issue has not been settled.

In large part, the 2006 Regulations adhere to the language and concepts of the Model Law. There are, however, several key distinctions:

- First, the 2006 Regulations vary from the Model Law to account for the British court system, the different forms of relief available under British insolvency law, and to clarify the provisions of the automatic stay following recognition.
- Second, the 2006 Regulations deny relief to numerous companies regulated or protected by separate legislation, such as certain public companies, insurance providers, U.K. credit institutions, and protected railway companies.
- Third, where permissible domestically under the U.K. Insolvency Act 1986, notification to foreign creditors of the ancillary proceeding may be made by advertisement in foreign newspapers chosen by the foreign representative.

Finally, unlike their U.S. counterpart, the 2006 Regulations do not preempt or exclude a foreign representative from applying for relief under the predecessor section 426 of the U.K. Insolvency Act 1986, *Co-operations Between Courts Exercising Jurisdiction in Relation to*

英国跨国界破产条例 2006

英国在 2006 年通过了《示范法》并据此订立了《跨国界破产条例 2006》(以下简称《2006 年条例》),旨在补充而非替代欧盟法规,截至 2019 年年中,它仍具有法律效力。如果《2006 年条例》与欧盟法规发生冲突,则以欧盟法规为准。但英国脱欧对此产生的影响尚未解决。

《2006 年条例》在很大程度上沿用了《示范法》的表述和概念,但仍有以下几个区别:

- 第一,《2006 年条例》不同于《示范法》,需要对英国法院体系、英国破产法下多种形式的救济手段以及承认程序后自动中止等作出规定。

- 第二,《2006 年条例》不适用于受特别立法规范和监管的公司,如上市公司、保险公司。

- 第三,英国 1986 年《破产法》允许外国破产管理人以报纸刊登广告的方式通知辅助程序中的外国债权人。

最后,与美国不同,《2006 年条例》并不禁止或排除外国破产管理人依据英国 1986 年《破产法》第 426 条向英国法院申请救济,也不排斥各法院依据破产法或普通法开展管辖权方面的合作。第 426 条也适用于澳大利亚、巴哈马、英属维京群岛、开曼群岛、海峡群岛、爱

Insolvency, or under the common law. Section 426 applies to insolvency proceedings in the courts of Australia, the Bahamas, the British Virgin Islands, the Cayman Islands, the Channel Islands, Ireland, the Isle of Man, and New Zealand, among others. Petitions for recognition and relief are often made in the alternative under the various statutory provisions in cross-border insolvencies.

International and Institutional Considerations

International Considerations

To enable the recovery of assets, a country's legal system should embody the recognized best practices of World Bank Principle C15 (box 5.1). A predictable and robust crossborder system is critical for the tracking and retrieval of stolen assets because these cases often involve multiple jurisdictions.

BOX 5.1 World Bank Principle C15: International Considerations

Insolvency proceedings may have international aspects, and a country's legal system should establish clear rules pertaining to jurisdiction, recognition of foreign judgments, cooperation among courts in different countries, and choice of law. Key factors relating to effective handling of cross-border matters typically include:

- A clear and speedy process for obtaining recognition of foreign insolvency proceedings;
- Relief to be granted upon recognition of foreign insolvency proceedings;
- Foreign insolvency representatives to have access to courts and other relevant authorities;
- Courts and insolvency representatives to cooperate in international insolvency proceedings; and
- Nondiscrimination between foreign and domestic creditors.

Cross-border insolvency agreements should be permitted and encouraged. World Bank Principle C17.5 on Cross-Border Insolvency

尔兰、马恩岛和新西兰等地法院的破产程序。依据不同的跨境破产规定，对外国程序的承认和救济措施也可视具体的情况进行选择。

国际层面和机构层面的考量

国际层面的考量

为了能够追回资产，一个国家的法律应收录目前公认最佳的世界银行准则 C15 的规定（见方框 5.1）。由于案件往往涉及多个国家，一个可预测且足够稳固的跨境系统对于追踪和检索腐败资产至关重要。

方框 5.1 世界银行准则 C15：国际层面的考量

破产程序常涉及国际方面，一个国家的法律体系应在管辖权确定，承认外国判决，开展跨国法院合作以及法律适用等问题上制定明确的规则。处理跨国案件的几个关键因素包括：

- 为承认外国破产程序制定明确、高效的流程；
- 承认外国破产程序后，授予必要的救济；
- 外国破产管理人可以诉诸法院或其他主管部门；
- 在跨国破产程序中，法院和破产管理人互助合作；
- 外国债权人与本国债权人互不歧视。

我们应当鼓励和认可跨境破产协议，世界银行关于跨境破产协议的原则 C17.5 规定：“当破产程序涉及不同国家的不同公司时，为了更

Agreements provides: "The system should permit insolvency representatives and other parties in interest to enter into crossborder insolvency agreements involving two or more enterprise group members in different States, in order to facilitate coordination of the proceedings. The system should allow the courts to approve or implement such agreements."

Institutional Considerations

Institutional capacity varies widely across jurisdictions. A country's legislative framework may be less important than the status of the judiciary and the rule of law (box 5.2).

BOX 5.2 World Bank Principle D1: Implementation—Institutional and Regulatory Frameworks

D1.1: Independence, Impartiality, and Effectiveness. The system should guarantee the independence of the judiciary. Judicial decisions should be impartial. Courts should act in a competent manner and effectively.

D1.2: Role of Courts in Insolvency Proceedings. Insolvency proceedings should be overseen and impartially disposed of by an independent court and assigned, where practical, to judges with specialized insolvency expertise. Nonjudicial institutions playing judicial roles in insolvency proceedings should be subject to the same principles and standards applied to the judiciary.

D1.3: Court Organization. The court should be organized so that all interested parties—including the attorneys, the insolvency representative, the debtor, the creditors, the public, and the media—are dealt with fairly, in a timely manner, objectively, and as part of an efficient, transparent system. Implicit in that structure are firm and recognized lines of authority, clear allocation of tasks and responsibilities, and orderly operations in the court.

The World Bank has issued principles for the development of adequate institutional frameworks (box 5.3).

好地协调推进破产程序，破产管理人和其他利益相关方可以签订破产协议并由法院批准执行。”

机构层面的考量

各个国家司法机构的能力相差甚远。比起国家的法律制度，法治水平和司法体系更为重要（见方框 5.2）。

方框 5.2　世界银行准则 D1：执行—机构和监管框架

D1.1: 独立、公正、实效。该系统应确保独立，公正裁决，法院恪尽职守。

D1.2: 破产程序中法院的职能。法院应公正审理、严格监督破产案件。若条件允许，选任专业的破产法官。在破产程序中，非司法机关履行与司法机关相似或相同的职能时，也应遵守相同的原则和标准。

D1.3: 组织庭审。法院应组织所有利益相关人参与庭审，包括律师、破产管理人、债务人、债权人、公众和媒体。确保庭审公正、及时、客观、透明和权威。这体现了各级法院明确的职权划分和有序运作。

为发展和构建完善的机构性框架，世界银行制定了一系列准则（见方框 5.3）。

BOX 5.3 World Bank Principles and Best Practices

In 2001, the World Bank and UNCITRAL, in consultation with the International Monetary Fund, designed the Insolvency and Creditor Rights Standard (the ICR Standard) to represent the international consensus on best practices for evaluating and strengthening national insolvency and creditor rights systems. The ICR Standard combines the World Bank Principles for Effective Insolvency and Creditor/Debtor Regimes (the World Bank Principles) and the UNCITRAL Legislative Guide on Insolvency Law (UNCITRAL 2004). The Financial Stability Board, which monitors and assesses vulnerabilities in the global financial system, has recognized the ICR Standard and designated the UNCITRAL and the World Bank as joint standard setters in the area of insolvency.

The World Bank Principles emphasize contextual, integrated solutions and the policy choices available for the development of those solutions. The World Bank Principles constitute the international best practices in the design of insolvency systems and creditor-debtor regimes. Adapting international best practices to the realities of individual jurisdictions requires an understanding of the market environments in which these systems operate, especially in developing jurisdictions, where common challenges include weak or unclear social protection mechanisms, weak financial institutions and capital markets, ineffective corporate governance and uncompetitive businesses, ineffective or weak laws, institutions and regulation, and a shortage of capacity and resources. These obstacles pose challenges to the adoption of systems that address the needs of developing countries while keeping pace with global trends and good practices. The application of the World Bank Principles in a jurisdiction will be influenced by domestic policy choices.

The effective functioning of the insolvency framework depends on both the substantive legal and regulatory systems and institutional factors. Institutions are the vital foundation on which the insolvency framework is based. Without effective institutions—judicial and administrative—the insolvency system can be unpredictable, slow, and unfair. The institutional framework has three main elements: (1) the institutions responsible for insolvency proceedings; (2) the operational system through which cases and decisions are processed; and (3) the requirements needed to preserve the integrity of those institutions, because the integrity of the insolvency system is the linchpin of its success. Several fundamental principles influence the design and maintenance of the institutions and participants with authority over insolvency proceedings.

方框 5.3 世界银行准则和实践范例

2001 年，世界银行、联合国国际贸易法委员会与国际货币基金组织进行磋商，制定了《破产和债权人权利标准》(以下简称 ICR 标准)，这代表国际上在评估和加强各国破产与债权人制度上达成了共识。ICR 标准结合了世界银行《关于有效破产及债权人债务人制度的准则》(以下简称《世界银行准则》) 和《联合国国际贸易法委员会破产法指南》(UNCITRAL 2004) 的内容。负责监管和评估全球金融体系薄弱环节的金融稳定委员会，高度认可 ICR 标准，并指定联合国国际贸易法委员会和世界银行为制定破产标准的权威机构。

《世界银行准则》强调全局性、综合性的解决办法和相应的配套政策。它是当前破产制度设计上的国际典范。将其在各国推广和应用还应考虑各国运行的实际市场和环境，特别是发展中国家面临许多共通的挑战，包括薄弱的、不清晰的社会保障机制，脆弱的金融体系和资本市场，低效的企业管理和缺乏竞争力的商业贸易，乏力或薄弱的法律、制度和监管，资源和产能严重短缺，等等。这些都为发展中国家采用该范例寻求与全球其他国家同步发展带来了阻碍。《世界银行准则》在一国的适用情况受该国政策的影响很大。

破产制度的有效运作取决于实质性的法律监管制度以及机构因素。机构是破产制度的重要基础。缺乏有效的运行机构，如司法机构和行政机构，就会造成破产制度变得不可预测、低效甚至有失公平。机构有三个组成部分：(1) 负责破产程序的机构；(2) 案件和裁决的执行操作机构；(3) 公正，这是破产运营成功的关键，所以确保以上机构公正运作的监督机构必不可少。这几项基本原则都会对破产机构设计和维护产生重要的影响。

The Conflict between State Confiscation of Criminal Assets and Insolvency Proceedings

Cross-border insolvency processes raise many complex issues. The pursuit of assets in a variety of jurisdictions requires careful strategic planning, especially when the laws of the different jurisdictions diverge. As a general rule, the location of assets will determine the applicable law. In some jurisdictions, assets held locally may be ring-fenced under local insolvency law giving creditors within that jurisdiction first priority.

In international corruption cases, assets may be the subject of a preservation order under the criminal law of a jurisdiction or under a mutual legal assistance treaty (MLAT) request from a foreign country. In such cases, assets may be held or "preserved" for years pending the conclusion of all criminal appeals abroad, removing the potential assets of an insolvent estate from the insolvency representative's balance sheet. Insolvency practitioners and law enforcement should attempt to cooperate to benefit both creditors and the victims of crime.

The conflict between criminal and bankruptcy proceedings was reflected in the wave of bankruptcies following the collapse of a series of Ponzi schemes in the United States in 2008 (Bernard Madoff—$18 billion; Tom Petters—$3.6 billion); 2009 (Robert Alan Stanford—$5.5 billion; Nevin Shapiro—$880 million; Scott Rothstein—$1 billion); and 2012 (Nikolai Battoo—$500 million). In these cases, conflicts arose between the U.S. federal criminal or civil asset forfeiture laws and the distributive regime of the U.S. Bankruptcy Code. For example, victims of fraud may be entitled to file a petition for remission of monies forfeited to the United States as the proceeds of crime entirely outside traditional bankruptcy proceedings. These

国家没收犯罪资产与破产程序间的冲突

跨国破产是一个很复杂的问题。在不同国家追回资产都需要仔细地规划和部署，尤其当各国法律不尽相同时。一般而言，资产的位置决定了适用的法律。根据某些国家的破产法，位于该国的资产可能会受到特定限制，使该国的债权人对负债资产享有优先权。

在国际腐败案件中，根据各国的刑法或跨国司法互助协定，相关资产有时受保全令的保护被冻结或扣押，直到外国刑事案件审结，才能将其从破产管理人的资产负债表中删除。破产从业人员应与执法部门通力合作，保护债权人和受害人的合法权益。

一系列庞氏骗局在美国引发的破产浪潮，体现了刑事诉讼与破产程序之间的冲突。众多金融大鳄被指控诈骗，涉案金额巨大。例如，2008 年，伯纳德 · 麦道夫涉案金额 180 亿美元；汤姆 · 佩特斯涉案金额 36 亿美元；2009 年，罗伯特 · 艾伦 · 斯坦福涉案金额 55 亿美元；内文 · 沙皮罗涉案金额 8.8 亿美元；斯科特 · 罗斯斯坦涉案金额 10 亿美元；以及 2012 年，尼古拉·巴图涉案金额 5 亿美元。在这些案件中，美国联邦刑事法律或民事财产没收法与美国破产法中的财产分配制度产生了冲突。例如，欺诈犯罪的受害人有权对美国没收的犯罪所得提起独立于破产程序的诉讼。这些诉求与美国破产法中“绝对优先”原则和比例分配原则产生了直接的冲突。同样，根据破产法，刑事案件

petitions may be in direct conflict with the policies of rateable distribution and "absolute priority" under the U.S. Bankruptcy Code. Also, a "victim" in a criminal case may be a "creditor" under bankruptcy law; but not all creditors are victims under criminal asset forfeiture law (compare, for example, a trade creditor with an investor in a Ponzi scheme).

A criminal asset forfeiture order can have the effect of removing assets from the pool of value available to an insolvency estate that would otherwise be available for rateable distribution to creditors. Likewise, assets held by third parties that would otherwise be subject to claw-back provisions under bankruptcy law may also be unavailable. In some cases, a debtor who is also a criminal defendant in pending proceedings may voluntarily turn over assets in settlement of a restitution action, fine, or penalty that are then used to compensate victims in preference to creditors who would have had rights under a bankruptcy distribution scheme.

When a debtor faces criminal charges, state forfeiture provisions can interfere with assets that would otherwise be subject to the jurisdiction of the court in which the insolvency or bankruptcy proceedings are being administered. State forfeiture provisions can also interfere with distributions from the bankruptcy estate. In many jurisdictions, upon commencement of an insolvency or bankruptcy case, all civil actions against the debtor are automatically stayed. The stay does not necessarily apply, however, to asset forfeiture proceedings commenced by the state. In the United States, for example, because forfeiture is considered punishment for a crime, forfeiture proceedings are not automatically stayed by a U.S. Bankruptcy Court filing by or against a debtor. The tension between insolvency proceedings and criminal asset forfeiture is illustrated by *Stanford International Bank* in box 5.4.

中的“受害人”可能是“债权人”。但并非所有债权人都是犯罪的受害人（例如，庞氏骗局中的债权人就区别于投资人）。

犯罪资产本可按照比例原则分配给债权人用于清偿，但一经没收，便从破产财产池中移除。第三方资产也可能面临同样的问题，本可依据破产法进行追讨，但一经没收，便无法清偿。在一些情况下，作为被告的债务人自愿移交资产用以履行恢复原状、罚金或其他刑罚，但依据破产分配的原则，它往往被优先用于清偿债权人。

若债务人面临刑事指控，国家没收程序可以干扰破产法院对资产的管辖和分配。许多国家在破产程序开始后，债务人相关的所有民事诉讼会自动中止，但中止并不适用于国家发起的资产没收程序。例如，在美国，由于没收被视为对犯罪的惩罚，因此美国破产法院也不会自动中止与债务人相关（债务人起诉或被起诉）的没收程序。方框 5.4 中，斯坦福国际银行对破产程序和没收犯罪资产之间的紧张关系做了详细的阐述。

BOX 5.4 The Stanford International Bank (in Liquidation)

Stanford International Bank (SIB), based in the Caribbean, went into receivership in 2009 when its parent company, the Stanford Financial Group was seized by U.S. authorities as part of the investigation into Allen Stanford (see the section titled *Claims against Corporate Officers, Agents, and Third-Party Facilitators* in chapter 3).

Under U.K. law, when a conflict arises between creditors' rights and the state's interest in confiscation of the proceeds of crime, victim creditors may be prejudiced if the state obtains a restraining order. A restraining order will prohibit the debtor from transferring assets to its victim creditors unless the creditors (or the insolvency representative) can establish a proprietary claim to the property stolen and bring themselves within the definition of a "third party" who "holds property" frozen by a restraining order. The restraining order will remain in force even if a debtor is prepared to repay all or part of the stolen funds. A preliminary decision of the English Court of Appeal of 2010 in *Re Stanford International Bank*[a] provisionally resolved the issue of whether $100 million in frozen sums should remain frozen or be released to foreign insolvency representatives acting on behalf of 22,000 creditor victims. The court held that the funds should remain frozen. The state was in a position to conduct an orderly distribution at the conclusion of the criminal proceedings, and a contrary policy could lead to a scramble by victims and insolvency representatives to secure the distribution of funds to satisfy their claims to the debtor's assets in preference to others.

In July 2011, however, Mrs. Justice Elizabeth Gloster of the English High Court released $20 million of the $100 million in frozen funds to the Antiguan insolvency representatives of SIB. These were considered "living expenses" needed to allow the Antiguan estate to preserve and pursue $5.5 billion in ancillary civil liability damages claims against certain banks, law firms, and other facilitators of the Stanford fraud before the statutes of limitation on such claims expired and to fund other asset recovery work. Mrs. Justice Gloster also indicated that the Antiguan insolvency representatives' claim to have been vested with the title to the remaining $80 million in frozen assets in London (by means of their appointment as insolvency representatives in April 2009 and by reason of the operation of Antiguan law vesting title to SIB's assets in the names of its insolvency representatives) prior to the July 30, 2009, issuance of an external Proceeds of Crime Act restraint order (upon an MLAT request from the U.S. Department of Justice (DOJ)), was likely to prevail.

方框 5.4　斯坦福国际银行（清算中）

斯坦福国际银行（SIB），总部位于加勒比海，2009 年进入破产程序。为了对艾伦·斯坦福进行调查，其母公司斯坦福金融集团被美国当局扣押。（详见第三章“针对公司员工、代理中介和第三方协助者的诉讼”一节。）

根据英国的法律，为债权人的权益与国家没收制度产生冲突时，如果国家发布限制令，则可能损害债权人的权益。限制令禁止将债务人的资产转让给债权人，除非债权人或破产管理人对资产享有特定权益，属于被限制令冻结的资产的“第三方”所有权人。即使债务人自愿从中偿还全部或部分债务，限制令仍然有效。2010 年英国上诉法院在斯坦福国际银行案[a]的初审裁决中就考虑了该如何处理 1 亿美元的涉案资产的问题，是将其继续处于没收被冻结状态还是将其解冻并交由代表 22,000 名债权人主张权益的外国破产管理人。法院最终裁决继续冻结有关资产。法院认为，国家有能力在刑事诉讼完结时对涉案资产有序分配，而相反的政策可能导致受害人和破产管理人互相争抢以确保自己的权益优先于对方获得赔偿。

然而，在 2011 年 7 月，英国高等法院的大法官伊丽莎白·高罗斯特将冻结的 1 亿美元中的 2000 万美元分配给了斯坦福国际银行在安提瓜岛的破产管理人。对于这被视为“生活费”的 2000 万美元，破产管理人可将其用于对相关银行、律所和斯坦福欺诈行为的协助者提请附带民事诉讼损害赔偿，申请保全和追查 55 亿美元相关资产或其他涉案资产直到诉讼时效终止。而早在 2009 年 4 月，破产管理人已依据安提瓜岛的法律获得斯坦福国际银行的资产所有权。所以在诉讼中，破产管理人主张，在 2009 年 7 月 30 日外国《犯罪所得法案》的限制令（美国司法部签署的一项司法协助协议）生效之前，就已经取得了位于伦敦的剩余 8000 万美元冻结资产的所有权。法官表示该主张很可能胜诉。

continued

In March 2013, the DOJ, the U.S. Securities and Exchange Commission (SEC), an SEC receiver, and the Antiguan insolvency representatives of SIB entered into a Settlement Agreement and Cross-Border Cooperation Protocol, which resolved the conflict between state-driven criminal asset forfeiture proceedings and the cross-border insolvency process. The DOJ, acting with the U.K.'s Serious Fraud Office, the Office of Justice in Bern, Switzerland, and the Attorney General of Ontario, sought to recover more than $300 million of bank deposits frozen in Canada, the United Kingdom, and Switzerland. The Antiguan insolvency representatives sought to use a portion of the available frozen funds to develop and pursue $5.5 billion in predominantly ancillary civil liability actions against banks, law firms, and other enablers of the fraud, including against Toronto-Dominion Bank for negligence and knowing assistance. Evidence has since been shared and cooperation is ongoing between the SEC receiver and the Antiguan insolvency representatives of SIB. The compromise between the parties may result in a substantially greater recovery.

a. [2010] EWCA Civ. 137.

In the United States, title to assets obtained through a criminal offense that are forfeited to the state are removed from the reach of bankruptcy because ownership of such assets is considered to have been transferred as of the date of the crime. A bankrupt estate consists of the assets of the debtor as of the date of commencement of bankruptcy (subject to the power to avoid fraudulent dispositions); assets forfeited as a result of a crime that occurred prior to the commencement of bankruptcy are not included. An order forfeiting funds in a bank account does not, however, forfeit funds that the debtor had previously paid from that account to third parties. A trustee in bankruptcy may assert claw-back claims and recover those funds. A criminal or civil asset forfeiture order does not divest a bankruptcy trustee of such claims. A claimant who can establish sufficient evidence of his legal interest in the property or who can establish that the property is subject to a constructive trust[29] may be able to supersede a forfeiture order.

A constructive trust is an equitable remedy imposed by a court to

续表

2013年3月，美国司法部、美国证券交易委员会（SEC）及其接管人和SIB的安提瓜破产管理人签署了和解协议和跨境合作协议，解决了国家没收犯罪所得与跨境破产程序之间的冲突。美国司法部与英国严重诈骗调查署、瑞士伯尔尼司法局以及加拿大安大略省总检察厅合作，追讨在加拿大、英国、瑞士的价值3亿加元的银行存款。安提瓜破产管理人利用部分可解冻的资金向其他银行、律所或其他欺诈协助人提起附带民事诉讼，追讨55亿加元的破产资产，其中就牵涉了多伦多道明银行的过失以及故意协助欺诈的行为。之后，美国证券交易委员会接管人和SIB安提瓜破产管理人共享证据互相合作，极大地促进了涉案资产的追回。 a. [2010] EWCA Civ. 137.

在美国，已被国家没收的犯罪财产不属于破产财产的范围。从犯罪之日起，财产所有权视为已经转移。破产财产由破产之日起的债务人资产组成（取决于撤销欺诈性交易的权力），破产开始前被没收的犯罪收益不计算在内。银行账户向第三方支付的资金不属于可被没收的资产，破产管理人可以申请撤销交易收回资产，刑事或民事的资产没收令无权剥夺破产管理人的这一主张。有充分的证据证明债权人对该财产享有合法权益或该财产属于表面委托的[29]，没收令失效。

表面信托是法律采取的一种公平救济措施。当一方因违反委托义

benefit a party that has been wrongfully deprived of its rights by another's obtaining or holding a legal property right through unjust enrichment or interference or through a breach of fiduciary duty. If the imposition of a trust is likely to affect the recovery of other victims from a limited pool of forfeiture assets, however, U.S. courts may conclude that the remedy is inequitable and refuse to allow the claimant to recover.[30]

In cases of corruption, the state may be the beneficial owner of public funds or assets that were misappropriated, including any profits derived from that property or any property into which it has been converted. Beneficial ownership adheres unless there is a bona fide purchaser for value without notice of the breach of trust. Saadi Qaddafi used funds belonging to Libya to purchase a $10 million property in London. The property was owned by a shell company of which Qaddafi was the beneficial owner. The English High Court found that Qaddafi held the house in constructive trust and ordered its transfer to Libya.[31]

Article 53 of the United Nations Convention Against Corruption (UNCAC) requires states to permit the initiation of civil actions by other state parties to establish ownership of property acquired through corruption and to recognize another state's claim as the beneficial owner. A successful state claimant in a property-based action will have priority over the defendant's other creditors (van der Does de Willebois and Brun 2013).

Criminal and civil asset forfeiture procedures have weaknesses; some jurisdictions lack a provision entitling general unsecured creditors, such as trade creditors, to be compensated from forfeited funds. Trustees and receivers can, however, seek to avoid certain asset transfers and may also seek recovery for damages. The benefits of having all assets (whether tangible or intangible, including the rights to sue facilitators of fraud or corruption) marshalled under the insolvency representative or the receiver

务或通过其他不正当的方式持有财产从而影响了财产合法所有权人的权益时，法院可以对其提供救济。但是，如果这种救济方式会影响其他受害人从有限的没收财产中获得清偿，那么美国法院可能会认定该救济违背公平而拒绝一方以此获得资产。[30]

在腐败案件中，国家可能是涉案资产（包括财产本身也包括其产生的收益）的实际所有人，除非有不知情的善意第三方，否则实际所有权人的权益将一直存在。萨迪·卡扎菲（Saadi Qaddafi）曾挪用利比亚的资金购买了位于伦敦的价值1000万美元的房产，并由空壳公司持有，而卡扎菲才是实际控制人。英国高等法院裁定，卡扎菲以表面信托的方式持有该房产，下令将其移交给利比亚。[31]

《联合国反腐败公约》（UNCAC）第53条要求各成员国允许互相提起确认腐败财产所有权的民事诉讼并承认国家是实际的所有权人。在财产诉讼中，胜诉的国家债权人相对于其他债权人享有优先权（埃米尔·威勒博伊斯和布伦，2013）。

刑事和民事的资产没收程序都存在一定的缺陷。一些国家并未允许无抵押的一般债权人从没收资产中获得赔偿，而破产管理人却可以撤销特定交易或获得相应的损害赔偿。法院认可将所有的财产（无论是有形的、无形的），包括对其他欺诈、腐败犯罪的第三方的起诉权都交由破产管理人统一安排。例如，在美国第七巡回上诉法院审理的美国诉弗吕克霍尔姆案[32]中，法官伊斯特布鲁克评论道：

have been recognized by courts, such as the Seventh Circuit Court of Appeals in *United States v. Frykholm*,[32] in which Judge Easterbrook commented:

> Neither side paid much attention to the effect of the fraudulent conveyance, likely because both sides are represented by forfeiture specialists and have focused on the language of § 853 and opinions interpreting that statute. Everything would have been clearer had the United States initiated an involuntary bankruptcy proceeding against Frykholm. That not only would have brought to the fore § 548 of the Bankruptcy Code but also would have provided a superior way to marshal Frykholm's remaining assets and distribute them to her creditors. Although § 853(n)(1) allows the Attorney General to use forfeited assets for restitution, it does not create a comprehensive means of collecting and distributing assets. Bankruptcy would have made it pellucid that Cotswold cannot enjoy any priority over the other victims and cannot reap a profit while Frykholm's other creditors go begging. Moreover, bankruptcy would have enabled the trustee to recoup the sums distributed to the first generation of investors, who received $5 million or so against $2.5 million paid in. Those payments could have been reclaimed under the trustee's avoiding powers and made available to all of the bilked investors.[33]

In *SEC v. Madoff*,[34] Judge Stanton, in commenting on the opposition to an application to modify a preliminary injunction to allow a group of creditors to file an involuntary bankruptcy petition against Mr. Madoff, stated:

> No opponent to the relief sought by the motion offers as familiar, comprehensive, and experienced a regime as does the

双方都没有过多地关注欺诈行为的影响，可能是因为双方都是没收专家，所以专注于第 853 条的表述和解释上。如果美国对弗里克霍姆发起强制破产程序，一切都会更加清楚。这不仅能发挥《美国破产法》第 548 条的作用，还是一种更好的分配弗里克霍姆资产的方式。尽管第 853（n）（1）条允许检察院将没收的资产用于清偿，但它并没有规定追回资产进行分配的具体手段。破产本可以明晰科茨沃尔德相较于其他债权人并不具有任何优先权，也不能在弗里克霍姆的其他债权人申请赔偿时获得任何额外的收益。此外，破产程序还能使破产管理人通过撤销交易的方式收回分配给第一批投资人的款项，即从 500 万美元的收益中收回 250 万美元，分配给所有的投资人。[33]

在美国证券交易委员会诉麦道夫案 [34] 中，一部分债权人为对麦道夫单独提起破产诉讼而申请法院变更预先禁令，斯坦顿法官拒绝该申请并评论道：

反对者并不能提供一个像《美国破产法》一样全面、熟练的方案来整合和抑制分散的针对麦道夫的独立诉讼，以管

> Bankruptcy Code for staying the proliferation of individual lawsuits against Mr. Madoff individually, marshaling his personal assets other than those criminally forfeitable, and distributing those assets among his creditors according to an established hierarchy of claims.
>
> A Bankruptcy Trustee has direct rights to Mr. Madoff's individual property, with the ability to maximize the size of the estate available to Mr. Madoff's creditors through his statutory authority to locate assets, avoid fraudulent transfers, and preserve or increase the value of assets through investment or sale, as well as provide notice to creditors, process claims, and make distributions in a transparent manner under the procedures and preferences established by Congress, all under the supervision of the Bankruptcy Court.[35]

Despite these rulings, conflicting interests continue to be an issue in forfeited property cases. Cooperation and coordination agreements between a trustee or receiver and a government have successfully mitigated some of the problems.[36] In *United States v. Petters*,[37] the court on its own motion chose to use the bankruptcy process over statemanaged restitution proceedings to redress the claims of victims, noting that "it would be a waste of resources to order restitution of pennies on the dollar (at best) when most victims have filed, or will be filing, parallel claims in bankruptcy proceedings."[38] The benefits of cooperation and coordination can extend beyond the sharing of information and the decision on what can be claimed and by whom to the preservation and maximization of value for the benefit of all creditors.

Cooperation was beneficial in the chapter 11 bankruptcy of California agribusiness giant SK Foods LP, a case involving a number of jurisdictional elements (see box 5.5).

理除没收犯罪收益外的个人资产，并将这些资产依据固定的顺序分配给债权人。

破产管理人对麦道夫的个人财产拥有直接处置权，为使债权人利益得到最大化满足，管理人依据法定授权可追讨资产、撤销欺诈性交易以及通过投资、出售等方式保有或增加资产价值和及时知会债权人等。同时，依据国会制定的程序和优先级，在破产法院的监督下以公开透明的方式将资产和收益分配给债权人。[35]

在没收财产的案件中，这些裁定尽管仍然存在利益冲突的问题，但破产管理人与政府之间的合作协调协议已经成功缓解了一些问题。[36]在美国诉佩特斯案[37]中，法院选择用破产程序而非国家没收程序来赔偿受害人，并提到“在大多数受害人已经或即将在破产程序中申请并行索赔的情况下，命令归还一美元中的几分钱（充其量），是一种资源的浪费”。[38]合作与协调的好处还包括信息共享，共同商讨决定起诉谁，以及以什么理由起诉，以便将全体债权人的利益最大化。

加利福尼亚农业巨头 SK 食品公司破产一案的判决书第十一章，充分体现了合作的益处。该案也涉及众多司法管辖的要素。（见方框 5.5）

BOX 5.5 SK Foods LP

SK Foods LP (SK Foods) was the second-largest processor of tomatoes for commercial use in the United States, with revenues of $270 million per year. Its customers included Heinz and Kraft. The business went into bankruptcy in the United States after the U.S. Federal Bureau of Investigation found evidence of price fixing, bribery, and sales of tainted tomato products. Scott Salyer, SK Foods' owner, was convicted of price-fixing and racketeering and sentenced to six years in federal prison.

SK Foods had owned several operating subsidiaries in Australia, collectively known as Cedenco. Bradley Sharp, the U.S. bankruptcy trustee, was advised bySK Foods' former management that SK Foods had transferred its interests in Cedenco to affiliates owned and controlled by Salyer. Audited financial statements corroborated this account. Cedenco was placed into Australian receivership shortly after the U.S. bankruptcy proceeding commenced. The Australian receivers sold its assets, paying all secured and unsecured debt in full and leaving a surplus of more than $50 million for Cedenco's owner.

Sharp determined, however, that the ownership of Cedenco had never been transferred and, therefore, Cedenco remained an asset of SK Foods. Sharp asserted ownership of Cedenco and the $50 million surplus. Salyer contested Sharp's claim and alleged that, as a result of subsequent transfers, Cedenco was owned and controlled by offshore asset-protection structures in the West Indies and the Cook Islands.

Sharp sought a determination of the ownership of Cedenco from the U.S. bankruptcy court and obtained an injunction against a series of defendants claiming an interest in Cedenco, including the offshore vehicles, thus preventing any further attempts to transfer interests in Cedenco outside the jurisdiction of the bankruptcy court. The Australian insolvency representatives refused to be bound by the U.S. injunction, risking the possibility that they would distribute assets to a Salyer entity, which would then transfer those assets to yet another entity beyond the jurisdiction of the Australian and U.S. courts.

In March 2012, Sharp obtained an order from the U.S. bankruptcy court appointing a receiver for the Salyer entities to hold any distribution received from the Australian insolvency representatives. He then sought and obtained an order from the Federal Court of Australia recognizing the U.S. bankruptcy court's receivership order. In August 2012, Sharp succeeded in obtaining a summary

方框 5.5　SK 食品公司

SK 食品公司是美国第二大西红柿加工企业，年收入达 2.7 亿美元，客户包括亨氏食品公司和卡夫食品公司。在美国联邦调查局发现其存在操纵价格、贿赂以及销售受污染的番茄产品等不法行为后，它在美国宣告破产。SK 食品公司的所有人斯科特 · 赛勒也因操纵价格和诈骗罪被判入狱 6 年。

SK 食品公司在澳大利亚拥有多个子公司，统称为 Cedenco。美国破产管理人布拉德利 · 夏普从公司前任管理层获悉，公司已将其在 Cedenco 的权益转让给了赛勒控制的其他关联公司。审计后的财务报表也证实了这一转让。在美国的破产程序启动后不久，Cedenco 也在澳大利亚进入破产程序，澳大利亚破产管理人将其资产出售，所获收益全额偿还了所有债务，并为 Cedenco 的所有人留下了超过 5000 万美元的盈余。

但美国破产管理人夏普认为，Cedenco 的所有权从未转让，因此仍然属于 SK 食品公司的资产并主张对 Cedenco 及 5000 万美元盈余的所有权。随后，实际控制人赛勒对破产管理人的主张提出异议。他认为，由于随后的转让，Cedenco 归西印度群岛和库克群岛的离岸资产保护公司所有和控制。

夏普向美国破产法院申请对 Cedenco 所有权的确认，并对其他主张 Cedenco 所有权的被告（包括离岸中介）申请禁制令，以防止 Cedenco 的资产被进一步转移到其他国家。澳大利亚破产管理人拒绝了美国禁令并冒险将资产分配给了赛勒掌控的其他公司，而这些公司随后将这些资产转移给澳大利亚和美国法院管辖范围外的另一家公司。

2012 年 3 月，夏普被美国破产法院任命为赛勒的破产管理人，有权获得澳大利亚破产管理人分配的资产。随后他就向澳大利亚法院申请对美国破产法院关于破产管理人任命的承认。2012 年 8 月，他又成功申请美国破产法院依据澳大利亚法律承认其作为破产管理人而享有 Cedenco 的所有权，理由是在破产程序启动前，他并没有将 Cedenco 的股份过户。

continued

judgment from the U.S. bankruptcy court that he, as trustee, owned Cedenco under Australian law because there had been no transfer of title to the shares of Cedenco prior to bankruptcy.

Because the Salyer entities and Australian insolvency representatives refused to acknowledge the judgment of the U.S. bankruptcy court as to his ownership, as trustee, of Cedenco, Sharp sought a judgment from the Federal Court of Australia recognizing his ownership rights. In 2013, the Australian Court found that the Salyer entities were estopped from relitigating the issues that had been decided by the U.S. bankruptcy court and recognized Sharp as the owner in trust of Cedenco.

It might have appeared that the Australian judgment cleared the way for the repatriation of the Cedenco proceeds. Prior to the court's decision, however, the Australian Federal Police made an application under the Australian Proceeds of Crime Act to prohibit the payment to Sharp, and declare the funds forfeit, claiming that they represented the proceeds of Salyer's criminal activity in the United States.

Had the criminal asset forfeiture action been successful, the creditors would have suffered because the Australian government would not have been required to use the proceeds to compensate victims of Salyer's crimes. The Australian Federal Police admitted that any forfeited funds would be used for other purposes. Sharp engaged in a concerted campaign to convince all parties that forfeiture would result in an injustice to the real victims, the creditors. He mobilized various U.S. senators and members of the California congressional delegation and conducted a forensic accounting analysis that showed the link between the funds and Salyer's criminal activities in the United States.

Before the initial forfeiture hearing, Sharp and the Australian Federal Police agreed to mediation and reached a settlement. Sharp convinced not only the Australian Federal Police, but also the DOJ, the U.S. Department of State, and legislators in California that the creditors would be hurt by the criminal asset forfeiture effort. The Australian Federal Police agreed to release 90 percent of the Cedenco proceeds, with the remainder to be deposited into the Commonwealth of Australia's Confiscated Assets Account. The Australian Federal Police also agreed to support Sharp's application to release the remaining proceeds for the benefit of SK Foods' creditors.

A cooperation agreement also helped resolve disputes in the bankruptcy of Banco Santos (see box 5.6).

续表

由于赛勒和澳大利亚破产管理人拒绝承认美国破产法院作出的夏普为 Cedenco 的破产管理人而享有所有权的判决，因此夏普又向澳大利亚联邦法院申请承认美国的判决。2013 年，澳大利亚法院裁定，禁止赛勒就美国法院已裁定的问题向该法院上诉，所以认可夏普为 Cedenco 的所有权人。 可见，澳大利亚法院的判决为 Cedenco 的清偿扫清了障碍。但是，在法院作出裁定前，澳大利亚联邦警局根据《澳大利亚犯罪收益法》没收了该资金并禁止向夏普支付，同时声称这笔资金是赛勒在美国的犯罪收益。 如果最终认定犯罪收益被成功没收，那么澳大利亚不得将其用于清偿赛勒的债务从而损害债权人的利益。澳大利亚联邦警局也承认，没收的资金将用于其他目的。为此，夏普组织了一场集中游说，向所有相关方力证没收财产对真正的受害人不公。他动员了许多美国参议员和加利福尼亚州国会代表团的成员，还开展了司法会计鉴定分析，显示了资金与赛勒在美国的犯罪活动之间的联系。 在没收听证会之前，夏普和澳大利亚联邦警局达成调解协议。成功说服了警局、美国司法部、美国国务院和加利福尼亚州的议员认同没收犯罪所得会损害债权人的利益。随后，澳大利亚联邦警局同意将 90% 的 Cedenco 的资产归还，剩余款项存入澳洲联邦没收资产账户。最后警局还同意夏普的申请，将剩余款项用于清偿 SK 食品公司的债权人。

合作协议也帮助解决了桑托斯银行破产一案的纠纷（详见方框 5.6）。

BOX 5.6 Banco Santos

Banco Santos, a Brazilian bank, became insolvent as a result of acts of fraud by its main shareholder, Edemar Cid Ferreira. Dr. Eronides Aparecido Rodrigues dos Santos, the Public Attorney, petitioned the bankruptcy court in Brazil for an order to pierce the corporate veil of Banco Santos and to extend the bankruptcy to several other entities, ultimately owned by Ferreira, that benefited from the diversion of assets from Banco Santos. Prosecutors had also filed a criminal complaint against Ferreira and obtained a seizure order against all the assets controlled by his entities, including those entities subject to the order piercing the corporate veil.

Those entities, now part of the bankruptcy estate, owned works of art in the United States that had previously been frozen pursuant to an MLAT issued by the Brazilian prosecutors. A conflict arose between the insolvency estate and the Brazilian criminal court. The insolvency estate sought to recover the art to compensate the victims of the bankruptcy, and the criminal court sought to confiscate the same assets for a state museum. Minister Massami Uyeada of the Superior Court of Brazil, the highest court for federal matters, ruled that the assets owned by the entities behind the corporate veil, although frozen by the criminal court, be transferred to the insolvency estate and used to compensate the victims of the bankruptcy. The court affirmed that frozen assets do not remain with the state, even if the seizure order was issued before the insolvency began.

After the judicial dispute in Brazil was resolved, the bankruptcy court and the criminal court had to collaborate to repatriate the assets to Brazil. Only the criminal court had the authority to carry out the MLAT. The bankruptcy court and the criminal court entered into a Term of Adjustment of Competencies and Mutual Cooperation. Under that agreement, the criminal court would fulfill the MLAT and, upon receiving the assets, transfer them to the insolvency estate.

方框 5.6 桑托斯银行

巴西桑托斯银行因其主要股东费雷拉的欺诈行为而宣告破产。检察官埃隆迪德斯向巴西破产法院申请揭开桑托斯银行的面纱，将破产财产的范围扩大到该银行转入费雷拉控制的其他公司的资产。检察官还对费雷拉提起了刑事指控并扣押了他控制的所有资产，包括被揭开面纱的公司。

这些实体是破产财产的一部分，他们在美国持有的一批艺术品依据先前巴西与美国的司法互助协定而被冻结，这使破产财产与巴西刑事裁定发生了冲突。破产程序试图追讨这批艺术品用于对受害人进行赔偿，而刑事法院则试图将其没收并交由州立博物馆。最终，巴西最高法院联邦事务部部长马萨米裁定，公司面纱背后的资产，即便被刑事法院冻结，仍属于破产财产，应用于受害人的赔偿。法院认为，即使冻结令在破产程序开始前签发，也不属于可没收的国家资产。

解决冲突后，由于只有刑事法院有权执行司法互助协定，破产法院与刑事法院合作将资产运回巴西。破产法院也与刑事法院订立了合作协议。根据该协议，刑事法院执行司法互助协定收到资产后，应将其转交给破产法院。

Key Points from this Chapter

- In many developing countries, outdated insolvency laws remain on the books, and there is limited or no local experience in conducting insolvency cases. These jurisdictions may face challenges in implementing insolvency as a tool to support cross-border asset recovery.
- Many countries have enacted legislation to ensure transnational consistency and proper oversight in the application and enforcement of crossborder insolvency laws.
- A country's legal system should ideally have clear rules pertaining to jurisdiction, recognition of foreign judgments, cooperation among courts in different countries, and choice of law.
- The pursuit of assets in a variety of jurisdictions requires careful strategic planning, especially where applicable laws diverge.

Notes

1. Although there can be overlap between offshore jurisdictions and developing countries, as used in this chapter offshore jurisdictions are those that provide financial services to nonresidents that are out of proportion to the size of their domestic economy, whether or not they would also be considered developing countries.

2. Using another indicator of court efficiency, resolving a contractual dispute takes, on average, 1,109 days in South Asia and 768.5 days in Latin America and the Caribbean (World Bank 2018).

3. UNCITRAL (United Nations Commission on International Trade Law), Status of Model Law on Cross-Border Insolvency with Guide to Enactment, UNCITRAL, Vienna (accessed August 5, 2019), http://www.uncitral.org/uncitral/en/uncitral_texts/insolvency/1997Model_status.html; Regulation (EU) 2015/848 of the European Parliament and of the Council of May 20, 2015, on Insolvency Proceedings, annex A, https://eur-lex.europa.eu/legal-content/EN/TXT/HTML/?uri=CELEX:32015R0848&from=en.

本章要点

- 许多发展中国家依然沿用落后的破产法且缺乏办理破产案件的经验。这些国家在将破产作为工具追查跨国资产时，可能面临极大的挑战。
- 许多国家制定了相应法律，即统一跨国破产案件适用的法律和执行程序并实施必要的监督。
- 理想情况下，一个国家的破产法律制度应在管辖权、承认外国判决、跨国法院合作以及适用法律选择等方面规定明确的细则。
- 跨国追查资产需要缜密的规划，特别是在各国适用不同法律的情况下。

注释

1. 尽管离岸司法管辖区于发展中国家之间可能存在重叠，但本章中离岸司法管辖区是指向非本地居民提供金融服务，并且其规模与国内经济实体不成比例的地区，与它们是否会被视为发展中国家无关。

2. 在南亚，使用另一个衡量法律效率的指标解决合同纠纷平均需要 1109 天，而在拉丁美洲和加勒比地区则需要 768.5 天（世界银行，2018）。

3. UNCITRAL（联合国国际贸易法委员会）《跨国界破产示范法现状与颁布指南》，维也纳（2019 年 8 月 5 日访问），http://www.uncitral.org/uncitral/en/uncitral_texts/insolvency/1997Model_status.html；2015 年 5 月 20 日欧洲议会和理事会第 2015/848 号条例，关于破产程序，附件 A，https://eur-lex.europa.eu/legal-content/EN/TXT/HTML/?uri=CELEX:32015R0848&from=en。

4. 11 U.S.C. §§ 1501–1532 (2019). These provisions repealed and replaced 11 U.S.C. § 304, *Cases Ancillary to Foreign Proceedings,* which had been in effect since 1978.

5. Federal Rule of Bankruptcy Procedure 1007.

6. 11 U.S.C. § 1517; 11 U.S.C. § 101.

7. Ibid. § 1506.

8. Ibid. §§ 1502(4), 1515–1517.

9. Ibid. § 1516(c).

10. In re Kemsley, 489 B.R. 346, 353 (Bankr. S.D.N.Y. 2013).

11. See, for example, In re Loy, 380 B.R. 154, 162 (Bankr. E.D. Va. 2007) (recognizing the United Kingdom as the COMI where a debtor had only temporary legal status in the United States, almost all the debtor's creditors were located in the United Kingdom, and English law governed the debtor's initial proposal for voluntary reorganization with his U.K. creditors, as well as a later bankruptcy proceeding); In re Chiang, 437 B.R. 397, 404 (Bankr. C.D. Cal. 2010) (recognizing a Canadian bankruptcy case as a foreign main proceeding because the debtor's permanent legal status in Canada and his strong personal ties indicated that Canada was his COMI).

12. 11 U.S.C. §§ 1502(5), 1515–1517.

13. Ibid. § 1502 (2).

14. In re Ran, 607 F.3d 1017 (5th Cir. 2010).

15. 11 U.S.C. § 1506.

16. H.R. Rep. No. 109-31 (2005).

17. In re British American Isle of Venice (BVI), Ltd., 441 B.R. 713, 717 (Bankr. S.D. Fla. 2010) (rejecting a public policy challenge to recognition based on allegations of purported procedural unfairness of foreign proceedings due to a claimed conflict of interest and confidentiality order with another creditor when the complaining party was afforded the

4. 11 U.S.C. § § 1501–1532 (2019). 该条款废除并取代了《美国法典》第十一编第 304 条从 1978 年开始生效的外国程序附带诉讼。

5. 联邦破产程序规则 1007。

6. 11 U.S.C. § 1517; 11 U.S.C. § 101.

7. Ibid. § 1506.

8. Ibid. § § 1502(4), 1515–1517.

9. Ibid. § 1516(c).

10. In re Kemsley, 489 B.R. 346, 353 (Bankr. S.D.N.Y. 2013).

11. 参见 In re Loy, 380 B.R. 154, 162 (Bankr. E.D. Va. 2007) 一案。（该案承认英国为主要资产所在地，债务人在美国只具有临时法律地位，几乎所有的债权人都位于英国，而英国法律对债务人的债务和破产程序具有管辖权。）在 In re Chiang, 437 B.R. 397, 404 (Bankr. C.D. Cal. 2010) 一案中，加拿大破产案件被认定为外国主要程序，因为债务人在加拿大具有永久居民身份，以及牢固的人际关系表明，加拿大是他的主要资产所在地。

12. 11 U.S.C. § § 1502(5), 1515–1517.

13. Ibid. § 1502 (2).

14. In re Ran, 607 F.3d 1017 (5th Cir. 2010).

15. 11 U.S.C. § 1506.

16. H.R. Rep. No. 109–31 (2005).

17. In re British American Isle of Venice (BVI), Ltd., 441 B.R. 713, 717 (Bankr. S.D. Fla. 2010)（以违背公共政策为由拒绝承认外国破产管理人必须基于外国不正当的委任程序，这造成了保密令保护的利益与另一方出庭及辩护权之间的冲突，尽管美国法律可以据此拒绝承认，但英属维京群岛没有类似规定）。

right to appear and defend in the foreign proceedings, and, although a conflict of interest may lead to disqualification under U.S. law, it did not under British Virgin Islands law).

18. Ibid. See also In re Fairfield Sentry Ltd., 714 F.3d 127 (2d Cir. 2013) (public policy exception cannot be invoked based on the argument that the British Virgin Islands proceedings were cloaked in secrecy and under seal because confidentiality does not offend U.S. public policy, the complaining party had the right in the British Virgin Islands to seek leave to access sealed documents, and "unfettered public access to court records is [not] so fundamental in the United States" as to justify denial of recognition); In re Millard, 501 B.R. 644 (Bankr. S.D.N.Y. 2013) (rejecting a § 1506 challenge based on a stay of judgment and potential rejection of default judgment for unpaid taxes by the Cayman Islands court when, among other things, similar laws applied under U.S. law and bad faith in allegedly seeking to avoid judgment, even if it could be found, rejecting as not ripe for consideration a § 1506 challenge based on a stay of judgment and potential rejection of default judgment for unpaid taxes by the Cayman Islands court, even if bad faith in allegedly seeking to avoid judgment under U.S. law could be found).

19. In re Qimonda AG, 462 B.R. 165, 183-84 (Bankr. E.D. Va. 2011) (denying a motion to excuse a trustee from compliance with a section 1522 of the Bankruptcy Code prohibiting cancellation of patent-licensee contracts on public policy grounds when the provision was enacted by Congress immediately following a decision allowing avoidance of such contracts; Congress's action was based on the effect avoidance of such contracts would have on American innovation and technology, which would impinge on a *statutory* protection fundamental to U.S. public policy). See also In re Gerova Financial Group, Ltd., 482 B.R. 86, 94–95 (Bankr. S.D.N.Y. 2012)

18. 同上。见 In re Fairfield Sentry Ltd., 714 F.3d 127 (2d Cir. 2013)（在该案中，并不能因为英属维京群岛的程序是秘密进行的而适用“公共政策例外”，因为“保密”程序本身并不违背美国的公共政策。诉讼方有权在法律程序中申请保密令，并且“完全公开庭审文件”也不属于美国法保护的“最基本的价值”，因此并不能据此拒绝承认外国程序）；In re Millard, 501 B.R. 644 (Bankr. S.D.N.Y. 2013)（即使存在恶意撤销诉讼的情况，如果美国有类似法律允许相同的情形存在，那么开曼群岛的程序中止或缺席审判就不构成第 1506 条的适用；但如果美国不存在类似的条款，那么不应该拒绝第 1506 条的适用）。

19. In re Qimonda AG, 462 B.R. 165, 183–84 (Bankr. E.D. Va. 2011)（拒绝免除破产管理人第 1522 条的义务，基于公共政策而禁止取消专利保护合同，该条款是美国国会在先前某决定允许撤销合同之后立即启动的。国会的行动是基于撤销此类合同会大大影响美国的创新和科技，进而损害最基本的保护公共政策的法定原则）。见 In re Gerova Financial Group, Ltd., 482 B.R. 86, 94–95 (Bankr. S.D.N.Y. 2012)（尽管美国法规定清算程序至少需要 3 个债权人提起，而百慕大法律允许本案只由 1 个债权人发起，但也不能据此适用第 1506 条的公共政策例外）。

(rejecting a § 1506 public policy objection to recognition notwithstanding that under U.S. law an involuntary petition requires at least three creditors while the winding up at issue was commenced by one creditor, as permitted by Bermuda law).

20. In re Toft, 453 B.R. 186 (Bankr. S.D.N.Y. 2011) (rejecting on §1506 grounds a request for access to debtor's emails held on two Internet service provider servers and a request to place a wiretap on such email servers without giving notice to debtor as violative of the Federal Wiretap Act, the Privacy Act, and notice requirements under the rules of bankruptcy); In re Gold & Honey, Ltd., 410 B.R. 357 (Bankr. E.D.N.Y. 2009) (denying relief to a creditor who, notwithstanding an automatic stay imposed by U.S. proceedings and a warning that proceeding abroad would be at his own risk, filed and prosecuted a proceeding in Israel as an end-run around, and in violation of, a § 362 automatic stay under the Bankruptcy Code); Jaffe v. Samsung Electronics Co., Ltd., 737 F.3d 1426, 28–29 (4th Cir. 2013) (denying a motion to excuse a trustee from compliance with a provision of Bankruptcy Code that prohibits cancellation of patentlicensee contracts on the basis of § 1522, though recognizing that by so holding it was furthering the public policy of the statutory provision that prevented cancellation of licenses) (affirming Qimonda).

21. 11 U.S.C. § 1520.

22. In re Daewoo Logistics Corp., 461 B.R. 175 (Bankr. S.D.N.Y. 2011).

23. 11 U.S.C. § 1521.

24. Federal Rule of Civil Procedure 2004.

25. See In re MMH Automotive Grp., LLC, 346 B.R. 229, 233 (Bankr. S.D. Fla. 2006) ("Rule 2004 does allow the Trustee to go on a general fishing expedition so long as the information sought relates to 'the acts,

20. 2011 年 Toft 公司破产案：债权人申请查阅债务人的邮件并在不通知债务人的情况下，对存储邮件的两个网络服务器进行窃听。法院以第 1506 条为由驳回了该申请，因其违反了《联邦窃听法》、《隐私法》及破产规则中的通知要求。2009 年 Gold & Honey 有限责任公司破产案：尽管美国自动中止了相关程序，也提醒债权人在外国提起诉讼风险自担，但债权人依旧在以色列提起终审审判，违反了《美国破产法》第 362 条自动中止的规定，因而法院拒绝对债权人提供司法救济。2013 年亚夫诉三星电子有限公司案：根据《美国破产法》第 1522 条的规定，法院驳回了破产管理人免于遵守"禁止取消专利授权合同"的申请。这样裁定也是为了推行相关公共政策，防止不当注销专利许可。（由奇梦达公司确认。）

21. 11 U.S.C. § 1520.

22. In re Daewoo Logistics Corp., 461 B.R. 175 (Bankr. S.D.N.Y. 2011).

23. 11 U.S.C. § 1521.

24. 2004 年联邦民事诉讼程序条例。

25. 参见 In re MMH Automotive Grp., LLC, 346 B.R. 229, 233 (Bankr. S.D. Fla. 2006)。（2004 年联邦民事诉讼程序条例允许破产管理人进行审前调查以获取与债务人经济状况、财产权益、相关行动或任何可能

conduct, or property or to the liabilities and financial condition of the debtor, or to any matter which may affect the administration of the debtor's estate.'"); In re Washington Mutual, Inc., 408 B.R. 45, 50 (Bankr. D. Del. 2009) ("A Rule 2004 examination is commonly recognized as more in the nature of a 'fishing expedition.'") (citing In re Bennett Funding, Inc., 203 B.R. 24, 28 (Bankr. N.D.N.Y. 1996)); In re Marathe, 459 B.R. 850, 858–59 (Bankr. M.D. Fla. 2011) (Rule 2004 discovery "is properly extended to creditors and third parties who have had dealings with the debtor").

26. 11 U.S.C. §§ 546–550.

27. Ibid. §§ 550–551.

28. Fogerty v. Petroquest Resources, Inc. (In re Condor Ins. Ltd.), 601 F.3d 319 (5th Cir. 2010).

29. See, for example, United States v. Shefton, 548 F.3d 1360, 1366 (11th Cir. 2008); United States v. $4,224,958.57, 392 F.3d 1002, 1004–05 (9th Cir. 2004); United States v. Schwimmer, 968 F.2d 1570, 1574, 1582 (2d Cir. 1992); United States v. Marx, 844 F.2d 1303, 1308 (7th Cir. 1988); United States v. Campos, 859 F.2d 1233, 1238–39 (6th Cir. 1988).

30. See, for example, United States v. Andrews, 530 F.3d 1232, 1238–39 (10th Cir. 2008); United States v. Durham, 86 F.3d 70, 73 (5th Cir. 1996).

31. Libya v. Capitana Seas Ltd. [2012] EWHC 602 (Com).

32. 362 F.3d 413 (7th Cir. 2004).

33. Ibid. 417.

34. SEC v. Madoff, 2009 U.S. Dist. LEXIS 30712 (S.D.N.Y. Apr. 10, 2009).

35. Ibid. at 3–4.

36. Article 57(5) of UNCAC provides that state parties may "give special consideration to concluding agreements or mutually acceptable arrangements on a case-by-case basis, for the final disposal of confiscated

影响债务人资产管理的信息。）In re Washington Mutual, Inc., 408 B.R. 45, 50 (Bankr. D. Del. 2009)（2004 条例中的检查权被广泛认为具有审前调查的性质）。[citing In re Bennett Funding, Inc., 203 B.R. 24, 28 (Bankr. N.D.N.Y. 1996)]; In re Marathe, 459 B.R. 850, 858–59 (Bankr. M.D. Fla. 2011)（2004 年条例中的调查允许扩展到债权人以及任何与债务人相关的第三方）。

26. 11 U.S.C. § § 546–550.

27. Ibid. § § 550–551.

28. Fogerty v. Petroquest Resources, Inc. (In re Condor Ins. Ltd.), 601 F.3d 319 (5th Cir. 2010).

29. 参见美国诉谢富顿案 548 F.3d 1360, 1366 (11th Cir. 2008); United States v. $4,224,958.57, 392 F.3d 1002, 1004–05 (9th Cir. 2004); 美国诉施维默案 968 F.2d 1570, 1574, 1582 (2d Cir. 1992); 美国诉马克斯案 844 F.2d 1303, 1308 (7th Cir. 1988); 美国诉坎波斯案 859 F.2d 1233, 1238–39 (6th Cir. 1988)。

30. 参见美国诉安德鲁案 530 F.3d 1232, 1238–39 (10th Cir. 2008); 美国诉达勒姆案 86 F.3d 70, 73 (5th Cir. 1996)。

31. 利比亚诉 Capitana Seas 有限公司案 . [2012] EWHC 602 (Com)。

32. 362 F.3d 413 (7th Cir. 2004).

33. Ibid. 417.

34. 美国证券交易委员会诉麦道夫案 2009 U.S. Dist. LEXIS 30712 (S.D.N.Y. Apr. 10, 2009)。

35. Ibid. at 3–4.

36.《联合国反腐败公约》第 57（5）条认为，国家在没收财产的过程中，应特别考虑签订相关协议，确定双方都接受的安排。

property."

37. United States v. Petters, 2010 U.S. Dist. LEXIS 55040 (D. Minn. June 3, 2010).

38. Ibid. 14–15.

References

UNCITRAL (United Nations Commission on International Trade Law). 2004.

Legislative Guide on Insolvency Law. Vienna: UNCITRAL.

———. 2014. *UNCITRAL Model Law on Cross-Border Insolvency with Guide to Enactment and Interpretation*. Vienna: UNCITRAL.

van der Does de Willebois, Emile, and Jean-Pierre Brun. 2013. "Using Civil Remedies in Corruption and Asset Recovery Cases." *Case Western Reserve Journal of International Law* 45 (3): 615.

World Bank. 2014. *Doing Business Report 2015: Going Beyond Efficiency*. Washington, DC: World Bank.

———. 2018. *Doing Business Report 2019: Training for Reform*. Washington, DC: World Bank.

37. 美国诉皮特案，2010 U.S. Dist. LEXIS 55040 (D. Minn. June 3, 2010)。

38. Ibid. 14–15.

参考文献

UNCITRAL (United Nations Commission on International Trade Law). 2004.

Legislative Guide on Insolvency Law. Vienna: UNCITRAL.

———. 2014. *UNCITRAL Model Law on Cross-Border Insolvency with Guide to Enactment and Interpretation*. Vienna: UNCITRAL.

van der Does de Willebois, Emile, and Jean-Pierre Brun. 2013. "Using Civil Remedies in Corruption and Asset Recovery Cases." *Case Western Reserve Journal of International Law* 45 (3): 615.

World Bank. 2014. *Doing Business Report 2015: Going Beyond Efficiency*. Washington, DC: World Bank.

———. 2018. *Doing Business Report 2019: Training for Reform*. Washington, DC: World Bank.

Appendix A. Country-Specific Regulations for Insolvency Representatives

This appendix contains an edited version of a Survey of the Law of Recognition of Foreign Insolvency Office Holders that was distributed to 15 different jurisdictions.[1] The survey, which was designed to be relevant to creditors in India,[2] was given to us by the authors with the permission to publish. Responses from 11 jurisdictions have been included in appendix A; some have been condensed.

a. Is recognition of foreign office holders permitted in your jurisdiction? What is the source and name or nature of the law governing the subject of recognition in your jurisdiction? Do you have one or more types of recognition (e.g., under [the United Nations Commission of International Trade Law] (UNCITRAL) there is foreign main and foreign nonmain recognition), and what are the principal differences between the two?

Belgium: Article 16 of Regulation 2015/848 installed a system of automatic mutual recognition of insolvency proceedings in other Member States. There is no need for exequatur proceedings. Under the International Private Law Code, the situation is somewhat different. A foreign court decision will be automatically recognized provided the debtor has its main establishment in the country where the foreign court decision has been rendered. In territorial proceedings, there will be an automatic recognition if the court decision was rendered by a court in a country where the debtor

附录 A　破产管理人的国际立法

本附录包含了外国破产办公室对 15 个国家或地区关于破产相关立法的问卷调查（编辑版本）。[1] 该调查的设计初衷与印度债权人有关，[2] 经作者授权发布，同时，本附录囊括了 11 个国家或地区的回复，部分经过精简。

a. 本国是否允许承认外国破产管理人？规范这一事项的法律名称、来源和性质分别是什么？是否存在多种类型的承认方式？［如根据联合国国际贸易法委员会（UNCITRAL），对外国承认的方式包括主要承认和非主要承认］，它们之间的区别是什么？

比利时：第 2015/848 号条例第 16 条规定，成员国间将自动相互承认破产程序，无需进行专门的承认程序。根据《比利时国际私法典》分情况而定。债务人的主要利益中心和判决地一致的，外国判决将自动得到承认。在管辖权诉讼中，如果法院的判决地是债务人的营业地，但非主要利益中心，判决也将自动获得承认。但这种情况下，确认的资产仅限于诉讼发生地的资产。除此以外的其他情形，外国法院的判决得到承认都必须经过专门的领事认证。在执行过程中，也必须提供领事证明书。例如，如果外国破产管理人需要出售比利时的资产，他

has an establishment, other than his main establishment. In such a case, the recognition will be restricted to assets located in the territory of the country where the proceedings were initiated. In all other cases, an exequatur must be obtained for the foreign court decision to be recognized. For enforcement, an exequatur must be obtained in all cases. For example, if a foreign trustee wants to sell Belgian assets, he will have to request an exequatur.

British Virgin Islands: Recognition and assistance is available only under Part XIX of the Insolvency Act 2003 to office holders of nine designated countries or economies (Australia; Canada; Finland; Hong Kong SAR, China; Japan; Jersey; New Zealand; the United Kingdom; and the United States). The British Virgin Islands High Court has ruled that the common law approach to recognition and assistance does not survive generally in the British Virgin Islands in parallel with the statutory scheme (although it may be afforded to office holders from the nine designated countries or economies). Part XVIII of the Insolvency Act contains provisions based on the UNCITRAL Model Law on Cross-Border Insolvency for giving and seeking assistance in insolvency proceedings, but this Part has not been brought into force.

Hong Kong SAR, China: Yes, recognition of foreign office holders is permitted. This is based on Common Law, as there are no statutory provisions governing the recognition of foreign insolvencies or requiring the Hong Kong SAR, China Courts to cooperate with foreign Insolvency Practitioners.

Jersey: In Jersey, there are two routes to recognition of foreign officer holders: under Article 49, Bankruptcy (Désastre) (Jersey) Law 1990 or Jersey customary (common) law. The United Kingdom, Guernsey, the Isle of Man, Finland, and Australia are prescribed jurisdictions under the Bankruptcy (Désastre) (Jersey) Order 2006 for their willingness to provide

必须提供领事证明书。

英属维京群岛：根据2003年《破产法》第XIX部分，对指定的9个国家或地区（澳大利亚、加拿大、芬兰、中国香港、日本、泽西岛、新西兰、英国和美国）的破产管理人提供承认和协助。英属维京群岛高等法院裁定，在英属维京群岛，普通法规定的承认和协助方式与该法案重叠的，无法生效（尽管可以向指定的9个国家或地区的破产管理人提供）。《破产法》第XVIII部分在联合国国际贸易法委员会《跨国界破产示范法》的基础上，制定了破产程序中提供协助的规定，但该部分尚未生效。

中国香港：是的。对外国破产管理人予以承认是被允许的。但这是基于普通法，因为并没有承认外国破产程序，或要求中国香港特区对外国从业人员予以协助的相关法律规定。

泽西岛：在泽西岛，有两种途径可以对外国破产管理人予以承认：一种是依据1990年《破产法》（泽西岛）第49条，另一种是依据泽西岛习惯法（普通法）。2006年《破产法》指定了英国、根西岛、马恩岛、芬兰和澳大利亚作为特定互惠司法协助地区，可依据第49条自动获得泽西岛对外国法院判决的承认。非上述国家或地区的外国破产

reciprocal assistance to Jersey. An Article 49 application for foreign recognition from a prescribed foreign court is usually granted automatically. Foreign office holders from nonprescribed jurisdictions can apply for recognition in Jersey under customary law as a matter of comity. Under both routes to recognition, the Jersey courts have regard to the rules of private international law and any UNCITRAL Model Law on Cross-Border Insolvency. Further, it has been suggested that the court take into account the following factors: jurisdiction; title to property for determination of the proper law in relation to that property; choice of law; and public policy. Generally, Jersey is prepared to accede to requests for foreign assistance insofar as these requests are consistent with its domestic laws and policies.

Singapore: Yes, recognition of foreign office holders is permitted. Such recognition may be based on common law and is at the discretion of the Singapore Courts. As of the date of publication, there are no statutory provisions governing the recognition of foreign insolvencies or holders of insolvent foreign companies. One exception to this is where a foreign company registered in Singapore goes into liquidation in its place of incorporation—the foreign liquidator in such a case has the powers and functions of a Singapore liquidator, until a Singapore liquidator is appointed by the court. Singapore has, as of the date of publication, not as yet adopted the UNCITRAL Model Law [on Cross-Border Insolvency], although it is likely to do so, along with proposing a new bill which would include provisions relating to the recognition of foreign insolvencies and office holders of foreign insolvent companies.

United States: Like the UNCITRAL Model Law [on Cross-Border Insolvency], there is foreign main and foreign nonmain recognition. Chapter 15 of Title 11 of the United States Code (Chapter 15) defines a "foreign main proceeding" as a "foreign proceeding pending in the country where

管理人可以依据习惯法向泽西岛法院申请承认。这两种承认途径，泽西岛法院都参考了国际司法规则和联合国国际贸易法委员会的《跨国界破产示范法》。此外，法院还会将下列引入内容纳入考量：管辖权、财产所有权（以决定与之相关的适用法律）、其他法律、公共政策的选择。一般而言，只要不违背本地法律与公共政策，泽西岛都愿意对外提供协助。

新加坡：是的。允许承认外国破产管理人。依据普通法给予认可，并由新加坡法院酌情决定。截至本书定稿之日，尚无与承认外国破产程序或外国破产管理人相关的法规。一个例外情况是，在新加坡注册的外国公司在其他营业地清算的情况下，外国破产管理人拥有新加坡破产管理人的权力和职能，直到法院指定新加坡破产管理人为止。截至定稿之日，新加坡尚未通过联合国国际贸易法委员会《跨国界破产示范法》，尽管未来可能会通过。同时，新加坡还提议了一项新法案，其中包括有关承认外国破产程序和破产管理人的规定。

美国：像联合国国际贸易法委员会的《跨国界破产示范法》分外国主要承认程序和非主要承认程序一样，《美国破产法》第十一编第1502（4）条将“外国主要程序”定义为“外国债务人的主要利益中心所在国的待决程序”，第1502(5）条将“外国非主要程序”定义为“债

the debtor has the center of its main interests." 11 U.S.C. § 1502(4). Chapter 15 defines a "foreign nonmain proceeding as a foreign proceeding, other than a foreign main proceeding, pending in a country where the debtor has an establishment." 11 U.S.C. §1502(5). The principal difference between the two types of recognition is that if a Bankruptcy Court recognizes a proceeding as a foreign main proceeding, then the automatic stay immediately springs into effect, the debtor may sell property of the debtor in the United States and can operate its business and exercise the rights of a trustee. If a Bankruptcy Court recognizes a proceeding as a foreign nonmain proceeding, then the petitioning party must specifically request additional specified relief from the Bankruptcy Court, which it has discretion to do so and must be satisfied that the relief relates to assets that, under U.S. law, should be administered in a foreign nonmain proceeding.

United Kingdom: In the United Kingdom (subject to minor variations between the countries forming the Kingdom as a whole), recognition of a validly appointed foreign insolvency office holder can be permitted. Recognition can be granted under the laws which implement the UNCITRAL Model Law [on Cross-Border Insolvency], the [European Union] Cross Border Insolvency Regulations, the Insolvency Act 1986, or the common law which predates each of the three more recent enactments. The United Kingdom recognizes an office holder of "main proceedings" and "secondary proceedings." Main proceedings are, in summary, those commenced in the sovereign state in which the entity or individual has its "center of main interests." An office holder recognized as the main proceedings practitioner will, in general, be afforded greater powers automatically than those appointed under secondary proceedings. That will include powers of investigation, asset seizure and sale, and powers to stay proceedings or bring litigation on behalf of the insolvent estate. A

务人营业地所在国的待决程序”。这两种承认的主要区别在于，如果破产法院将某程序确认为外国主要程序，“自动中止”立即生效，债务人可以出售在美国的财产，破产管理人可以依据职权行事。如果经破产法院确认为外国非主要程序，则申请方必须向破产法院专门申请特定救济，法院可自行裁决并确保该程序下资产的相关救济符合美国法律。

英国：在英国（各地区之间可能存在微小差异），允许对外国委任的破产管理人予以承认。可依据联合国国际贸易法委员会的《跨国界破产示范法》、欧盟《跨国界破产条例》、《1986年破产法》或三个法案之后的普通法予以承认。英国对破产管理人的承认程序也包括“主要程序”和“次要程序”。简单来说，主要程序是公司或个人在主要利益中心所在国进行的程序。一般而言，主要程序的破产管理人将自动获得比次要程序更大的权力，包括调查、扣押和出售资产的权力以及提起诉讼或中止诉讼的权力。次要程序则必须专门向英国法院提出授权申请，获得授权后，才可开展活动。

recognized office holder of secondary proceedings might have to apply specifically to court in the United Kingdom to take certain actions that a main proceedings office holder could take as of right once recognized.

Switzerland: Switzerland does not recognize the foreign trustees of foreign entities in bankruptcy. The foreign office holder can, however, apply before the civil judge (or the [Financial Market Supervisory Authority] in case of banks) for recognition of the foreign bankruptcy decree or any equivalent insolvency measures. There is only one type of recognition of foreign bankruptcies in Switzerland, which does not follow the UNCITRAL Model Law [on Cross-Border Insolvency]. Once the foreign bankruptcy decree is recognized, an ancillary bankruptcy, the so-called minibankruptcy, is opened in Switzerland. A Swiss liquidator is appointed to conduct the activities of the ancillary bankruptcy. The ancillary bankruptcy is strictly conducted in accordance with Swiss bankruptcy law (with some modifications provided for at Articles 170–174 of the [Swiss private international law act] (PILA); see below our answers to question (*g*)). The Federal Banking Act provides, however, for a simplified procedure of recognition of foreign banks in bankruptcy before the [Financial Market Supervisory Authority], where, as an alternative to the ancillary bankruptcy, the foreign trustee may be allowed to be remitted with the assets located in Switzerland (see below our answers to question (*d*)). On January 1, 2019, a revised law on cross-border insolvency—Chapter 11 of the Swiss Federal Code on Private International Law (CPIL)—entered into force in Switzerland. The amendments to the CPIL will facilitate the recognition of foreign bankruptcy proceedings and composition agreements. It will also foster international cooperation between the various courts and other competent authorities in such matters. The restrictive recognition requirements of the prior law, in particular the principle of reciprocity and

瑞士：（在 2019 年 1 月 1 日之前）瑞士并不承认外国破产程序中的破产管理人。但是，外国破产管理人可以向民事法官（在银行案件中，对应的是金融市场监督管理局）申请承认外国破产程序或其他等效的破产措施。瑞士对外国破产程序的承认只有一种，它并不遵循联合国国际贸易法委员会《跨国界破产示范法》。外国破产程序一经承认，即可启动辅助破产程序，也被称为“迷你破产程序”，是指委任瑞士破产管理人辅助破产行动。辅助破产是严格按照瑞士破产法进行的［《瑞士国际私法》（PILA）第 170–174 条进行了修正，请参见下文问题（g）的回复］。但是，瑞士《联邦银行法》规定，在金融市场监督管理局对外国破产银行案件予以承认之前，作为辅助破产的替代办法，允许外国破产管理人和瑞士的资产一并转移［参见问题（d）的回复］。2019 年 1 月 1 日，修订后的《瑞士联邦国际私法法典》（CPIL）第十一章关于跨国破产程序的法规在瑞士生效。这项修订将有助于瑞士对外国破产程序与和解协议的承认，同时，还将促进各法院与其他主管部门在该问题上的国际合作。先前限制承认的相关法律，特别是对等原则和强制性辅助破产程序，曾阻碍和拖延对外国程序的承认。修订后法律已将其取消，而债务人在国外的主要利益中心启动的破产程序在瑞士已正式得到承认。

the mandatory ancillary bankruptcy proceedings, have in the past impeded or delayed Swiss recognition of foreign insolvencies. Under the new law, these requirements are lifted—insolvency proceedings that were opened at the debtor's center of main interest abroad will now be recognized in Switzerland.

Australia: In Australia, a "foreign representative" can apply for recognition of foreign insolvency proceedings under the Cross-Border Insolvency Act 2008 (Cth), which implements the UNCITRAL Model Law [on Cross-Border Insolvency] in Australia.

A foreign representative is defined as a person or body, including one appointed on an interim basis, authorized in a foreign proceeding to administer the reorganization or the liquidation of the debtor's assets or affairs or to act as a representative of the foreign proceeding. A "foreign proceeding" is defined as a collective judicial or administrative proceeding in a foreign State, including an interim proceeding, pursuant to a law relating to insolvency, in which proceeding the assets and affairs of the debtor are subject to control or supervision by a foreign court, for the purpose of reorganization or liquidation. Pursuant to the Model Law [on Cross-Border Insolvency], foreign proceedings may be recognized as "foreign name proceedings" or "foreign nonmain proceedings." The form of recognition impacts upon the relief a court will grant upon recognition. When a court recognizes a proceeding as a "foreign main proceeding," certain relief (including stays of proceedings against the debtor and execution against the debtor's assets) follows automatically. On recognizing a proceeding as a "foreign nonmain proceeding," relief may be awarded at the court's discretion and the court must take into account whether the assets subject to the relief should be dealt with in the foreign nonmain proceeding (as opposed to a different insolvency proceeding, whether main or nonmain).

澳大利亚：在澳大利亚，“外国破产管理人”可以依据《2008年跨境破产法案》申请对外国破产程序的承认。该法也是联合国国际贸易法委员会《跨国界破产示范法》在澳大利亚实施的体现。

外国破产管理人，是指在外国程序中被任命管理债务人资产、业务，进行重组或清算的个人或机构，也包括临时任命的个人或机构。“外国程序”，是指依据破产相关的法律，在外国进行的司法或行政的诉讼集合，也包括临时程序。在该程序中，债务人的资产和事务将由法院监督或控制以完成重组或清算。根据《跨国界破产示范法》，外国程序可以分为“外国主要程序”和“外国非主要程序”两种形式。不同承认形式会影响法院给予的救济权限。当法院将某程序确认为“外国主要程序”时，某些救济（包括针对债务人的诉讼中止和资产执行）将立即生效。而在“外国非主要程序”中，法院可以酌情决定是否给予救济，并且会考虑救济所涉及的资产是否应该由非主要程序处理（相对于其他破产程序而言，不论主要或非主要）。此外，1966年《破产法》第29（2）条规定，澳大利亚法院必须为“指定国家”的破产管辖权法院提供必要的协助（针对个人破产）。而2001年《公司法》第581（2）条对公司破产作出了相应的规定。尽管这些规定并没有明确承认外国破产管理人，但他们提供的救济措施一般意味着对外国破产管理人和破产程序的承认，如依据第29条允许破产资产转交给外国破产管理人。在澳大利亚，关于承认外国破产管理人的普通法还不够完善，也许可以通过执行普通法中对外国裁判的认可，或通过某些法院的对等管辖来达到承认外国破产管理人的目的，但这很少见。就我

In addition, section 29(2) of the Bankruptcy Act 1966 (Cth) provides that Australian courts must act in aid of the courts of "prescribed countries" that have jurisdiction in bankruptcy (that is, insolvency of an individual) and may act in aid of courts of other countries that have jurisdiction in bankruptcy. An equivalent provision with regard to companies can be found in section 581(2) of the Corporations Act 2001 (Cth). Although those provisions do not expressly contemplate recognition of foreign office holders, the remedies they provide tend to imply recognition of the foreign office holders and proceedings. For example, section 29 has been used to transfer assets to a foreign trustee in bankruptcy. The common law relating to the recognition of foreign insolvency officers is not well developed in Australia. It is possible for the appointment of a foreign insolvency practitioner to be recognized in Australia by operation of the common law of the recognition of foreign judgments, or by operation of the equitable jurisdiction of some courts, but this is very rare and (as far as we know) unheard of subsequent to the enactment of the Model Law [on Cross-Border Insolvency].

United Arab Emirates: No, although there are limited exceptions for the Dubai International Financial Centre (DIFC) area. The DIFC has a separate insolvency law from the rest of the United Arab Emirates, DIFC Law No. 3 of 2009. United Arab Emirates (non-DIFC) law is based on Arab Civil Law, a mixture of French Civil Code with Islamic principles from the Ottoman Majelle. There are no statutory provisions governing the recognition of foreign insolvencies or requiring the United Arab Emirates courts to cooperate with foreign insolvency practitioners. The DIFC law, which applies only to insolvency of companies and assets within the DIFC geographical area, is a common law–based jurisdiction.

Cayman Islands: Foreign office holders can be recognized in the

们所知，在《跨国界破产示范法》公布后也没有相关案例。

阿联酋：不承认。尽管迪拜国际金融中心（DIFC）地区存在少数例外，因其破产法与阿联酋其他地区不同。2009 年第 3 号 DIFC 法以阿联酋民法规范为基础，结合了法国民法以及奥斯曼帝国的伊斯兰教法原则。这里并没有承认外国破产程序以及协助外国破产管理人的相关法律法规。以普通法为基础的 DIFC 破产法仅适用其区域内的破产公司与资产。

开曼群岛：外国破产管理人可以在开曼群岛得到承认，大部分情

Cayman Islands and have commenced and participated in proceedings before the Grand Court of the Cayman Islands (a superior court of record, the Grand Court) without difficulty on many occasions. Although the UNCITRAL Model Law [on Cross-Border Insolvency] is not applicable in the Cayman Islands, there are two avenues for recognition: (1) common law recognition and (2) statutory recognition. The common law jurisdiction is set out in a substantial body of local case law and is similar to that of England, the case law of which is of persuasive value in the Cayman Islands due to its legal status as a British Overseas Territory. The statutory basis for recognition is by way of the International Cooperation provisions of Part XVII of the Cayman Islands' Companies Law (as revised) (the Companies Law), which provides a convenient statutory mechanism for the recognition of foreign trustee, liquidator, or other official (a foreign representative) appointed in respect of a foreign corporation or other foreign legal entity (a debtor) for the purposes of a foreign bankruptcy proceeding, including proceedings for the purpose of reorganizing or rehabilitating an insolvent debtor (a foreign bankruptcy proceeding), in the country of its incorporation or establishment. The purpose of Part XVII is to provide foreign representatives with a convenient and expeditious method of establishing their credentials and right to act on behalf of a debtor in a way that will have universal effect within the Cayman Islands, without the need to establish their right separately as against every individual counterparty.

b. What elements are required to be proven or established for a foreign office holder to successfully seek recognition in your jurisdiction?

Belgium: See response to question (*a*).

British Virgin Islands: The foreign office holder will need to establish that the proceedings in which he or she is appointed are a collective judicial or administrative proceeding in one of the designated countries,

况下，外国破产管理人都可向开曼群岛高等法院申请承认。尽管联合国国际贸易法委员会《跨国界破产示范法》在开曼群岛不适用，但仍有两种确认途径：（1）普通法承认；（2）法定承认。普通法承认体现在大量的地方判例中，与英国的判例法相似，由于开曼群岛是英国的海上地区，英国的判例法在开曼群岛同样具有法律效力。而法定承认则源于开曼群岛《公司法》（修订版）第XVII部分关于国际合作的规定，它为外国破产管理人、委托人或其他外国破产公司委任的人员，提供了方便、快捷的法律程序，以便于他们代表债务人行使职权。这在开曼群岛内具有普遍的法律效力，不需要依据不同的诉讼对象分别确立他们的职权。

b. 外国破产管理人需要具备什么条件或要素，才能成功获得本国的承认?

比利时：详见问题（a）的回复。

英属维京群岛：外国破产管理人首先需要在特定国家通过集体司法诉讼或行政诉讼（也包括破产法的临时程序）获得委任资格，并受外国法院的控制和监督，以完成破产重组或清算。随后可向本国法院

including an interim proceeding, pursuant to a law relating to insolvency, in which proceeding the property and affairs of the debtor are subject to control or supervision by a foreign court, for the purpose of reorganization, liquidation, or bankruptcy. Once that is established, in determining an application for recognition and assistance, the court shall be guided by what will best ensure the economic and expeditious administration of the foreign proceeding to the extent consistent with: (1) the just treatment of all persons claiming in the foreign proceeding; (2) the protection of persons in the [British] Virgin Islands who have claims against the debtor against prejudice and inconvenience in the processing of claims in the foreign proceeding; (3) the prevention of preferential or fraudulent dispositions of property subject to the foreign proceeding, or the proceeds of such property; (4) the need for distributions to claimants in the foreign proceedings to be substantially in accordance with the order of distributions in a [British] Virgin Islands insolvency; and (5) comity.

Hong Kong SAR, China: Application is made by letter of request in the foreign jurisdiction requesting the High Court in Hong Kong SAR, China seeking judicial assistance. The letter of request must be from a common law jurisdiction with a similar substantive insolvency law; and, the request must be for an order of a type that is available to liquidators under Hong Kong SAR, China's insolvency regime. By way of example, in the recent *African Minerals* case, English administrators were denied recognition to enforce a moratorium against disposal of assets, which was available to the administrators in England pursuant to the Insolvency Act [1986], as no equivalent statutory remedy was available in Hong Kong SAR, China.

Jersey: See response to question (*a*). In respect of an Article 49 application under the Bankruptcy (Désastre) (Jersey) Law 1990 made by

申请承认和协助，法院将以最为经济、快速的流程对外国程序进行确认，确保其符合以下条件：(1) 原外国诉讼应对所有的诉讼主体公平对待；(2) 在英属维京群岛提出索赔申请的债权人在原外国程序中也受到公平的对待；(3) 原外国程序对破产资产及其收益并无优先清偿、欺诈处置等不当行为；(4) 外国程序中对债权人的资产分配应基本符合英属维京群岛的分配顺序；(5) 各国相互礼让。

中国香港：外国法院以书面申请的方式向中国香港高等法院寻求司法协助。具有相关实质性破产法的普通法国家才可申请。同时，申请的协助必须是中国香港破产法制度中可提供的法令。例如，在非洲矿产案中，英国破产管理人在英国可依据 1986 年《破产法》申请暂停资产处置的强制令。但由于在香港的破产制度中并没有相对应的救济手段，所以香港法院驳回了该申请。

泽西岛：请参阅对问题 (a) 的答复。对于指定国家的外国法院，根据 1990 年《破产法》(泽西岛) 第 49 条提出申请，该申请本身即被

the foreign court of a prescribed country, the request itself is deemed as sufficient authority for a Jersey court to exercise its jurisdiction to grant foreign recognition. When assisting a foreign court in this way, a Jersey court may have regard to any UNCITRAL model law on cross-border insolvency to the extent that it considers it appropriate to do so. Further, the Royal Court has discretion as to whether it applies Jersey law or the law of the requesting country when granting assistance. For applications made by foreign office holders to whom Article 49 does not apply, applications are made by way of a letter of request from the foreign court administering the insolvency. Typically, the applicant consults with the Viscount's Department (the enforcement officer of the Royal Court in Jersey) before an application is issued in Jersey in order to ensure that the order sought is drafted in suitable terms. To establish an application for foreign recognition, there has to be a valid connection between the debtor and the law under which the insolvency occurred.

Singapore: Recognition is at the discretion of the Singapore Courts and must be consistent with justice and public policy of Singapore, including that the interests of domestic creditors would not be prejudiced. There are otherwise no specific elements to be met.

United States: To seek recognition, the foreign office holder must file a petition for recognition under Chapter 15 with the Bankruptcy Court. The elements required to seek recognition under Chapter 15 are as follows: (1) a certified copy of the decision commencing such foreign proceeding and appointing the foreign representative; (2) a certificate from the foreign court affirming the existence of such foreign proceeding and of the appointment of the foreign representative; or (3) in the absence of evidence referred to in paragraphs (1) and (2), any other evidence acceptable to the court of the existence of such foreign proceeding and of the appointment of the foreign

视为泽西岛法院对外国程序的充分承认与授权，此时，外国法院可适当参考联合国国际贸易法委员会《跨国界破产示范法》。皇家法院在给予协助时，可自行决定适用泽西岛法律或申请国的法律。而对于不适用第 49 条的外国破产管理人，应通过外国法院提出书面申请，通常，在申请之前应先咨询泽西岛皇家法院的下属执行部门，确保以适当的条款提起申请。此外，对外国程序的承认还需要确保债务人与破产地国家的法律存在实质性的关联。

新加坡：新加坡法院可自行裁决承认与否，一般要求是，必须与新加坡的司法与公共政策保持一致，不损害国内债权人的利益。除此以外，没有特定的要求。

美国：为了获得承认，外国破产管理人必须依据第十五章向破产法院提交承认申请书，以及如下文件：（1）外国破产程序以及外国破产管理人任命的认证副本；（2）外国法院签发的证明外国程序以及外国破产管理人任命的证书原件；（3）在无法提供前述两项证明时，法院可接受的其他证据［《美国法典》第十一编 1515（b）条（1）–（3）］。另外，还应附上一份声明书，表明外国破产管理人确认知晓与债务人相关的所有外国诉讼程序。

representative (11 U.S.C. § 1515(b)(1)–(3)). Also, “a petition for recognition shall also be accompanied by a statement identifying all foreign proceedings with respect to the debtor that are known to the foreign representative.” 11 U.S.C. § 1515(c).

United Kingdom: This differs slightly depending on whether recognition is sought by a European Union, Commonwealth, or other overseas office holder. In broad summary, you must show that the office holder is validly appointed in respect of a legitimate “collective” insolvency process in the foreign jurisdiction. You must also explain whether the foreign insolvency process is a main or secondary process. You must also provide a number of certified copies (or originals) of supporting documentation to prove the authority and scope of the foreign proceedings.

Switzerland: Article 166 (PILA) lists five cumulative requirements for the recognition of foreign insolvency measures: (1) proper jurisdiction of the foreign bankruptcy authority; (2) enforceability in the state in which the decision was taken (the measure does not need to be final); (3) legal standing of the applicant; (4) absence of grounds for refusal of recognition according to article 27 PILA; and (5) reciprocity rights in the state in which the decision was taken (see our answer to question (*j*)). Grounds for refusal of recognition according to Article 27 PILA are the following: (1) the foreign bankruptcy decree is manifestly incompatible with Swiss public order (see our answer to question (*e*)) (this legal requirement is applied ex officio by the judge); (2) a party establishes that it did not receive proper notice under either the law of its domicile or that of its habitual residence, unless such party proceeded on the merits without reservation; (3) a party establishes that the decision was rendered in violation of fundamental principles pertaining to the Swiss conception of procedural law, including the fact that said party did not have an opportunity to present its defense (see below

英国：对外国程序的承认，依据外国破产管理人来自欧盟、英联邦或其他国家而有所不同。概括地说，必须证明外国“集合”破产程序对破产管理人的有效任命。同时必须说明外国破产程序为主要程序还是非主要程序，以及提供诸多证明外国程序及其职权范围的文件的正本或副本。

瑞士：第 166 条（PILA）列出了承认外国破产程序的五项要求：（1）外国破产管理机构具有合法管辖权；（2）所在州作出承认决定具有可执行性（未必是最终措施）；（3）申请人的合法地位；（4）不存在 PILA 第 27 条中拒绝承认的事由；（5）所在州与相关国家存在互惠关系［详见对问题（j）的回复］。根据 PILA 第 27 条，拒绝承认的理由包括：（1）外国破产法令明显违背瑞士的公共政策［该项由法官自行判定，参考我们对问题（e）的回复］；（2）一方没有获得永居地或常住地法律的通知，除非该方本身充分掌握案情信息；（3）一方确认一旦承认，会违反瑞士程序法中某些基本原则，包括该方被剥夺抗辩机会等［参考下文对问题（e）的回复］；（4）一方确定双方争议的标的与瑞士其他待决诉讼的标的重合，或者已经在瑞士获得裁决，又或者在第三国获得裁决且瑞士承认该裁决的效力。瑞士不得根据案情审查外国裁决。

our answer to question (*e*)); (4) a party establishes that a dispute between the same parties and with respect to the same subject matter is the subject of pending proceedings in Switzerland or has already been decided there, or that such dispute has previously been decided in a third state, provided that the latter decision fulfills the prerequisites for its recognition. A foreign decision may not be reviewed on the merits.

Australia: *Pursuant to the [UNCITRAL] Model Law [on Cross-Border Insolvency]*: In order to obtain recognition of a foreign proceeding, the foreign representative must prove that he satisfies the definition of "foreign representative" in the Model Law. That is, he must be authorized in a foreign proceeding to administer the reorganization or the liquidation of the debtor's assets or affairs, or to act as a representative of the foreign proceeding. Article 15 of the Model Law requires the foreign representative to adduce at the time of application: (1) a certified copy of the decision commencing the foreign proceeding and appointing a foreign representative; (2) a certificate from the foreign court affirming the existence of the foreign proceeding and of the appointment of the foreign representative; or (3) in the absence of evidence of (1) and (2), any other evidence acceptable to the court of the existence of the foreign proceeding and of the appointment of the foreign representative. This Article has not been the subject of jurisprudence in Australia, and as yet there is no guidance from Australian courts as to what other evidence of the foreign proceeding will be acceptable. The foreign representative will also need to establish that the foreign proceeding is either a foreign main proceeding or a foreign nonmain proceeding. In order for a proceeding to be characterized as a foreign main proceeding, the foreign representative will need to prove that the proceeding is taking place in the jurisdiction where the debtor has the "center of its main interests." Article 16 of the Model Law provides that absent evidence to the contrary, the

澳大利亚： 根据（联合国国际贸易法委员会）《跨国界破产示范法》（以下简称《示范法》），对外国程序的承认，要求外国破产管理人证明其满足《示范法》对“外国破产管理人”的定义，即获得外国程序的授权以管理债务人的资产或事务，完成破产重组或清算，或代理外国诉讼。《示范法》第 15 条要求外国破产管理人在申请时应提交：（1）外国破产程序启动，外国破产管理人获得任命的证明副本；（2）外国法院签发的确认外国程序存在以及外国破产管理人任命的证明原件；（3）在无法提供前述两项证明的情况下，其他法院可以接受的证据。在澳大利亚，尚未有对该事项的具体规定，澳大利亚法院也还未明确可被接受的其他证据具体包括什么。此外，外国破产管理人还需要确定该外国程序属于主要程序还是非主要程序。主要程序中，需要证明破产程序受债务人的“主要利益中心”所在国管辖。《示范法》第 16 条规定，未提出相抗证据，推定债务人注册地或个人常住地是债务人的主要营业地。在非主要程序中，则需要证明该程序是在债务人营业地的国家进行的，这表示“债务人在此的营业活动并非暂时性的经济活动”。

debtor's registered office, or habitual residence in the case of an individual, is presumed to be the center of the debtor's main interests. In order to establish that a proceeding is a foreign nonmain proceeding, the foreign representative will need to prove that the proceeding is taking place in a State where the debtor has an "establishment," which means "a place of operations where the debtor carries out non-transitory economic activity."

Pursuant to the Bankruptcy Act and the Corporations Act: Assistance under the Bankruptcy Act and the Corporations Act must be sought by letter of request from a foreign court that the Australian court act in aid of an external administration. Under the statutes, there is nothing further that is required. However, the precise form of the assistance to be provided by the Australian court would likely depend on the evidence before the court.

United Arab Emirates: A foreign office holder cannot successfully seek recognition in the United Arab Emirates courts. The authorities (non–Dubai International Financial Centre) will accept control of a foreign entity through a power of attorney if issued before a notary in accordance with the corporate law of such country.

Cayman Islands: Under the common law rules applicable in the Cayman Islands, a representative of a company, appointed by a court in its country of incorporation (that is, someone equivalent to an official liquidator or trustee in bankruptcy), is entitled to recognition automatically, without special formalities. The procedure for recognition under Part XVII is set out in the Cayman Islands' Foreign Bankruptcy (International Cooperation) Rules 2008, pursuant to which an application for recognition must be supported by evidence of, inter alia, an affidavit of foreign law that explains the powers and duties of the foreign representative under the law of the place of his appointment.

根据 1996 年《破产法》和 2001 年《公司法》：必须由外国法院书面申请澳大利亚提供两法规定的协助，即澳大利亚法院在外部行政管理层面予以协助，法律对此并无额外要求。但协助的具体形式可依据澳大利亚法院收到的证据决定。

阿联酋：外国破产管理人无法在阿联酋法院获得承认。除非通过依据外国公司法公证后的委任书，本国（除迪拜国际金融中心以外）才可以对外国公司采取控制措施。

开曼群岛：依据开曼群岛适用的普通法，公司注册国法院委任的公司代表（相当于破产管理人）无需专门的手续，自动获得承认。根据 2008 年《开曼群岛外国破产（国际合作）条例》第 XVII 部分中关于承认程序的规定，承认申请必须提交一份声明书，阐明外国程序所委任的破产管理人的职责与权力。

c. In some jurisdictions there are special rules governing the recognition of insolvency office holders of foreign financial institutions or insurance companies (such as under the Financial Markets Supervisory Authority in Switzerland). Do you have any such special rules in your jurisdiction? If so, what is required to obtain recognition?

Belgium: No.

British Virgin Islands: No.

Hong Kong SAR, China: No.

Jersey: No.

Singapore: No.

United States: To qualify under Chapter 15, you must meet certain requirements. Chapter 15 does not apply to entities identified as being excluded from seeking relief under the Bankruptcy Code in section 109(b), which excludes, inter alia, foreign banks and insurance companies.

United Kingdom: There are special rules in the United Kingdom relating to insolvency proceedings concerning insurance undertakings, credit institutions, holding investment undertakings, or collective investment undertakings. These apply especially within the European Union. However, those rules relate more significantly toward the conduct of an insolvency proceeding involving a relevant entity, to ensure that a single set of proceedings will govern the winding up within the European Union, rather than the process of obtaining recognition per se. This is a complex area outside the scope of this high-level summary.

Switzerland: In respect of foreign banks in bankruptcy, the ordinary requirements for recognition described above at question (*c*) apply. Instead of the civil judge, however, the Swiss Financial Markets Supervisory Authority (FINMA) is competent to recognize foreign banks in bankruptcy. With the entry into force of Article 37g [of the Banking Act] on January

c. 在某些国家或地区，针对外国金融机构或保险公司破产管理人的承认，有专门的规定（如瑞士金融市场监督管理局），在您所在的国家或地区是否也存在类似的特殊规则？如果有，获得承认需要满足什么条件？

比利时：无。

英属维京群岛：无。

中国香港：无。

泽西岛：无。

新加坡：无。

美国：要符合第十五章的规定，必须满足以下条件，即第十五章不适用于根据《美国破产法》第 109（b）条被排除在救济之外的外国银行和保险银行。

英国：针对保险公司、信贷机构、控股投资公司或集中投资公司的破产程序，英国存在特殊规则。这些规则专门适用于欧盟内部。然而，这些规则更关注破产程序中的任何一项操作是否确保在欧盟内部完成，而不关注承认本身。这是另一个难以就此概括的复杂领域。

瑞士：对破产外国银行的承认，一般适用问题（c）所述的要求，由瑞士金融市场监督管理局（FINMA）代替了民事法官，对破产外国银行行使承认权。《联邦银行法》第 37g 条于 2011 年 1 月 1 日正式生效，金融市场监督管理局不仅可以承认外国的破产程序，还可以承认外国任命的破产管理人。如果满足以下两个附加条件，外国破产管理人甚

1, 2011, FINMA is now allowed to recognize not only foreign insolvency measures but also trustees appointed abroad. Instead of the opening of a Swiss ancillary bankruptcy, the foreign trustee is allowed to be directly remitted with the assets of the bank in bankruptcy that is located in Switzerland, when two additional requirements are met: (1) equal treatment in the foreign proceedings of bankruptcy of secured claims and privileged claims pursuant to the Swiss Federal Act on Debt Collection and Bankruptcy of the creditors domiciled in Switzerland; and (2) the other Swiss creditors are duly taken into account in the foreign proceedings of bankruptcy. FINMA will particularly pay attention to the possibility that the State where the foreign bankruptcy is open gives a particular privilege to the claims held by the State (such as taxes, justice costs), which could jeopardize the recovery of the privileged and secured claims of the Swiss creditors.

Australia: Regulation 9 of the Cross-Border Insolvency Regulations 2008 (Cth) provides that the UNCITRAL Model Law [on Cross-Border Insolvency] does not apply to certain banks under the Banking Act 1959 (Cth), general insurance businesses under the Insurance Act 1975 (Cth), or life insurance companies under the Life Insurance Act 1995 (Cth). The result of this is that there is no way for insolvency office holders of those institutions to be recognized under Australia's cross-border insolvency laws. However, those entities would be covered by Australia's domestic insolvency laws.

United Arab Emirates: No.

Cayman Islands: There are no special rules to differentiate insolvency office holders in this way.

d. Will the court (or other relevant adjudicating body) charged with considering applications for recognition in your country likely refuse such an application if the foreign office holder was appointed ex parte or in a way which is incompatible with principles of natural justice or of

至可以将瑞士银行账户中的相关资产直接汇出，而不需要在瑞士另走辅助破产程序：(1)瑞士《联邦债务与破产法》中对居住在瑞士的债权人的担保债权和特权债权应在外国程序中受到平等对待；(2)外国破产程序也会充分考虑其他瑞士债权人的权益。对于外国破产国家作为债权人所拥有的债权（如税收、司法成本），瑞士金融市场监督管理局将特别研究是否存在给予特权的可能性，但这可能会造成对其他瑞士担保债权人的损害。

澳大利亚：《2008年跨境破产条例》第9条规定，联合国国际贸易法委员会《跨国界破产示范法》并不适用于1959年《银行法》规范的某些银行，1975年《保险法》所规定的一般保险业务，以及1995年《人寿保险法》规定的人寿保险公司。所以，上述机构的破产管理人无法依据澳大利亚的跨境破产法获得承认，但可受澳大利亚国内破产法的保护。

阿联酋：无。

开曼群岛：并无专门规则区分这类破产管理人。

d. 如果外国破产管理人被单方面任命，或以违背实质正义或程序公平的方式任命，您国家负责承认的法院（或其他对应判决机构）是否会拒绝对其承认？

procedural fairness?

Belgium: Yes. Due process rules must have been complied with.

British Virgin Islands: As the court is exercising a discretion in deciding what, if any, assistance to provide to the foreign court through its officer, such matters will likely be taken into account in the exercise of the court's discretion.

Hong Kong SAR, China: As the application is made by Letter of Request, it would be presumed valid. If the order is obviously made in breach of principles of natural justice, it is likely that this would be taken into consideration in deciding whether the order should be granted. The fact an appointment was made ex parte would not affect its validity.

Jersey: Yes. Public policy exceptions are not codified in Jersey law but in applying its discretion when considering an application for foreign recognition under Article 49 or common (customary) law, the Jersey courts are likely to take into account principles of procedural fairness and natural justice. The UNCITRAL Model Law on Cross-Border Insolvency, which the Jersey courts may consider when dealing with an Article 49 application for recognition, provides for a "public policy" exception. It states that "the receiving court retains the ability to refuse to take any action covered by the Model Law … if to take that action would be 'manifestly contrary' to the public policy of the State in which the receiving court is situated."

Singapore: The Singapore Courts will take into consideration the fact that the order appointing the foreign office holder was obtained in breach of natural justice or procedural fairness, and be less inclined to recognize that foreign office holder. The mere fact that an appointment was made ex parte should not in and of itself be a material factor against recognition.

United States: Bankruptcy courts can inquire as to procedural fairness and consider principles of natural justice in granting or denying recognition.

比利时：是的。必须遵守正当程序。

英属维京群岛：由于法院在决定对外国法院提供何种协助时，拥有自由裁量权，可能会适当考量上述事项。

中国香港：由于通常是通过书面申请书的方式提出申请，所以会被推定为有效。但如果明显违反公平正义原则，在决定是否给予承认时会将其纳入考量。但单方面的任命并不会影响承认的效力。

泽西岛：是的。尽管公共政策例外的原则并没有被纳入泽西岛的法律，但法院在根据第 49 条或普通法（习惯法）行使自由裁量权时，很可能会考虑公平公正的原则。法院也会考虑联合国国际贸易法委员会《跨国界破产示范法》中的公共政策例外原则，“在明显违反受理国的公共政策时，受理国法院保留拒绝履行《示范法》的权力”。

新加坡：若任命外国破产管理人违反实质正义或程序公平，新加坡法院会因此拒绝承认该国破产管理人，但单方面委任并不会成为拒绝的重要因素。

美国：破产法院会将程序公正与实质正义纳入考量，并决定对外国程序给予承认或拒绝。《美国破产法》第 1506 条规定：“如果该诉讼

Section 1506 [of the Bankruptcy Code] provides that "[n]othing in this chapter prevents the court from refusing to take an action governed by this chapter if the action would be manifestly contrary to the public policy of the United States." 11 U.S.C. § 1506. A Chapter 15 petition recognizing office holders cannot proceed ex parte, but there is no per se rule preventing recognition of foreign office holders that were appointed ex parte.

United Kingdom: The court would not necessarily refuse an application solely because the appointment was made ex parte. However, it would be likely to do so if it found that there has been a material breach of procedure or a failure to give full and frank disclosure of all relevant facts. There are also rules that oblige the office-holder seeking recognition to explain what the effect of recognition would be in the United Kingdom on any third parties as part of their application. This is mainly aimed at avoiding "unfairness" if, for example, recognition would result in an automatic stay of on-going proceedings that could affect a third party.

Switzerland: Switzerland will not recognize foreign decisions which are rendered ex parte since this does not comply with article 27 of PILA. However, this has to be established by any concerned party and the judge will not refuse to recognize the foreign bankruptcy decree for this particular reason ex officio. Among the grounds for denial of recognition of a foreign bankruptcy decree is its manifest incompatibility with Swiss material public policy. This exception is rarely applied. In bankruptcy matters, a violation of Swiss public policy will be realized, for instance: (1) when the foreign decision on bankruptcy has a confiscatory or discriminatory nature; (2) when a creditor applies for recognition only to try to locate assets of a common debtor in Switzerland for reasons unrelated to the bankruptcy; or (3) when the nature of the claim which led to the bankruptcy violates the Swiss conception of public policy. This will be typically the case for

明显违反美国的公共政策，那么没有什么可以阻止法院拒绝本章规定的诉讼程序。”第十五章也规定，外国破产管理人不能单方面提出申请，但并没有任何规定表明可拒绝承认单方委任的外国破产管理人。

英国：法院并不会仅仅因为单方面申请而拒绝承认，但如果存在严重违反程序的行为或没有如实、充分地披露相关事实，则可能会拒绝承认。还有一些规定要求外国破产管理人在申请时必须说明在英国申请承认对任何第三方是否会造成影响。这主要是为了避免“不公平”的发生。例如，如果承认将导致某个正在进行的诉讼自动中止，从而可能影响第三方的相关权益。

瑞士：瑞士不会承认单方面委任的外国破产管理人，这违背了PILA 第 27 条的规定，但这必须由其他相关方来决定，法院不会直接依据职权拒绝承认外国破产裁决。直接拒绝承认外国破产程序的理由之一是，其与瑞士重大公共政策存在明显不兼容的情况。但这种例外在实践中较为罕见。违反瑞士公共政策的情形如：（1）外国破产裁决是为了没收资产充公的，或带有歧视性质的；（2）债权人申请破产承认是出于与破产无关的原因，如仅为了定位瑞士普通债务人的资产；（3）对债权人进行赔偿，会严重违反瑞士的公共政策。惩罚性赔偿就是典型的情形。

punitive damages.

Australia: Pursuant to the [UNCITRAL] Model Law [on Cross-Border Insolvency]: On its face, if a "foreign representative" can show that he was appointed by the foreign court to manage the insolvency, the Model Law does not permit the exercise of any discretion by an Australian court to refuse recognition on grounds that the office holder was appointed in a way that was incompatible with principles of natural justice or procedural fairness. However, Article 6 of the Model Law provides that a court may refuse to take any action under the Model Law if the action would be manifestly contrary to the public policy of Australia. Depending on the gravity of the circumstances, it may well be found that the recognition of a foreign representative who was appointed contrary to the principles of natural justice and procedural fairness would be contrary to public policy. In addition, the court retains considerable discretion in the relief that may be awarded upon recognition. The court must be satisfied, in granting relief, that the interests of Australian creditors are adequately protected. In our view, if a court were satisfied that a foreign representative had been appointed other than in accordance with principles of natural justice and procedural fairness, it would most likely exercise its discretion to refuse substantive relief to facilitate the foreign proceeding and in that way, stymie the effect of the recognition.

Pursuanttothe Bankruptcy Actand Corporations Act: Under section 29(2) ofthe Bankruptcy Act and section 581(2) of the Corporations Act, an Australian Court must assist the court of a "prescribed country." The prescribed countries are the United Kingdom, New Zealand, Jersey, Singapore, Switzerland, Malaysia, Papua New Guinea, and the United States (and their colonies, overseas territories, or protectorates), although the Australian court retains the discretion as to what assistance it should

澳大利亚：根据联合国国际贸易法委员会《跨国界破产示范法》，理论上，如果"外国破产管理人"可以表明他是由外国法院任命而执行破产的，则《示范法》不允许澳大利亚法院以违背公平正义为由拒绝对其承认。但是，《示范法》第6条又规定，如果承认程序明显违背澳大利亚的公共政策，则法院可以拒绝《示范法》规定的行动。事实上，根据情况的严重程度，是有可能发现违反公共政策的不当任命的。此外，法院对其救济措施也享有保留权，可酌情决定是否给予承认。在给予救济时，法院必须确保澳大利亚的债权人利益得到充分的保护。我们认为，如果认为外国破产管理人并不是依据正当程序任命的，则它很可能会拒绝对外国程序提供实质性的便利，从而限制承认的实际效力。

根据《破产法》第29（2）条和2001年《公司法》第581（2）条，澳大利亚法院必须协助"指定国家"的法院。"指定国家"具体包括英国、新西兰、泽西岛、新加坡、瑞士、马来西亚、巴布亚新几内亚和美国（及其殖民地、海外领土和保护国）。尽管澳大利亚法院对其提供协助有保留权，但只能针对在澳大利亚本国发生的事项，法院才可行使该权利。对于"指定国家"外的国家，澳大利亚法院可自行决定是否提供协助。通过违反公正原则或不当程序而委任外国破产管理人

provide. The Australian court may exercise only such powers with respect to the matter as it could exercise if the matter had arisen within its own jurisdiction. For countries other than "prescribed countries," the Australian court retains discretion as to whether it should assist. The fact that a foreign office holder had been appointed contrary to the principles of natural justice and procedural fairness would be a significant factor weighing against the exercise of discretion in favor of a request for assistance. Even if an Australian court was bound to assist, any assistance ultimately provided would be heavily constrained if the court was of the view that the foreign officer had been appointed other than in accordance with principles of natural justice or procedural fairness. The mere fact that an appointment was made ex parte is unlikely to be a material consideration weighing against recognition under the Model Law or assistance under the Bankruptcy Act and the Corporations Act.

United Arab Emirates: Not relevant.

Cayman Islands: Not relevant.

e. Can interim office holders like provisional liquidators or interim receivers seek recognition in your jurisdiction or does an order of appointment have to be a final order at first instance?

Belgium: The order must be final and enforceable. However, pursuant to the International Private Law Code one can obtain an exequatur for provisional measures on the basis of the foreign decision that can still be appealed.

British Virgin Islands: Recognition and assistance is open to any "foreign representative" from the designated countries. A foreign representative is defined as a person or body, including one appointed on an interim basis, authorized in a foreign proceeding to administer the reorganization or the liquidation of the debtor's property or affairs or to act

的，对法院作出协助决定有巨大的负面影响。即使澳大利亚法院有义务提供协助，但在这种情况下，提供协助会受到严重的限制。此外，依据《破产法》和《公司法》，单方面委任不会成为法院决定协助与否的重要考量。

阿联酋：不相关。

开曼群岛：不相关。

e. 诸如临时清算人或临时接管人这类临时破产管理人能否在您的国家申请承认？在申请时，委任令必须是最终的委任吗？

比利时：破产令必须为最终裁决并且可以执行。但是依据《国际私法典》，允许依据仍可上诉的外国法令，获得临时的保障措施。

英属维京群岛：指定国家的任何“外国破产管理人”均可获得承认和协助。外国破产管理人，是指在外国程序中被授权管理债务人财产、事务，以达到重组或清算目的的代理人或机构，包括临时任命的个人或机构。

as a representative of the foreign proceeding.

Hong Kong SAR, China: If the office holder has authority to represent the insolvent company in the foreign court of his appointment, and requires judicial assistance to support that liquidation, he may apply for judicial assistance through his own court to the Hong Kong SAR, China court. If there is any doubt, in appropriate circumstances (urgency, risk of dissipation), assets may similarly be preserved through injunctive relief pending the formal appointment of liquidators or receivers.

Jersey: Provisional liquidators are not a feature of Jersey insolvency law but the Royal Court is flexible and prepared to consider innovative solutions where there has been fraud or debtors have sought to conceal assets from lawful creditors.

Singapore: If the office holder has authority to represent the insolvent company in the foreign court of his appointment, the fact that such appointment is interim in nature should not, by itself, be a bar toward recognition by the Singapore courts.

United States: Yes, interim office holders can seek recognition in the United States. A "foreign representative means a person or body, including a person or body appointed on an interim basis, authorized in a foreign proceeding to administer the reorganization or the liquidation of the debtor's assets or affairs or to act as a representative of such foreign proceeding." 11 U.S.C. § 101(24).

United Kingdom: In general, an interim insolvency measure such as provisional liquidation is capable of recognition. This is not a straightforward question, though, and depends upon the basis of recognition (whether European Union, Commonwealth, or UNCITRAL). As a general rule, if the foreign insolvency proceeding is a formal, collective, process properly enacted in the country of origin, it is likely to be capable of

中国香港：如果该破产管理人在外国的任命下代表破产公司，并需要司法协助以支持破产行动，则可以通过其本国法院向中国香港法院申请司法协助。如果有任何疑问，在正式任命破产管理人之前的适当情况下（紧急情况、具有财产流失风险时），可以通过禁止令等救济措施保全财产。

泽西岛：临时破产管理人并不是泽西岛破产法承认的对象，但皇家法院通常是灵活变通的，在存在欺诈行为，或债务人试图向合法债权人隐瞒资产的情形下，法院可以考虑运用变通、创新的解决方法。

新加坡：如果破产管理人在外国法院中获得授权，代表破产公司履行职权，那么临时性任命本身并不会成为新加坡法院认可的障碍。

美国：是的，临时破产管理人可以在美国申请承认。“外国破产管理人，是指在外国程序中被授权管理债务人资产、事务，以实现重组或清算的个人或机构，包括临时任命的个人或机构。”［《美国法典》第十一编第 101（24）条］

英国：一般而言，临时破产程序（如临时清算）能够得到认可。但是，这不能一概而论，它取决于认可的依据是欧盟、英联邦还是联合国国际贸易法委员会。一般来说，如果外国破产任命程序是通过其本国权威机构以正当程序作出的，一般予以承认。如果任命并不是依托全体债权人的权益，而仅仅是为了任命方的利益，则“破产管理人”很可能无法得到承认。

recognition one way or another. A "receiver" may not be capable of recognition if the appointment is not a collective one for the benefit of all creditors, but instead solely for the benefit of the appointing party.

Switzerland: Yes. Foreign insolvency measures can be recognized (see above our answer to question (*c*)) in Switzerland provided that they are enforceable (and not final) and that they are not rendered ex parte. However, the foreign trustee (whether interim or not) will never replace the Swiss ancillary liquidator. Even in cases of interim measures, an ancillary bankruptcy has to be formally opened in Switzerland (and can be revoked later depending on the final measures abroad). The applicant can apply, in its application for recognition, for conservatory measures pursuant to Articles 162–165 and 170 of the [Federal Act on Debt Collection and Bankruptcy], namely for: (1) the inventory of the assets of the debtor located in Switzerland (which equals a freeze of the assets); and (2) any conservatory measures that the judge considers to be in the interest of the creditors.

Australia: Pursuant to Article 2(d) of the [UNCITRAL] Model Law [on Cross-Border Insolvency], interim office holders can seek recognition in Australia. The fact that a foreign office holder was provisional on its own would not impact the foreign court's ability to seek the assistance of an Australian court under section 29 of the Bankruptcy Act or section 581 of the Corporations Act.

United Arab Emirates: There is no concept of provisional liquidator or interim receiver in United Arab Emirates law. Any liquidator appointed in accordance with United Arab Emirates law needs to be confirmed by a final judgment of the United Arab Emirates courts (unless there is a notarized shareholders' resolution of 100 percent of the shareholders of the company in question).

Cayman Islands: The Grand Court is unlikely to recognize foreign

瑞士：是的。只要是可强制执行的（非最终决定）并且非单方面申请的外国破产程序就可以在瑞士得到承认［请参见对问题（c）的回复］。但是，外国破产管理人（无论是否临时）都不会取代瑞士辅助破产管理人。即使在采取临时措施的情况下，辅助破产也必须在瑞士被正式宣告（但之后可以根据外国最终裁决而撤销）。申请人可以依据《联邦债务与破产法》第 162–165 条和第 170 条申请保护措施，须提交:（1）位于瑞士的债务人的资产清单（等同于资产冻结）;（2）法官认为的任何有利于保障债权人权益的措施。

澳大利亚：根据《跨国界破产示范法》第 2（d）条，临时破产管理人可以在澳大利亚申请承认。根据《破产法》第 29 条或《公司法》第 581 条，临时的外国破产管理人并不会影响澳大利亚的协助决定。

阿联酋：在阿联酋的法律中，没有临时破产管理人的概念，任何破产管理人都必须为阿联酋法院最终确认任命的，除非经过公司全体股东的认可。

开曼群岛：法院不太可能承认临时任命的外国破产管理人，除非

office holders appointed on a provisional basis, unless there are compelling reasons to do so. Further, the Grand Court's recognition will only go as far as the extent to which the foreign appointing order exists—if the appointment is subsequently superseded in the foreign jurisdiction, the former appointee will no longer be recognized by the Grand Court.

f. Can a foreign office holder get recognized on his own or does he have to seek a joint appointment with a locally licensed insolvency practitioner in your jurisdiction?

Belgium: If recognition is necessary (see response to question (*a*)), the request must be signed by a Belgian lawyer.

British Virgin Islands: A foreign office holder does not need to be jointly appointed together with a local insolvency practitioner.

Hong Kong SAR, China: He can be recognized on his own, for purposes of carrying out his duties as an office holder. In appropriate circumstances, (such as proof of sufficient connection, and that the company carries on business in Hong Kong SAR, China) he may also apply to the court for the liquidation of the company in the Hong Kong SAR, China courts.

Jersey: There is no requirement that a foreign office holder be jointly appointed with a Jersey insolvency practitioner.

Singapore: It will be at the discretion of the Singapore Courts whether: (1) the foreign office holder may be recognized on his own; (2) he is required to be appointed jointly with a locally licensed insolvency practitioner; or (3) he must apply to appoint a locally appointed insolvency practitioner and only the latter will be recognized.

United States: A foreign office holder may get recognition on his own. "A foreign representative may commence a case under section 1504 by filing directly with the court a petition for recognition of a foreign

有特别充分的理由需要这么做。此外，法院的承认仅限于外国法院的委任范围，如果之后外国程序更改任命，则不再承认前任外国破产管理人。

f. 外国破产管理人可以单独获得承认吗？还是必须与本国的破产管理人联合而获得承认？

比利时：申请承认必须具备比利时律师的签字［请参见对问题（a）的答复］。

英属维京群岛：外国破产管理人无需与当地破产从业人员共同申请承认。

中国香港：为了行使职权，可以单独予以承认。在适当的情况下（如有充分证明表明或者公司在香港开展业务时），他还可以向香港法院申请对香港公司的清算。

泽西岛：无需与泽西岛破产从业人员共同任命。

新加坡：新加坡法院可酌情自行决定：（1）外国破产管理人可自行获得承认；（2）须与具有本地执照的破产从业人员联合任命；（3）外国破产管理人申请任命本地的破产从业人员，而只有本地破产从业人员获得承认。

美国：外国破产管理人可自行获得承认。“外国破产管理人可以依据第 1504 条的规定，直接向法院申请对外国程序的承认。”［《美国法典》第十一编第 1509（a）条］

proceeding under section 1515." (11 U.S.C. § 1509(a))

United Kingdom: The foreign office holder can be recognized on his own and then take action in his own name once recognized.

Switzerland: The foreign office holder has legal standing to apply for recognition of the foreign bankruptcy in Switzerland but cannot ask to be appointed jointly with the Swiss ancillary liquidator, which is the sole person in charge of the ancillary bankruptcy. Note, however, that the foreign bankruptcy can bring a claw-back action before Swiss courts (Article 171 PILA). The procedure concerns only the assets located in Switzerland. All the assets of the foreign bankrupt entity that are located in Switzerland will be subject to the payment of the Swiss creditors' secured and privileged claims within the meaning of Article 219 of the [Federal Act on Debt Collection and Bankruptcy]. Once the schedule of secured and privileged claims of the ancillary bankruptcy is in force, the ancillary trustee liquidates the assets of the minibankruptcy. Once the proceeds of the liquidation have been distributed to the Swiss secured and privileged creditors, any balance remaining is distributed to the foreign bankruptcy only after a formal application before the civil judge on recognition of the foreign schedule of claims by the foreign trustee or a creditor. If the draft bill that the Swiss government circulated on October 14, 2014, is adopted, it will be possible for a foreign trustee to be recognized in Switzerland and to be remitted with the assets of the bankruptcy located in Switzerland, provided that the requirements of equal treatment of the Swiss privileged and secured creditors and the taking into account of other Swiss creditors are met (see the answer to question (*d*)).

Australia: A foreign representative may seek recognition of a foreign proceeding in Australia without being jointly appointed with an Australian practitioner. As part of the discretionary relief available upon recognition,

英国：外国破产管理人可以自行获得承认，一旦承认，便可以自己的名义行使职权。

瑞士：外国破产管理人具有申请承认外国破产程序的资格，但无权要求与瑞士辅助破产管理人共同任命，瑞士破产管理人是辅助破产程序的唯一责任人。但注意，外国破产人可以申请撤回诉讼（PILA 第 171 条）。该程序只适用于瑞士的资产。外国破产公司位于瑞士的所有资产都应按照《联邦债务与破产法》第 219 条的规定，用于清偿瑞士担保债权人的债务。辅助破产管理人会依据担保债权人的追偿时间表，启动辅助破产清算程序。一旦清算程序中，资产被分配给担保债权人或其他享有优先权的债权人，剩余的资产可在正式向民事法官申请对外国破产清偿计划承认之后，分配给外国破产管理人或债权人。当时认为，如果 2014 年 10 月 14 日政府发布的草案获得正式通过，则外国破产管理人可能在瑞士获得承认，并连同位于瑞士的破产资产一起转移，但同时也要求对瑞士的担保债权人给予同等的对待，其他瑞士债权人的权益也应获得满足［请参阅对问题（d）的答复］。*

澳大利亚：外国破产管理人可在澳大利亚自行申请承认，无需联

* 经查证瑞士国际私法的相关法律条文，可合理推测该草案已获得正式通过。——译者注

the [UNCITRAL] Model Law [on Cross-Border Insolvency] provides that the court may appoint an Australian representative. This is usually done for the sake of convenience when there are a large number of assets in Australia to be realized. Australian courts also have a general discretion to appoint a receiver to assets in appropriate cases, but there is no requirement for a local receiver to be appointed in circumstances of a foreign insolvency.

United Arab Emirates: The United Arab Emirates courts will appoint only a United Arab Emirates registered practitioner (usually a locally registered accountant also registered with the court in question) as liquidator in the jurisdiction. The Dubai International Financial Centre (DIFC) courts will accept only a DIFC "registered practitioner."

Cayman Islands: A foreign office holder can be recognized on his own, without the need for a joint appointment with a licensed Cayman Islands Insolvency Practitioner.

g. What powers can a foreign office holder exercise in your jurisdiction once he is recognized locally? In some legal systems (such as the English common law of recognition) a local court can only permit a foreign office holder to exercise powers which are no greater than what he has been given in the place of his initial appointment. Is that true of your jurisdiction?

Belgium: Pursuant to [European Union] Regulation 2015/848, the liquidator appointed by a court which has jurisdiction pursuant to Article 3(1) (main proceedings) may exercise all the powers conferred on him by the law of the State of the opening of proceedings in another Member State, as long as no other insolvency proceedings have been opened there, nor any preservation measure to the contrary has been taken there, further to a request for the opening of insolvency proceedings in that State. He may in particular remove the debtor's assets from the territory of the Member State in which they are situated. The liquidator appointed by a court which

合澳大利亚破产管理人。获得承认后，法院可依据情况提供必要的救济手段。根据《跨国界破产示范法》，当需要在澳大利亚处置大量资产时，为了方便起见，法院可以委任一名澳大利亚代表予以协助。在适当的情况下，澳大利亚还可任命资产的接管人。但在外国破产程序中，无需任命本地资产接管人。

阿联酋：阿联酋法院仅接受阿联酋注册的破产从业人员（通常为法院所在地的注册会计师）担任破产管理人。迪拜国际金融中心（DIFC）的法院仅接受其辖区内的“注册从业人员”。

开曼群岛：外国破产管理人可单独获得承认，无需与本地破产从业人员共同任命。

g. 外国破产从业人员在获得承认后可行使何种权力？在某些法律制度中（如英国普通法的承认制度），地方法院规定外国破产管理人的职权不得超过其最初委任时的范围，您的国家也是这样吗？

比利时：根据欧盟第 2015/848 号条例第 3（1）条的规定，具有管辖权的法院任命的破产管理人（主要程序）享有与之在启动外国破产程序的成员国相同的所有权力，只要该成员国并无启动其他破产程序，也没有任何与该程序相违背的保全措施，则可在其他成员国启动破产程序。特别是，允许破产管理人将位于成员国的债务人资产一并转移。法院依据本条例第 3（2）条任命的破产管理人（非主要程序），可于破产程序开始后，向任何其他成员国法院或庭外申请将资产从破产程序启动国转移到该国。他也可以采取任何有利于债权人的司法行动。在履行职权时，必须遵守该国的法律，特别是在资产变现的程序方面，

has jurisdiction pursuant to Article 3(2) (secondary [nonmain] proceedings) may, in any other Member State, claim through the courts or out of court that moveable property was removed from the territory of the State of the opening of proceedings to the territory of the other Member State after the opening of the insolvency proceedings. He may also bring any action to set aside, which is in the interests of the creditors. In exercising his powers, the liquidator must comply with the law of the Member State within the territory in which he intends to take action, in particular with regard to procedures for the realization of assets. Those powers may not include coercive measures or the right to rule on legal proceedings or disputes. Pursuant to the Belgian International Private Law Code, the powers are those granted to him by the appointment decision.

British Virgin Islands: The orders which the British Virgin Islands court can make in aid of foreign proceedings are extremely wide and include orders: (1) restraining the commencement or continuation of any proceedings, execution, or other legal process or the levying of any distress against a debtor or in relation to any of the debtor's property; (2) restraining the creation, exercise, or enforcement of any right or remedy over or against any of the debtor's property; (3) requiring any person to deliver up to the foreign representative any property of the debtor or the proceeds of such property; (4) granting such relief as it considers appropriate to facilitate, approve, or implement arrangements that will result in a coordination of a [British] Virgin Islands insolvency proceeding with a foreign insolvency proceeding in respect of a debtor; (5) appointing an interim receiver of any property of the debtor for such term and subject to such conditions as it considers appropriate; (6) authorizing the examination by the foreign representative of the debtor or of any person who could be examined in a [British] Virgin Islands insolvency proceeding in respect of a debtor; (7) staying

这些权力不包括某些强制措施或者对法律程序、争议进行裁决的权力。根据《比利时国际私法典》，其享有的职权与外国委任的一致。

英属维京群岛：英属维京群岛法院可以对外国诉讼提供广泛的协助，包括：（1）法院可限制任何与债务人或其财产有关的诉讼程序，包括启动、中止和征收；（2）限制利用债务人财产以实现盈利、执行或救济目的的行动；（3）要求相关人将债务人的资产移交给外国破产管理人；（4）提供必要的协助、批准或施行，以便利外国破产诉讼，使英属维京群岛的外国破产程序与之相协调；（5）任命债务人的临时破产管理人，规定适当的任期与条件；（6）授权外国破产管理人检查债务相关人及资产；（7）如有必要，可中止或终结与破产程序相关的其他法令；（8）其他适当的救济。英属维京群岛法院在作出上述命令时，可适用英属维京群岛的法律或该外国程序的法律，但仅依靠英属维京群岛对外国破产管理人的承认，其并不自然具有依据《破产法》任命的本国破产管理人一样的权力。

or terminating or making any other order it considers appropriate in relation to a [British] Virgin Islands insolvency proceeding; or (8) granting such other relief as it considers appropriate. In making any of the orders set out above the British Virgin Islands court may apply the law of the [British] Virgin Islands or the law applicable in respect of the foreign proceeding. However, the mere fact that a foreign office holder is recognized by the British Virgin Islands court will not result in his or her having the general rights and powers of a domestic office holder appointed under the Insolvency Act.

Hong Kong SAR, China: All of the powers granted in his own jurisdiction, to the extent that such powers coexist in Hong Kong SAR, China.

Jersey: All of the powers granted in his own jurisdiction. Recognition will normally be limited to the extent to which the foreign office holder needs to exercise such powers in Jersey and to the extent that the powers requested are consistent with Jersey's insolvency laws. Applicants are required to consult with the Viscount's Department (the enforcement officer of the Royal Court in Jersey) before an application is issued in Jersey in order to ensure that the order sought is drafted in suitable terms; requests need to be specific. The types of powers that have been granted to foreign office holders in the past have included the right to exercise authority over assets based in Jersey following a foreign insolvency or winding up, that is, protection and recovery of assets.

Singapore: All of the powers granted in his own jurisdiction, to the extent that such powers are recognized under Singapore law.

United States: Once a foreign office holder and foreign proceeding have been recognized either as a foreign main proceeding or a foreign nonmain proceeding, different provisions of Chapter 15 of the Bankruptcy

中国香港：在中国香港的协助范围内，外国破产管理人的职权均来自其本国的授权。

泽西岛：所有的权力均来自其本国的司法授权。承认是允许其在泽西岛范围内行使该职权，同时必须与泽西岛的破产法相一致。在泽西岛法院授予承认之前，申请人必须咨询泽西岛皇家法院的执行官，确保以适当的条款提出申请。过去授予外国破产管理人的权力包括依据外国破产程序对位于泽西岛的资产进行保全或追回。

新加坡：在新加坡法律许可的范围内，其本国授予的所有权力。

美国：外国破产管理人和外国程序被分为外国主要程序和外国非主要程序。《美国破产法》第十五章对此有不同的规定。参见《美国法典》第十一编第 1509 条以及第 1519-1521 条。这些权力不一定局限于

Code will be at the foreign office holder's disposal. See 11 U.S.C. §§ 1509 and 1519–1521. Those powers are not necessarily limited to the powers that are available in the foreign jurisdiction, but the Bankruptcy Court can take these issues into consideration when granting appropriate relief. The impact would be greater in a case in which only nonmain recognition has been granted. When recognition is granted as a foreign main proceeding, certain powers, listed above, come into effect automatically with only certain other relief requiring court authorization. Conversely, when recognition is granted as a foreign nonmain proceeding, the foreign representative will have to seek court approval for most activities, which allows the court greater discretion in determining what powers the foreign office holder will have.

United Kingdom: This is a complex issue. Some powers are available pursuant to the legislation under which the office holder is recognized, and dependent on whether recognition is of a main or secondary proceeding. Those powers can include investigatory powers, bringing proceedings, and execution against assets of the insolvent estate. There is, however, recent authority which suggests that in the United Kingdom (and certain Commonwealth and common law jurisdictions), the powers afforded to a foreign office holder at common law can be no greater than those that would have been available in their home jurisdiction.

Switzerland: As mentioned above (see the response to question (*a*)), Switzerland does not recognize the foreign trustees of a foreign bankruptcy but a Swiss ancillary liquidator is appointed. Therefore, the Swiss ancillary liquidator will have the powers provided for by the [Federal Act on Debt Collection and Bankruptcy]. In banking matters, the foreign trustee has the powers that the [Financial Market Supervisory Authority] granted. In practice, Article 37g [of the Banking Act] being quite new, there is no precedent where a foreign trustee was allowed to carry out broader activities

外国程序中规定的权利，但破产法院会在提供救济时适当参考这些事项。在确认为非主要承认的情况下，这一影响会更大。如果承认为外国主要程序，则上述权力自动生效，只有个别情况需要法院专门授权。相反，当承认为外国非主要程序时，外国破产管理人必须就大多数行动申请法院的授权，法院在决定其权力范围时拥有更大的空间。

英国：这是一个复杂的问题，根据承认外国破产管理人的法律规定，可行使某些权力，这取决于承认是主要程序还是次要程序。这些权力包括调查权、起诉权或执行破产资产的权力。但是，近期官方也认为，在英国（以及部分英联邦或普通法国家），根据普通法授权外国破产管理人的权力不得超过其本国的授权范围。

瑞士：如同对问题（a）的答复，瑞士不承认外国破产管理人，需要任命瑞士本土的辅助破产管理人。因此，瑞士辅助破产管理人具有《联邦债务和破产法》所规定的权力。在银行破产事务中，外国破产管理人可获得金融市场监督管理局的授权。但实际上，《联邦银行法》第37条是新规定，在瑞士境内，还没有外国破产管理人超出其原有职权范围行动的先例，大概因为瑞士法官认为其无权对外国破产管理人授予比原外国程序更大的权力。

on Swiss soil than the powers that the foreign decree grants to the foreign trustee. However, a Swiss judge would probably consider that he is not competent to give greater powers in Switzerland to a trustee appointed by a foreign authority.

Australia: Pursuant to the [UNCITRAL] Model Law [on Cross-Border Insolvency], the foreign representative has access to Australian courts and the authority to commence or participate in a proceeding pursuant to Australia's insolvency laws if the conditions for commencing such a proceeding are otherwise met. Otherwise, the exercise of the office holder's powers in relation to Australian assets or creditors are generally conditioned on a requirement that the interests of Australian creditors remain adequately protected. Under section 29 of the Bankruptcy Act and section 581 of the Corporations Act, the court may exercise only such powers in relation to the foreign proceeding as it would have if the matter arose in its own jurisdiction.

United Arab Emirates: None, not normally possible under United Arab Emirates law. Within the Dubai International Financial Centre (DIFC) however, cooperation with foreign jurisdictions is encouraged when a foreign company is the subject of insolvency proceedings in the jurisdiction of incorporation (the DIFC courts are allowed to assist the foreign courts in gathering and remitting amounts maintained within the DIFC pursuant to Article 82 of DIFC Law No. 3 of 2009).

Cayman Islands: A foreign office holder has direct access to the Grand Court and may commence whatever proceeding may be necessary to collect a foreign company's assets or otherwise enforce its rights in the Cayman Islands. Upon the successful application of a foreign representative made pursuant to Part XVII of the Companies Law, the Grand Court may make orders ancillary to the foreign bankruptcy proceedings for the purposes of

澳大利亚：根据联合国国际贸易法委员会《跨国界破产示范法》，满足条件的外国破产管理人有权依据澳大利亚《破产法》启动破产程序。此外，外国破产管理人行使与资产或债权人有关的职权时，必须充分保障澳大利亚债权人的权益。根据《破产法》第29条和《公司法》第581条，法院对外国程序的授权不得超出其本国的授权范围。

阿联酋：不适用阿联酋的法律。但在迪拜国际金融中心（DIFC），当外国公司成为该区域破产程序的管辖对象时，与外国司法机关互助合作是受到鼓励的（依据2009年第3号DIFC法第82条规定，允许法院为外国破产程序提供征收、转账等协助）。

开曼群岛：外国破产管理人可以直接通过法院启动任何必要的程序，以追回外国破产资产或以其他方式在开曼群岛上履行职权。根据《公司法》第XVII部分，外国破产管理人申请成功后，法院可为外国破产程序提供一些附加命令，目的在于：（1）承认外国破产管理人代表债务人或以债务人名义在开曼群岛上采取行动；（2）启动或中止任何针对债务人的司法程序；（3）中止任何针对债务人的执行行动；

(1) recognizing the right of a foreign representative to act in the Cayman Islands on behalf of or in the name of a debtor; (2) enjoining the commencement or staying the continuation of legal proceedings against a debtor; (3) staying the enforcement of any judgment against a debtor; (4) requiring a person in possession of information relating to the business or affairs of a debtor to be examined by and produce documents to its foreign representative; and (5) ordering the turnover to a foreign representative of any property belonging to a debtor.

h. Oftentimes, a foreign office holder does not need to seek a formal order of recognition abroad if all he wishes to do is to gather in some information by for instance resort to a right of any person to seek a disclosure order (such as a Norwich Pharmacal/Bankers Trust order under the English common law model or 28 U.S.C. § 1782 [Discovery in Aid of Foreign Litigation] in the [U.S. District Court]). Or if he wishes to sue a defendant in a foreign jurisdiction for relief in the civil courts and in the ordinary course (e.g., to sue an account debtor to collect monies owed to the estate he administers). All he needs to show in these instances is the standing to sue in the name of the insolvent debtor for which or whom he acts as agent. Is this option of avoiding the law of recognition altogether available to office holders in your jurisdiction where he does not need to use the special powers of an insolvency office holder, or where he does not need to set up a local ancillary estate or to seek special protections like an insolvency stay or moratorium of actions against the estate that he administers?

Belgium: As the recognition is automatic, the liquidator's appointment shall be evidenced by a certified copy of the original decision appointing him or by any other certificate issued by the court which has jurisdiction. A translation into one of the official languages in Belgium may be required. No legalization or other similar formality shall be required.

（4）可要求其他相关方提交信息或文件，供外国破产管理人查阅；
（5）命令将债务人的资产移交给外国破产管理人。

h. 通常，外国破产管理人为了收集信息，例如，只需要申请信息披露令（如英国普通法制度下的第三方披露令或《美国法典》第二十八编“对外国程序的司法协助”中规定的银行信托令）而无需在外国申请正式的承认。抑或他在国外起诉只是为了在民事法院或其他程序中获得救济（如只是为了收回欠款而起诉债务人）。在这些情况下，他需要的只是借债务人的名义提起诉讼，并不真的需要行使破产管理人的权力，也不需要申请寻求任何诸如中止、延期等资产保护令，这种情形也是被允许的吗?

比利时：由于自动承认，所以破产管理人应提交原始任命原件和认证副本，还需要任一比利时官方语言的译本。除此之外，不需要其他的手续。

British Virgin Islands: Yes.

Hong Kong SAR, China: Yes.

Jersey: Yes.

Singapore: Yes.

United States: Under 28 U.S.C. § 1782, if there is foreign litigation pending or reasonably contemplated, then the foreign office holder may seek documentary and testimonial evidence in the United States. As to substantive claims, subject to there being appropriate jurisdiction and standing, a foreign office holder may bring actions in the United States on behalf of the insolvent debtor. Section 1509 expressly provides that the failure of a foreign representative to commence a case or to obtain recognition does not affect any right the foreign representative may have to sue in a court in the United States to collect on or recover for a claim or debt which is property of the debtor.

United Kingdom: Yes. A foreign office holder could pursue a stand-alone claim or application for relief in some circumstances without seeking formal recognition.

Switzerland: The foreign trustee will always have to make the foreign insolvency measures recognized in Switzerland and will not be entitled to obtain directly information in Swiss civil proceedings. However, the foreign trustee that is not recognized in Switzerland can lodge a criminal complaint, on behalf of the bankrupt company, before Swiss criminal authorities when, before or after the bankruptcy, cross-border criminal behavior took place (such as fraud, embezzlement, or criminal mismanagement). Under Swiss Code of Penal Procedure (CPP), an entity who has been harmed by a crime may participate in the Swiss criminal investigation into those crimes in support of the prosecution, even if it has no claim for damages against the perpetrator. This allows the foreign legal representatives of the bankrupt

英属维京群岛：是的。

中国香港：是的。

泽西岛：是的。

新加坡：是的。

美国：依据《美国法典》第二十八编第1782条，如果存在外国待决案件或其他合理原因，外国破产管理人可以在美国申请相关的文件和证据。而对于实质性的债务诉讼，在具有管辖权和法律地位的前提下，外国破产管理人可以代表破产债务人在美国提起诉讼。第1509条明确规定，外国破产管理人未获得承认或未启动某个案件，不影响其作为破产管理人向美国法院申请追讨债务人的财产。

英国：是的。在某些情况下，外国破产管理人可以单独提出索赔或者救济的申请，不必获得正式的承认。

瑞士：外国破产管理人必须在瑞士获得对外国破产程序的承认，且无权在瑞士民事诉讼中直接获取信息。但是，在瑞士境内未获得承认的外国破产管理人可以在破产程序之前或之后发生跨国犯罪时（如欺诈、贪污、渎职等），代表破产公司提起刑事诉讼。依据瑞士《刑事诉讼法》（CPP），受害人有权参与刑事调查，即便他并不打算对被告提起损害赔偿。这使得外国破产管理人可以在获得承认之前就提起刑事诉讼并参与调查。包括原告在内的所有当事方都可以查阅文件，最迟截止到嫌疑人第一次听证时，其他主要证据也都要收集完毕（《刑事诉讼法》第101条）。为防止该权利被滥用，可能对其施加时间限制（《刑事诉讼法》第108条）。原则上，允许将文件的副本用于瑞士或国外的其他刑事或民事诉讼程序。

entity to lodge a criminal complaint and to participate in the criminal investigation, even before recognition of the foreign insolvency. The right to consult the file exists for all the parties, including the plaintiff, at the latest at the moment when the suspect has been heard for the first time and the other main evidence has been gathered (art. 101 CPP). This right may be restricted for a limited time to prevent abuses (art. 108 CPP). The use of the copies levied from the file for use in other criminal or civil proceedings, in Switzerland or abroad, is, in principle, allowed.

Australia: Yes.

United Arab Emirates: The United Arab Emirates (non–Dubai International Financial Centre [DIFC]) courts have no concept of "disclosure order." It is, however, possible for a foreign office holder to use the DIFC courts to obtain a disclosure order (*Norwich Pharmacal* or *Bankers Trust*) depending upon whether the DIFC courts have jurisdiction for such order (that is, is the defendant or asset in question within the DIFC's jurisdiction?).

Cayman Islands: See the answer to question (*g*).

i. Does your law of recognition require any form of reciprocity to be shown in the legal system of an office holder's place of appointment? If so, what kind of reciprocity is required to be shown?

Belgium: No

British Virgin Islands: Only to the extent that the need for reciprocity could be said to be relevant to considerations of comity.

Hong Kong SAR, China: See [various responses] above.

Jersey: The countries prescribed under the Bankruptcy (Désastre) (Jersey) Order 2006 have, through their own domestic insolvency regimes, offered reciprocal treatment to Jersey. In the case of other jurisdictions, Jersey will recognize a foreign office holder on the basis of comity. Jersey does not demand absolute reciprocity, and it is not a requirement that has

澳大利亚：是的。

阿联酋：阿联酋［除了迪拜国际金融中心（DIFC）］法院没有“披露令”的概念。但外国破产管理人有可能可以向迪拜法院申请“披露令”（第三方披露令或银行信托令），这取决于迪拜法院是否对该命令具有管辖权（被告或其资产是否属于迪拜管辖）。

开曼群岛：详见对问题（g）的答复。

i. 您的承认，是否要求破产管理人的原任命国与您的国家达成任何形式的对等互惠？

比利时：不需要。

英属维京群岛：互惠的要求仅只达到礼让、尊重的程度即可。

中国香港：详见上文所有答复。

泽西岛：依据2006年《破产法》（泽西岛）所指定的国家，其国内的破产制度已经为泽西岛提供了互惠待遇。对于其他国家或地区，泽西岛法院会秉承尊重、礼让的原则对外国破产管理人予以承认。泽西岛并不要求绝对的对等，这也不是明确的法定要求，但在某些情况下，法院会审阅外国律师的说明，表明如果泽西岛提出类似要求，请

been codified or for which a legal test has been articulated by the courts. Nevertheless, there have been instances where the Jersey courts have considered a note from foreign counsel which states that the requesting foreign jurisdiction would offer similar assistance if Jersey were to make a similar request.

Singapore: There is no requirement for reciprocity, but its existence will be a factor toward the exercise of the Singapore court's discretion.

United States: To qualify for recognition, a foreign office holder must satisfy the provisions of section 1515 [of the Bankruptcy Code]. That section does not have a reciprocity requirement.

United Kingdom: Not as such, but it could be a factor in an unusual case involving an unusual jurisdiction.

Switzerland: Swiss law requires that reciprocity be granted in the State where the bankruptcy decree was granted. The requirement of reciprocity is not interpreted in a strict manner. The applicant will have to show that the foreign law provides for significantly similar rules but not that the foreign law provides for strictly the same rules. Generally, legal advice on recognition of foreign bankruptcy in the State where the bankruptcy decree was rendered will suffice. Reciprocity will usually be given for decrees coming from a country that adopted a law following the UNCITRAL Model Law [on CrossBorder Insolvency].

Australia: There is no requirement for reciprocity.

United Arab Emirates: Yes, "reciprocity" is usually required but even in circumstances of "reciprocity," an office holder appointed abroad would be unlikely to be accepted by the United Arab Emirates (non–Dubai International Financial Centre) authorities unless armed with an appropriate notarized power of attorney as formal legal representative of the company in question.

Cayman Islands: No.

求的外国法院也会提供类似的协助。

新加坡：没有互惠的硬性要求，但它会成为法院考量的因素之一。

美国：外国破产管理人获得承认必须满足《美国破产法》第 1515 条的规定，该条并无互惠性的要求。

英国：并非如此，但在涉及特殊司法管辖的案件中，它可能成为一个影响因素。

瑞士：瑞士法律要求宣告破产的国家或地区提供互惠，但没有严格定义互惠的细则。申请人必须证明外国法律规定了不完全相同但非常相似的规则。一般来说，宣告破产的国家提供有关承认外国破产程序的法律建议就足够了。一般对通过联合国国际贸易法委员会《跨国界破产示范法》的国家施行互惠原则。

澳大利亚：并无互惠要求。

阿联酋：是的。通常需要“互惠”。但即使在“互惠”的情况下，除非外国任命的破产管理人具有经过公证的公司委托书，否则也不大可能获得阿联酋（除迪拜国际金融中心外）的承认。

开曼群岛：不要求。

Notes

1. The contributors to the survey were: Emmanuel France, Field Fisher Waterhouse LLP (Belgium); Shane Donovan, Martin Kenney & Co., Solicitors (British Virgin Islands); Jeff Lane, Tanner De Witt Solicitors (Hong Kong SAR, China); Stephen Baker, Baker & Partners (Jersey); Sanjeev Ghurburrun, Geroudis (Mauritius); Danny Ong, Rajah & Tan Singapore LLP (Singapore); Edward Clarkson, Munsch Hardt Kopf & Harr (United States); Alex Jay, Gowling WLG (United Kingdom); Yves Klein and Antonia Mottironi, Monfrini Crettol & Associes (Switzerland); John Mitchell, Arnold Bloch Leibler (Australia); Richard Briggs, Hadef & Partners (United Arab Emirates); Collette Wilkins, Walkers Global (Cayman Islands); Karishma Beegoo, Appleby Global (Seychelles); Athina Chatziadamou, Andreas Neocleous & Co. LLC (Cyprus); and Kees van de Meent, Höcker Advocaten (Netherlands).

2. The survey was conducted by Martin Kenney & Co., Solicitors (British Virgin Islands), as the lead member of a consortium consisting of Aarna Law (Bangalore and New Delhi), Husch Blackwell (Kansas City, MO), and certain members of ICC FraudNet.

注释

1. 下列人员对本调查均有贡献：Emmanuel France, Field Fisher Waterhouse LLP（比利时）；Shane Donovan, Martin Kenney & Co., Solicitors（英属维京群岛）；Jeff Lane, Tanner De Witt Solicitors（中国香港）；Stephen Baker, Baker & Partners（泽西岛）；Sanjeev Ghurburrun, Geroudis（毛里求斯）；Danny Ong, Rajah & Tan Singapore LLP（新加坡）；Edward Clarkson, Munsch Hardt Kopf & Harr（美国）；Alex Jay, Gowling WLG（英国）；Yves Klein and Antonia Mottironi, Monfrini Crettol & Associes（瑞士）；John Mitchell, Arnold Bloch Leibler（澳大利亚）；Richard Briggs, Hadef & Partners（阿联酋）；Collette Wilkins, Walkers Global（开曼群岛）；Karishma Beegoo, Appleby Global（塞舌尔）；Athina Chatziadamou, Andreas Neocleous & Co. LLC（塞浦路斯）；以及 Kees van de Meent, Höcker Advocaten（荷兰）。

2. 该问卷由 Martin Kenny 律师事务所（英属维京群岛）设计，该事务所也是 Aarna Law 法律事务所（班加罗尔 & 新德里）、Husch Blackwell 律师事务所（堪萨斯城，密苏里州）联会的核心成员，同时是国际商会反欺诈组织（ICC FraudNet）的成员。

Appendix B. Website Resources

International Organizations and Bodies

World Bank Group

- World Bank: http://www.worldbank.org
  - World Bank Insolvency: http://www.worldbank.org/en/topic/financialsector/brief/insolvency-and-debt-resolution
  - Financial Market Integrity Group: http://www.worldbank.org/en/topic/financialmarketintegrity
- World Bank Doing Business: http://www.doingbusiness.org/

Stolen Asset Recovery (StAR) Initiative

- StAR: http://star.worldbank.org

United Nations

- United Nations: https://www.un.org
- United Nations Office on Drugs and Crime: https://www.unodc.org
- United Nations Convention Against Corruption (UNCAC): https://www.unodc.org/unodc/en/treaties/CAC/
- United Nations Convention Against the Illicit Traffic in Narcotic Drugs and Psychotropic Substances, 1988: https://www.unodc.org/unodc/en/treaties/illicit-trafficking.html
- United Nations Convention Against Transnational Organized Crime (UNTOC): https://www.unodc.org/unodc/en/organized-crime/intro/UNTOC.html

附录B 网络资源

国际组织和机构

世界银行集团

- 世界银行：http://www.worldbank.org
  - 世界银行破产项目：http://www.worldbank.org/en/topic/financialsector/brief/insolvency-and-debt-resolution
  - 金融市场诚信项目：http://www.worldbank.org/en/topic/financialmarketintegrity
- 世界银行经商项目：http://www.doingbusiness.org/

被盗资产返还倡议

- StAR: http://star.worldbank.org

联合国

- 联合国：https://www.un.org
- 联合国毒品和犯罪问题办公室：https://www.unodc.org
- 《联合国反腐败公约》：https://www.unodc.org/unodc/en/treaties/CAC/
- 《1988年联合国禁止非法贩运麻醉药品与精神药物公约》：https://www.unodc.org/unodc/en/treaties/illicit-trafficking.html
- 《联合国打击跨国有组织犯罪公约》(UNTOC): https://www.unodc.org/unodc/en/organized-crime/intro/UNTOC.html

United Nations Commission on International Trade Law

- UNCITRAL: https://uncitral.un.org/
- Working Group Documents: https://uncitral.un.org/en/working_groups
- UNCITRAL Colloquia Materials: https://uncitral.un.org/en/colloquia

Organisation for Economic Co-operation and Development Convention on Combating Bribery of Foreign Public Officials in International Business

Transactions: http://www.oecd.org/corruption/oecdantibriberyconvention.htm

Inter-American Convention against Corruption: http://www.oas.org/en/sla/dil/inter_american_treaties_B-58_against_Corruption.asp

Council of Europe Conventions and Groups: http://conventions.coe.int

Civil Law Convention on Corruption, November 4, 1999: https://www.coe.int/en/web/conventions/

Convention on Jurisdiction and the Enforcement of Judgments in Civil and Commercial Matters (Convention of Lugano): https://curia.europa.eu/common/recdoc/convention/en/c-textes/lug.htm

GRECO Group of States Against Corruption: https://www.coe.int/in/web/greco/home

Decisions and Regulations from the Council of the European Union: https://eur-lex.europa.eu

African Union Convention on Preventing and Combating Corruption, 2003: https:// au.int/en/treaties/african-union-convention-preventing-and-combating-corruption

Financial Action Task Force (FATF) on Money Laundering: http://www.fatf-gafi.org

联合国国际贸易法委员会

- 联合国国际贸易法委员会：https://uncitral.un.org/
- 工作组文件：https://uncitral.un.org/en/working_groups

- 联合国国际贸易法委员会会议讨论纪要：https://uncitral.un.org/en/colloquia

《经济合作与发展组织关于打击国际商业交易中行贿外国公职人员的公约》

交易： http://www.oecd.org/corruption/oecdantibriberyconvention.htm

《美洲反腐败公约》： http://www.oas.org/en/sla/dil/inter_american_treaties_B-58_against_Corruption.asp

欧洲理事会公约与团体： http://conventions.coe.int

1999 年 11 月 4 日通过的《反腐败民法公约》： https://www.coe.int/en/web/conventions/

《民商事司法管辖权和判决执行公约》(《卢加诺公约》)： https://curia.europa.eu/common/recdoc/convention/en/c-textes/lug.htm

反腐败国家集团： https://www.coe.int/in/web/greco/home

欧盟理事会的决定与条例： https://eur-lex.europa.eu

2003 年《非洲联盟预防与打击腐败公约》： https:// au.int/en/treaties/african-union-convention-preventing-and-combating-corruption

反洗钱金融行动特别工作组： http://www.fatf-gafi.org

Organizations, Rating Agencies, and Bar Associations that Track Asset Recovery Attorneys

International Chamber of Commerce: https://www.iccwbo.org/ U4, The Anti-Corruption Resource Centre: https://www.u4.no/ FraudNet: http://www.icc-ccs.org/home/fraudnet

The World Bank International Corruption Hunters: https://www.worldbank.org/en/about/unit/integrity-vice-presidency/brief/International-Corruption-Hunters-Alliance

Chambers and Partners: https://www.chambers.com

Online Sources for Case Law

StAR Corruption Cases DataBase: https://star.worldbank.org/corruption-cases/?db=All

British and Irish Legal Information Institute (BAILII): https://www.bailii.org

French legal framework and case laws (Legifrance): https://www.legifrance.gouv.fr (English translation available)

追踪资产返还的律师协会、评级机构及相关组织

国际商会： https://www.iccwbo.org/ U4，反腐败资源中心：https://www.u4.no/FraudNet: http://www.icc-ccs.org/home/fraudnet

世界银行国际腐败猎手联盟： https://www.worldbank.org/en/about/unit/integrity-vice-presidency/brief/International-Corruption-Hunters-Alliance

钱伯斯国际法律评级机构： https://www.chambers.com

线上案例资源

资产返还计划腐败案例数据库： https://star.worldbank.org/corruption-cases/?db=All

大不列颠与爱尔兰法律信息学院： https://www.bailii.org

法国法律制度与判例（破产）： https://www.legifrance.gouv.fr（有英文译本）

图书在版编目(CIP)数据

走向破产 ：跨国反腐败资产追查的策略 / (加) 吉恩 - 皮尔里 · 布鲁恩，(美) 莫莉 · 西尔弗著 ；王秀梅，林洁莹译. -- 北京 ：法律出版社，2024

书名原文：Going for Broke：Insolvency Tools to Support Cross-Border Asset Recovery in Corruption Cases

ISBN 978 - 7 - 5197 - 8674 - 8

Ⅰ. ①走… Ⅱ. ①吉… ②莫… ③王… ④林… Ⅲ. ①贪污贿赂罪 - 研究 Ⅳ. ①D914.392

中国国家版本馆 CIP 数据核字(2024)第 014391 号

走向破产：跨国反腐败资产产追查的策略
ZOUXIANG POCHAN: KUAGUO FANFUBAI ZICHAN ZHUICHA DE CELÜE

[加]吉恩 - 皮尔里 · 布鲁恩
[美]莫莉 · 西尔弗 著
王秀梅 林洁莹 译

责任编辑 孙东育 刘梦瑀
装帧设计 鲍龙卉

出版发行 法律出版社
编辑统筹 学术 · 对外出版分社
责任校对 王 丰
责任印制 胡晓雅 宋万春
经 销 新华书店

开本 A5
印张 13 **字数** 291 千
版本 2024 年 3 月第 1 版
印次 2024 年 3 月第 1 次印刷
印刷 天津嘉恒印务有限公司

地址：北京市丰台区莲花池西里 7 号(100073)
网址：www. lawpress. com. cn
投稿邮箱：info@ lawpress. com. cn
举报盗版邮箱：jbwq@ lawpress. com. cn

销售电话：010 - 83938349
客服电话：010 - 83938350
咨询电话：010 - 63939796

书号：ISBN 978 - 7 - 5197 - 8674 - 8 **定价**：68.00 元

凡购买本社图书，如有印装错误，我社负责退换。电话：010 - 83938349